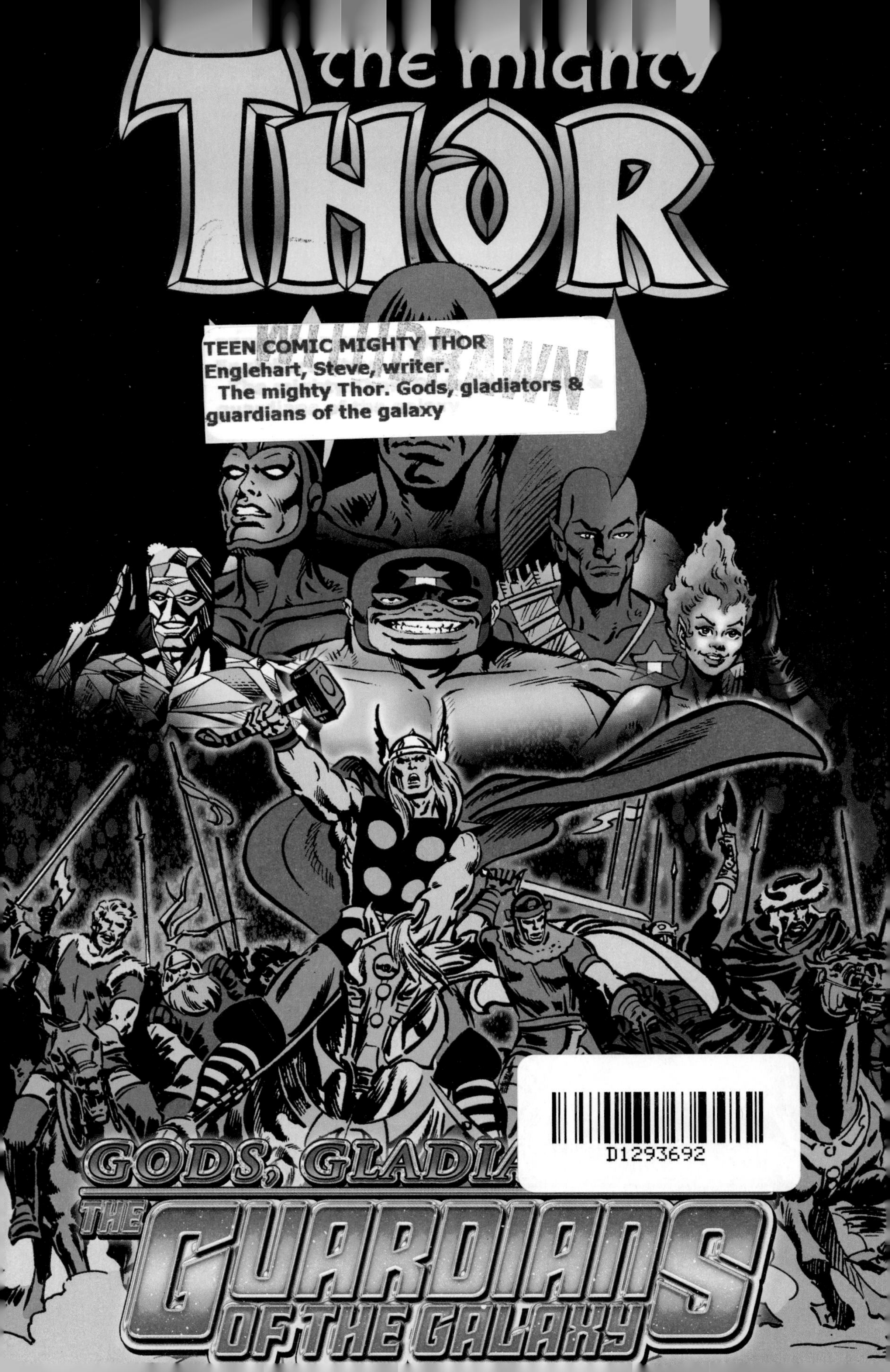
the mighty
THOR
GODS, GLADIA
THE
GUARDIANS
OF THE GALAXY

THE MIGHTY THOR

WRITERS
STEVE ENGLEHART,
ROGER STERN & LEN WEIN

PENCILERS
JOHN BUSCEMA,
SAL BUSCEMA &
WALTER SIMONSON

INKERS
TONY DEZUÑIGA &
KLAUS JANSON

COLORISTS
DON WARFIELD &
GLYNIS WEIN

LETTERERS
TONY SAN JOSE &
JOE ROSEN

EDITORS
ARCHIE GOODWIN &
LEN WEIN

FRONT COVER ARTISTS
JOHN BUSCEMA,
JOE SINNOTT &
THOMAS MASON

BACK COVER ARTISTS
WALTER SIMONSON,
JOE SINNOTT &
TOM SMITH

COLLECTION EDITOR & DESIGN: NELSON RIBEIRO
ASSISTANT EDITOR: ALEX STARBUCK
EDITORS, SPECIAL PROJECTS: MARK D. BEAZLEY & JENNIFER GRÜNWALD
SENIOR EDITOR, SPECIAL PROJECTS: JEFF YOUNGQUIST
RESEARCH: DANA PERKINS LAYOUT: JEPH YORK
PRODUCTION: COLORTEK, RYAN DEVALL & JOE FRONTIRRE
SVP OF PRINT & DIGITAL PUBLISHING SALES: DAVID GABRIEL

EDITOR IN CHIEF: AXEL ALONSO
CHIEF CREATIVE OFFICER: JOE QUESADA
PUBLISHER: DAN BUCKLEY
EXECUTIVE PRODUCER: ALAN FINE

GODS, GLADIATORS & THE GUARDIANS OF THE GALAXY. Contains material originally published in magazine form as THOR #267-271 and THOR ANNUAL #5-6. First printing 2013. ISBN# 978-
d by MARVEL WORLDWIDE, INC., a subsidiary of MARVEL ENTERTAINMENT, LLC. OFFICE OF PUBLICATION: 135 West 50th Street, New York, NY 10020. Copyright © 1976, 1977, 1978 and 2013 M
ights reserved. All characters featured in this issue and the distinctive names and likenesses thereof, and all related indicia are trademarks of Marvel Characters, Inc. No similarity between a
s, persons, and/or institutions in this magazine with those of any living or dead person or institution is intended, and any such similarity which may exist is purely coincidental. **Printed in**
P - Office of the President, Marvel Worldwide, Inc. and EVP & CMO Marvel Characters B.V.; DAN BUCKLEY, Publisher & President - Print, Animation & Digital Divisions; JOE QUESADA, Chief Crea
RT, SVP of Publishing; DAVID BOGART, SVP of Operations & Procurement, Publishing; C.B. CEBULSKI, SVP of Creator & Content Development; DAVID GABRIEL, SVP of Print & Digital Publishing Sal
erations & Logistics; DAN CARR, Executive Director of Publishing Technology; SUSAN CRESPI, Editorial Operations Manager; ALEX MORALES, Publishing Operations Manager; STAN LEE, Chairm
on regarding advertising in Marvel Comics or on Marvel.com, please contact Niza Disla, Director of Marvel Partnerships, at ndisla@marvel.com. For Marvel subscription inquiries, please ca
tured between 5/22/2013 and 6/24/2013 by R.R. DONNELLEY, INC., SALEM, VA, USA.

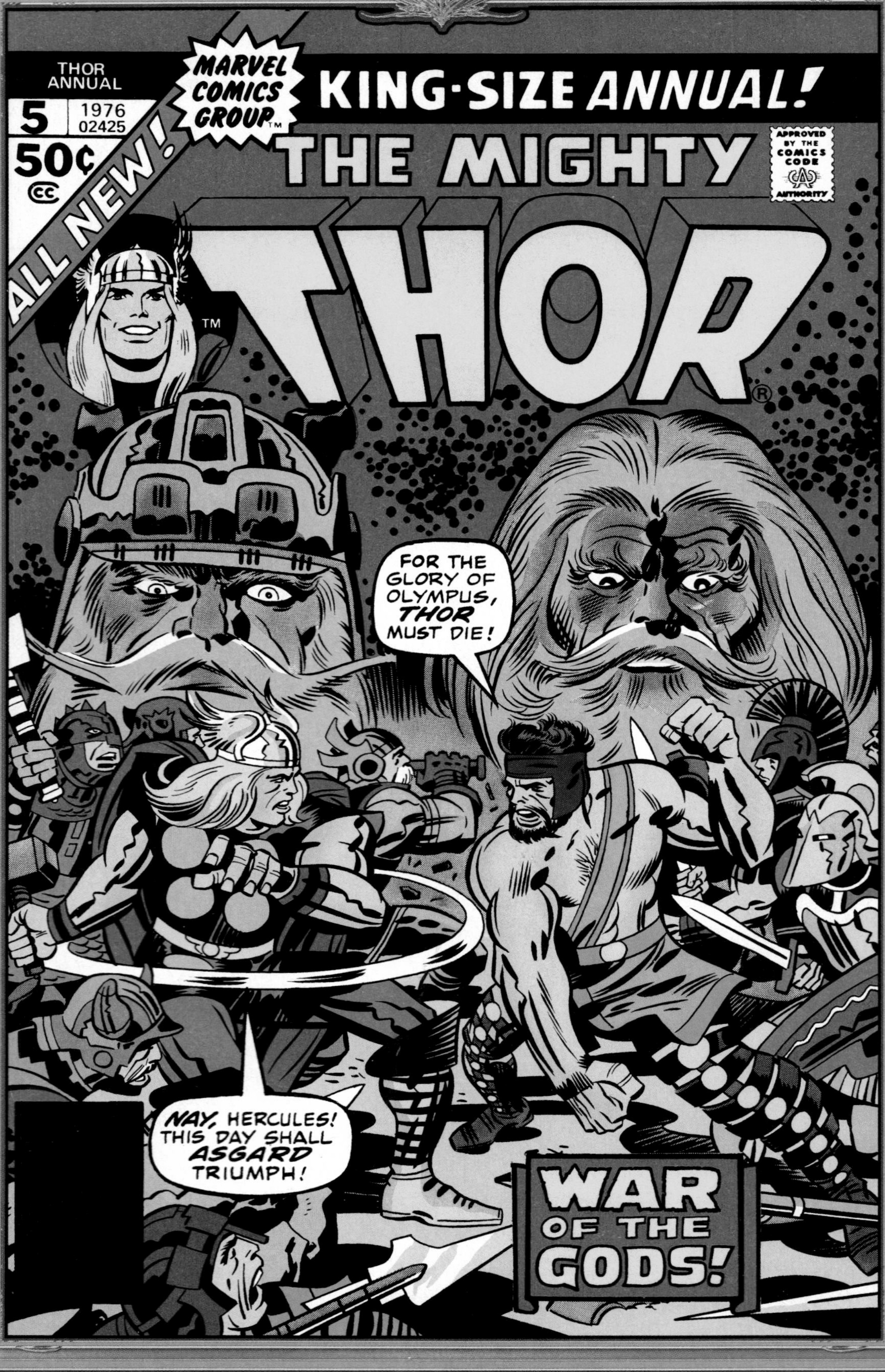
THOR ANNUAL
5
1976
02425
50¢
CC
MARVEL COMICS GROUP
KING-SIZE ANNUAL!
ALL NEW!
THE MIGHTY
THOR
APPROVED BY THE COMICS CODE AUTHORITY
FOR THE GLORY OF OLYMPUS, THOR MUST DIE!
NAY, HERCULES! THIS DAY SHALL ASGARD TRIUMPH!
WAR OF THE GODS!

When lame Dr. DONALD BLAKE strikes his wooden walking stick upon the ground, it becomes the mystic mallet MJOLNIR—and Blake is transformed into the Norse God of Thunder, Master of the Storm and the Lightning, Heir to the Throne of Immortal Asgard...

Stan Lee PRESENTS: THE MIGHTY THOR! ™

PRESENTING! A NOVEL-LENGTH MELDING OF MYTH, LEGEND, AND SHEER MARVEL WONDERMENT!

WAR of THE GODS!

A SAGA STIRRINGLY TOLD BY:

STEVE ENGLEHART ✱ **JOHN BUSCEMA** & **TONY DEZUNIGA**
WRITER   ARTISTS

SAN JOSE ✱ **DON WARFIELD** ✱ **A. GOODWIN**
LETTERER   COLORIST   EDITOR

PROLOGUE: DAWN OF THE GODS!

Once, there was **NOTHING**... neither the **EARTH** nor the **SKY ABOVE**, nor **SUN**, nor **MOON**, nor **LIFE**!

There was only the endless **ABYSS**.

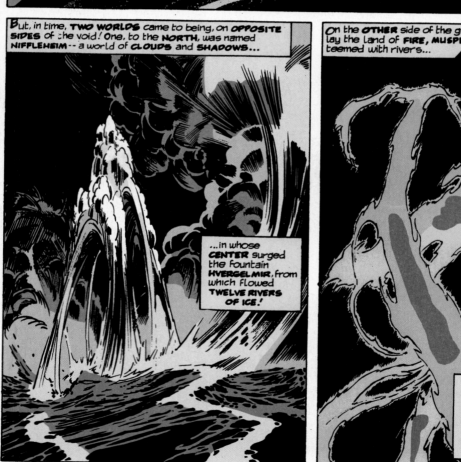

But, in time, **TWO WORLDS** came to being, on **OPPOSITE SIDES** of the void! One, to the **NORTH**, was named **NIFFLEHEIM** -- a world of **CLOUDS** and **SHADOWS**...

...in whose **CENTER** surged the fountain **HVERGELMIR**, from which flowed **TWELVE RIVERS OF ICE**!

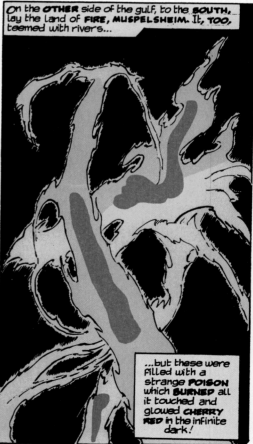

On the **OTHER** side of the gulf, to the **SOUTH**, lay the land of **FIRE**, **MUSPELSHEIM**. It, **TOO**, teemed with rivers...

...but these were filled with a strange **POISON** which **BURNED** all it touched and glowed **CHERRY RED** in the infinite dark!

6

Each land's rivers ran toward the **OTHER'S**, till they met halfway between in **CATACLYSMIC GRANDEUR**--

--whereupon the northern **ICE COVERED** and **SOLIDIFIED** the southern streams, so that their combined mass partially **FILLED** the abyss...for a **TIME!**

Before **LONG**, the **WARM AIR** blowing in from the south began to **MELT** the all conquering ice...

...and from the half-frozen mixture which **RESULTED**, stepped the first form of **LIFE**--

-- THE **FROST-GIANT**, **YMIR!**

Ymir was the **FATHER OF ALL GIANTS**. Later, when he chanced to **SLEEP**, the warm winds melted **HIM** somewhat...

...and from his form were born the **FIRST** of his many **CHILDREN!**

Moreover, as the slumbering ymir **CONTINUED** to melt, a **COW** was conceived, and this was **AUDUMBLA** the giants' **WET-NURSE**. From that day forward, all giants quenched their thirst on the four streams of **MILK** which they sucked from her udders...

...while audumbla **HERSELF** was content to find sustenance in licking the endless **ICE**. So it was that, in time, she **WORE DOWN** the ice...

...to reveal a **NEW** being, called **BURI**-- the first of the **GODS!**

Buri **INTRIGUED** the giants, so they allowed him to **LIVE** -- much to their future **CHAGRIN**. For Buri had a **SON**, named **BOR**, and Bor married one of the giant's **DAUGHTERS**. This union brought to life **THREE SONS** they called the **AESIR**, and whose **GIVEN** names were --

--ve--

--vili--

--and **ODIN!**

Odin grew to **HATE** the giants of his mother's race! When his brothers reached **FULL GROWTH**, he led them in a **WAR** against their ancestors!

The **FIRST** giant they attacked was **YMIR HIMSELF** --

--and after fierce struggle, Odin **SLEW** the aged creature!

Ymir **FELL**, and the seas of **BLUE BLOOD** which had filled his mighty frame coursed into the **ABYSS**, drowning all **OTHER** giants --

--or so it was **THOUGHT!**

At the **END**, however, a giant named **BERGELMIR** and his wife found a **SMALL BOAT** bobbing on the stormy waves and **ESCAPED!** The race of giants would **LIVE ON!**

But Odin and his brothers knew **NOTHING** of this, for with **YMIR'S** death, they turned their thoughts from the **DESTRUCTION OF THE OLD** to the **CREATION OF THE NEW!**

They raised the frost-giant's **BODY** from the **SEA**, to form a land they called **MIDGARD** -- the **"MIDDLE ABODE"** between Niffleheim and Muspelsheim --

--a land **WE** call the **WORLD!**

From Ymir's **BONES** they carved the **MOUNTAINS**, and from his **HAIR**, they made the **TREES!**

Then, they took his **SKULL**, and placed it atop **FOUR PILLARS** which they raised to the sky, to form the **VAULT OF THE HEAVENS!**

Within that vault, they confined the random **SPARKS** which blew out of **MUSPELSHEIM** -- and thus created the **SUN**, the **MOON** and the countless **STARS!**

EONS passed as they **REGULATED** the passage of these heavenly fires to fix the succession of **DAYS** and **NIGHT** as well as the length of the **YEAR...**

...and when midgard was **COMPLETED**, they built **THEMSELVES** a home **ABOVE** it-

--**ASGARD**, the abode of the **AESIR!**

BETWEEN the two, they stretched the **RAINBOW** -- and called this world-bridge **BIFROST!**

In time, there came to be **MANY** gods in Asgard, though **NONE** more powerful than mighty **ODIN**, whom they named their **CHIEFTAIN!**

Still, they were not **CONTENT.** They felt **ALONE** in the abyss, and longed for **OTHER BEINGS** like **THEMSELVES...**

...so they assembled in Odin's **GREAT HALL** to debate their course of **ACTION!**

Looking down on **MIDGARD**, they saw that **GRUBS** were beginning to form in **Ymir's** rotting **CORPSE...**

...and these they made **TROLLS**, to dwell, like **GRUBS**, beneath the **STONE** the giant's body had become!

But this was not **ENOUGH.**

Still, the **SOLUTION** to their solitude **ELUDED** them, until the day Odin and two other Asgardians, **HOENIR** and **LODUR**, went **RIDING** on the **MIDGARD** plains.

They came upon two **TREE TRUNKS...**

...and **ODIN**, in his wisdom, decided to give them **BREATH! HOENIR** then honored them with **SOULS** and **REASON**, while **LODUR** touched them with **WARMTH** and the colors of **LIFE!**

The **MAN** they called **ASKE**, and the **WOMAN EMBLA** -- and they were the **FIRST HUMANS!**

Humans quickly sprang up **EVERYWHERE**, to fill the midgard plains-- but they soon saw that they were **LESSER** than the **GODS**. In the sea which **SURROUNDED** the world in the abyss lurked the **MIDGARD SERPENT**, whose coils were **EVER READY** to encircle unwary **SAILORS**...

...and **BENEATH** the world now rested **NIFFLEHEIM**, the land of **MISTS** and **SHADOWS**, where the **DEAD** were obliged to **DWELL**.

The reborn race of **GIANTS** lived there, too, with renegade **TROLLS** and renegade **GODS**, and other, less **NAMEABLE** terrors...

...all of them under the iron hand of **HELA**, who followed in the path of Odin and **REAPED** what he had **SOWN**!

NO ONE escaped her final touch! At Niffleheim's bridge to the green world above stood a slavering **HOUND** to **INSURE** that the dead stayed dead-- for men were not **MEANT** to be **IMMORTAL** like their **MAKERS**!

And yet, the early men were **NOT AFRAID**! they were **WARRIORS**, and determined not only to **SURVIVE** but to **FORGE AHEAD**!

Thus it was that they turned their eyes back to the **SKIES**, to find a **COMRADE IN ASGARD**--

--a **CHAMPION**!

11

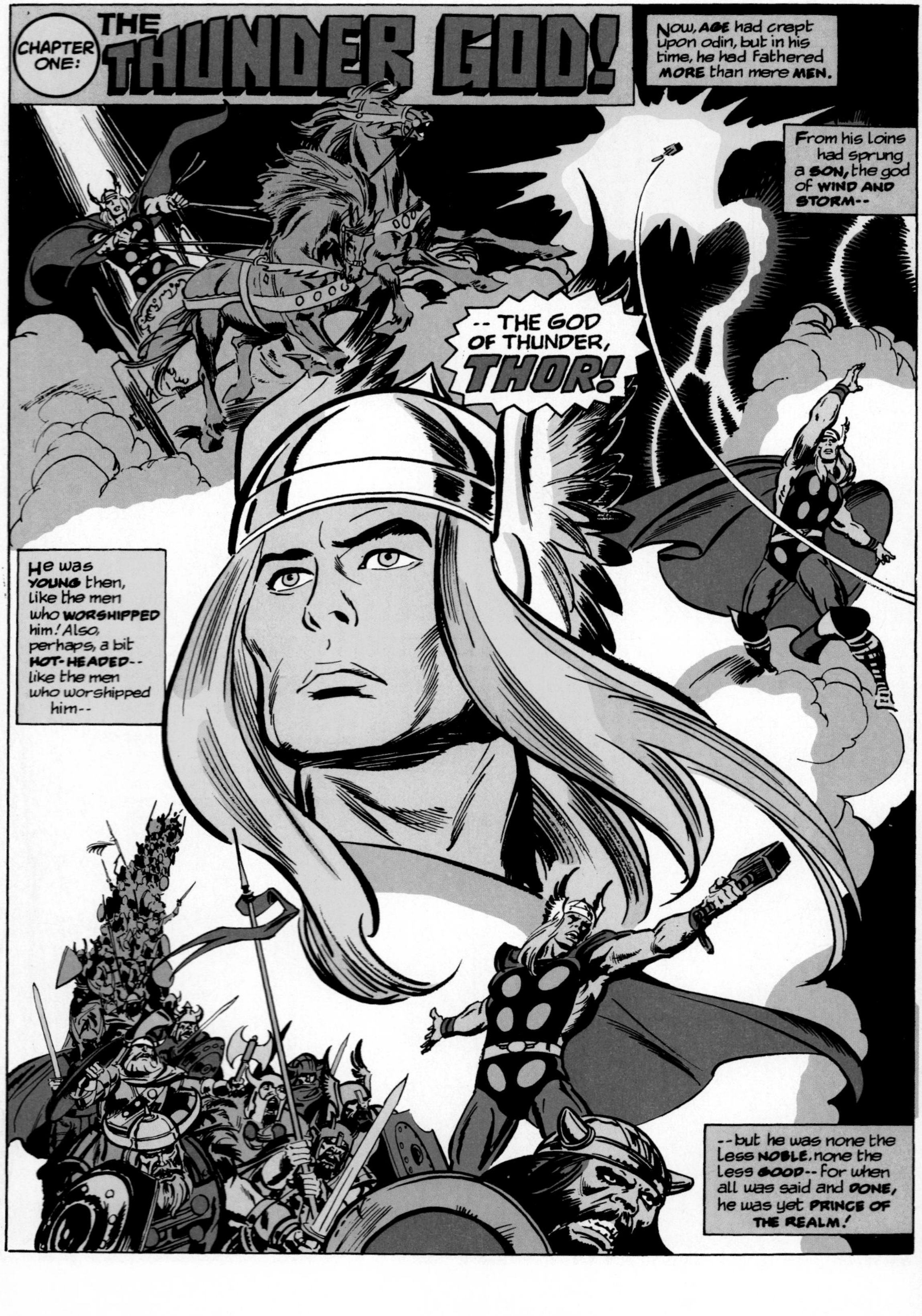
CHAPTER ONE:
THE THUNDER GOD!
Now, AGE had crept upon odin, but in his time, he had fathered MORE than mere MEN.
From his loins had sprung a SON, the god of WIND AND STORM--
-- THE GOD OF THUNDER, THOR!
He was YOUNG then, like the men who WORSHIPPED him! Also, perhaps, a bit HOT-HEADED-- like the men who worshipped him--
--but he was none the less NOBLE, none the less GOOD-- for when all was said and DONE, he was yet PRINCE OF THE REALM!

The early men REVERED the Thunder God--SOME, indeed, moreso than his FATHER! ODIN was chieftain over ALL THAT LIVED--

--GOD OF ASGARD and MAN OF MIDGARD ALIKE--

--but THOR was specifically concerned with the CONFLICT that colored the men's DAILY LIVES!

In essence, he was ONE of them--

--and as the YEARS swiftly mounted, his LEGENDS grew ever more GLORIOUS! EVERY midgardian knew of his VALOR in the face of DANGER--

--of his STAMINA, his STRENGTH-- his inevitable VICTORY!

And all of this was done with but a SINGLE WEAPON! Disdaining others' SWORDS and AXES--

--THOR chose a great stone HAMMER, forged in the furnace of the troll, Geirrodur.

He called it MJOLNIR, which meant "THE DESTROYER"! It never missed its MARK when hurled--

BLAM!!!

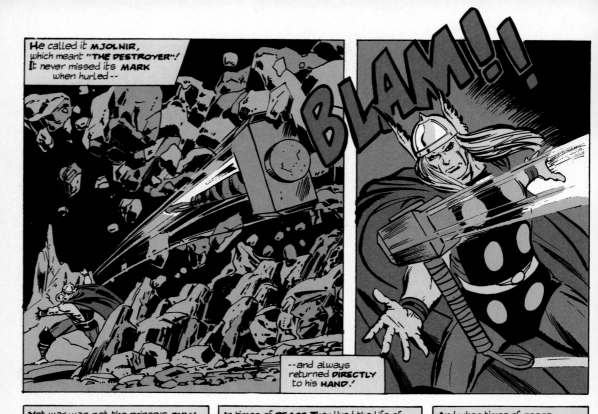

--and always returned DIRECTLY to his HAND!

Yet war was not the prince's ONLY interest. In times of PEACE, the power of the mystic mallet was used to CONSECRATE TREATIES--

--and more especially, MARRIAGES.

In times of PEACE, Thor lived the life of LUXURY in his MANSION, the palace of BILSKIRNIR, on the FIELD OF STRENGTH!

Its 540 CHAMBERS made it the LARGEST in all ASGARD!

And when times of peace became too STIFLING, he took to the SKIES in his golden CHARIOT--

--drawn without rest by two roaring HE-GOATS!

But times of peace never **LASTED** long beyond the **R**ainbow **B**ridge. **MISCHIEF** -- or, some said, **EVIL** -- was forever fomenting behind the locked doors of **LOKI'S** mansion!

LOKI -- Odin's **ADOPTED SON**, Thor's **HALF-BROTHER** --

--was a god **NO** other God could **TRUST!**

His **OPPOSITE NUMBER** was **B**alder -- noble, kind, beloved of **ALL!** It was no surprise that Balder came to be Thor's **BEST FRIEND!**

Together with **HOGUN THE GRIM, FANDRAL** the **DASHING**, and the voluminous **VOLSTAGG**, they fought **MANY** a fine **FOE** --

-- **FOR THE GREATER GLORY OF THE REALM!**

15

This, then, was the Thunder God-- THOR THE MIGHTY--!

--in the days of OLD...!

THOR!

NO, HEIMDALL! HOW DOTH THE RAINBOW'S GUARDIAN FARE THIS CHEERY SUMMER'S MORN?

AS WELL AS ONE MIGHT, WHOSE EYES MAY NEVER REST FROM THEIR ENDLESS VIGIL.

I SEE THY SISTER DOTH DISTURB THY LABOR, TO FROLIC IN THY PRESENCE.

G-GOOD MORROW, SON OF ODIN!

GOOD MORROW, SIF!

METHINKS THE LASS HATH ENAMORED HERSELF OF THEE, MILORD!

I THANK THEE MOST KINDLY, MILADY--BUT THERE BE MANY YEARS AHEAD ERE THOU SHOULDST CONCERN THYSELF WITH SUCH WEIGHTY MATTERS.

NOW, EXCUSE ME, BOTH--

--BUT PRAYERS TO MY NAME HAVE BEEN OFFERED BY MEN SORE BESET, AND I'VE MADE THE DECISION TO SEE TO THEIR WANTS!

FAREWELL! I JOURNEY TO MIDGARD!

On a dawn-lit field of **GLEAMING RED ICE**, somewhere near the **ARCTIC CIRCLE**...

...a **STORM-CLOUD** seems to swirl to earth, and birth a silent looming **FIGURE**!

BATTLE -- THE VIKINGS AGAINST SOME **UNFAMILIAR** FOE!

I SHOULD NOT HAVE DELAYED EVEN TO SPEAK TO **HEIMDALL**! THESE MEN STAND IN NEED OF **AID**!

When Thor went into **COMBAT** his voice did **TREMBLE** the **TREES**!

ONWARDS MEN OF MIDGARD!

FOR EVERY VIKING SLAIN, TEN OF THESE SHALL WEEP FOR THEM OUTSIDE VALHALLA'S WALLS!

YET **WHO** CAN THESE STRANGE MEN **BE**? I HAVE NEVER SEEN THEIR **LIKE**!

The amazement is **MUTUAL**, godling! At this selfsame **INSTANT**, in the frosty cavern used by the invading **GENERALS**...

MINE EYES DO **DECEIVE** ME! **NEVER** HAVE I SEEN SUCH STRENGTH SAVE ON THE **ISLES**!

ERE ALL IS **LOST**, WE MUST CALL UPON **OUR** CHAMPION--

--HERCULES THE MAGNIFICENT!

WHAT DO YOU **WISH**, MEN OF GREECE?

Swiftly, the startling tale is told--

--and two minutes **LATER**, a meeting destined to **CHANGE THE UNIVERSE** takes place beneath the **AURORA BOREALIS**!

HOLD, LONGHAIR!

NO LONGER SHALT THOU WAGE WAR UPON MY PEOPLE!

ART THOU **MAD**, FELLOW? A **PRINCE OF ASGARD** IS NO **GOATHERD** TO BE ORDERED ABOUT BY FOOLISH **MEN**!

18

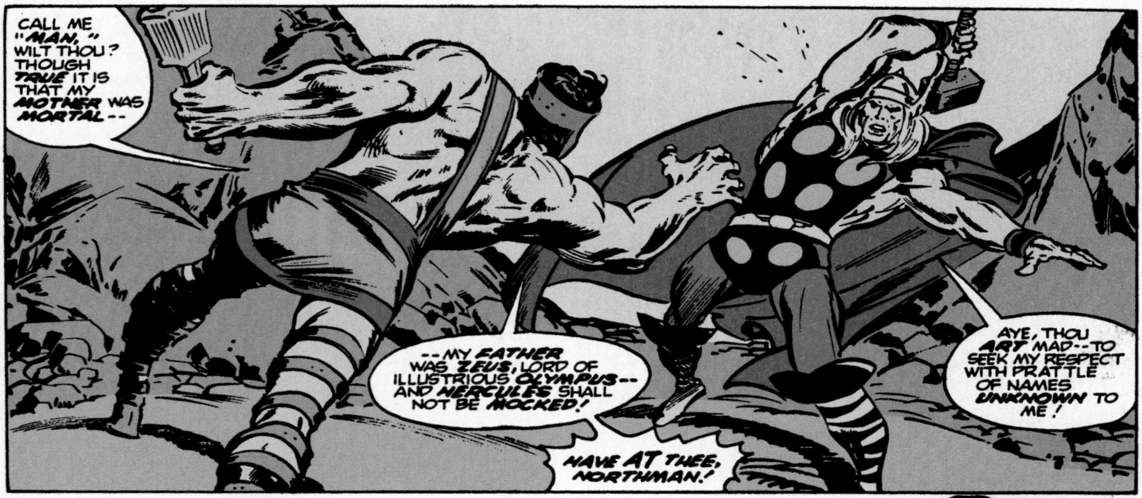
CALL ME "MAN," WILT THOU? THOUGH TRUE IT IS THAT MY MOTHER WAS MORTAL--
--MY FATHER WAS ZEUS, LORD OF ILLUSTRIOUS OLYMPUS-- AND HERCULES SHALL NOT BE MOCKED!
HAVE AT THEE, NORTHMAN!
AYE, THOU ART MAD--TO SEEK MY RESPECT WITH PRATTLE OF NAMES UNKNOWN TO ME!

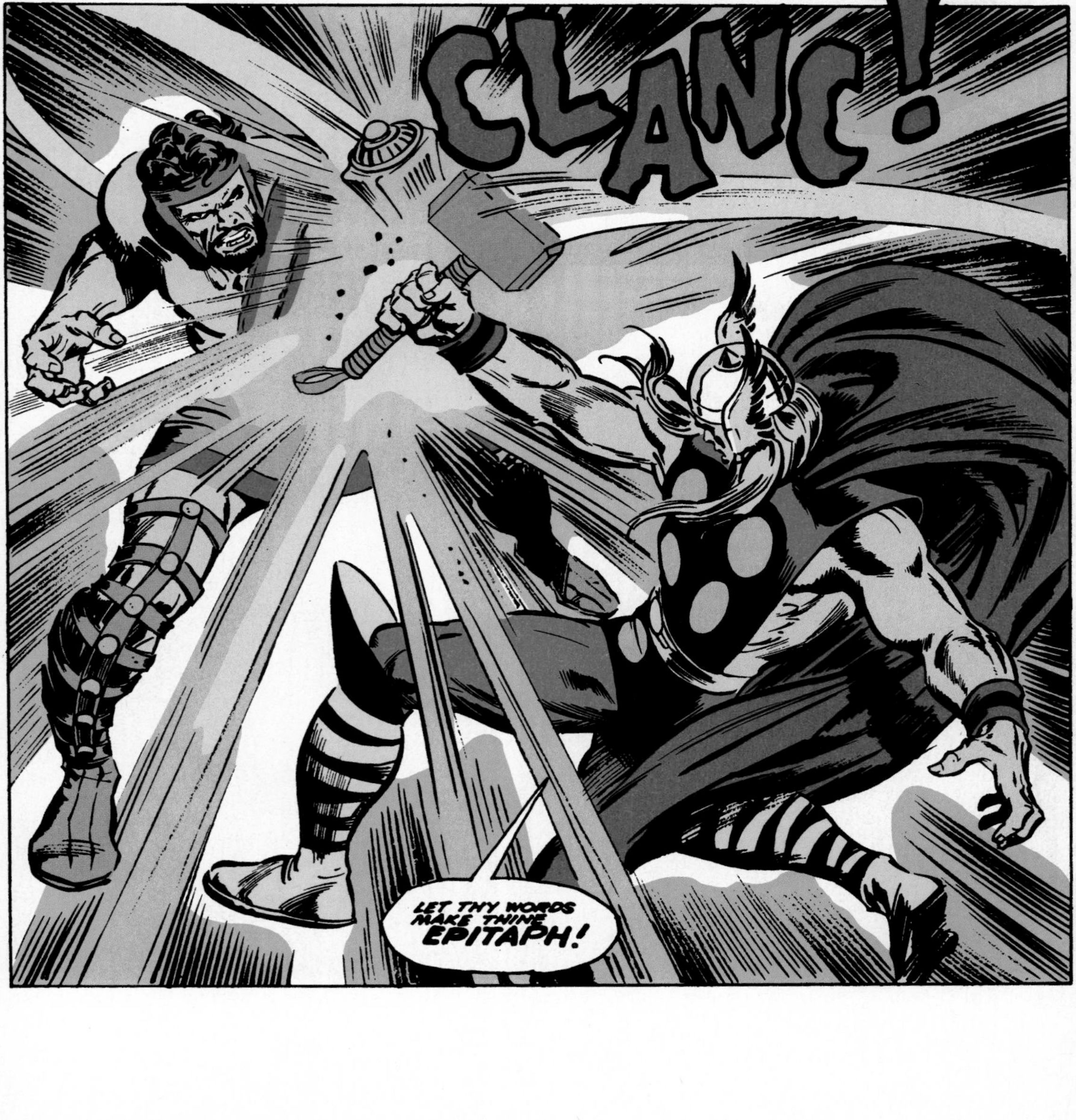
CLANC!
LET THY WORDS MAKE THINE EPITAPH!

Some say this meeting took place **OTHERWISE**, at **OTHER TIMES**--but who among us knows for certain **NOW**?

The glory of **THOR**-- the might of **HERCULES**--these have been writ with the lyrics of **LEGEND**--

--and legends are **TRUTHS** growing **MORE** true with **TIME**! legends tell of those who were **MORE THAN MEN**--

--and so, **UNLIKE** men, they know neither **DEATH** nor **DEFINITION**!

UNSPEAKABLE CHURL!

CRUMP

TO ATTACK THOR THE MIGHTY IS TO MEET THY DOOM!

BAR-ROOM!

ODIN'S BLOOD! WHAT HAVE WE HERE UNLEASHED?

REMAIN TO SEEK THE ANSWER IF THOU WHILST NORTHMAN!

A WISE MAN SEEKETH SHELTER!

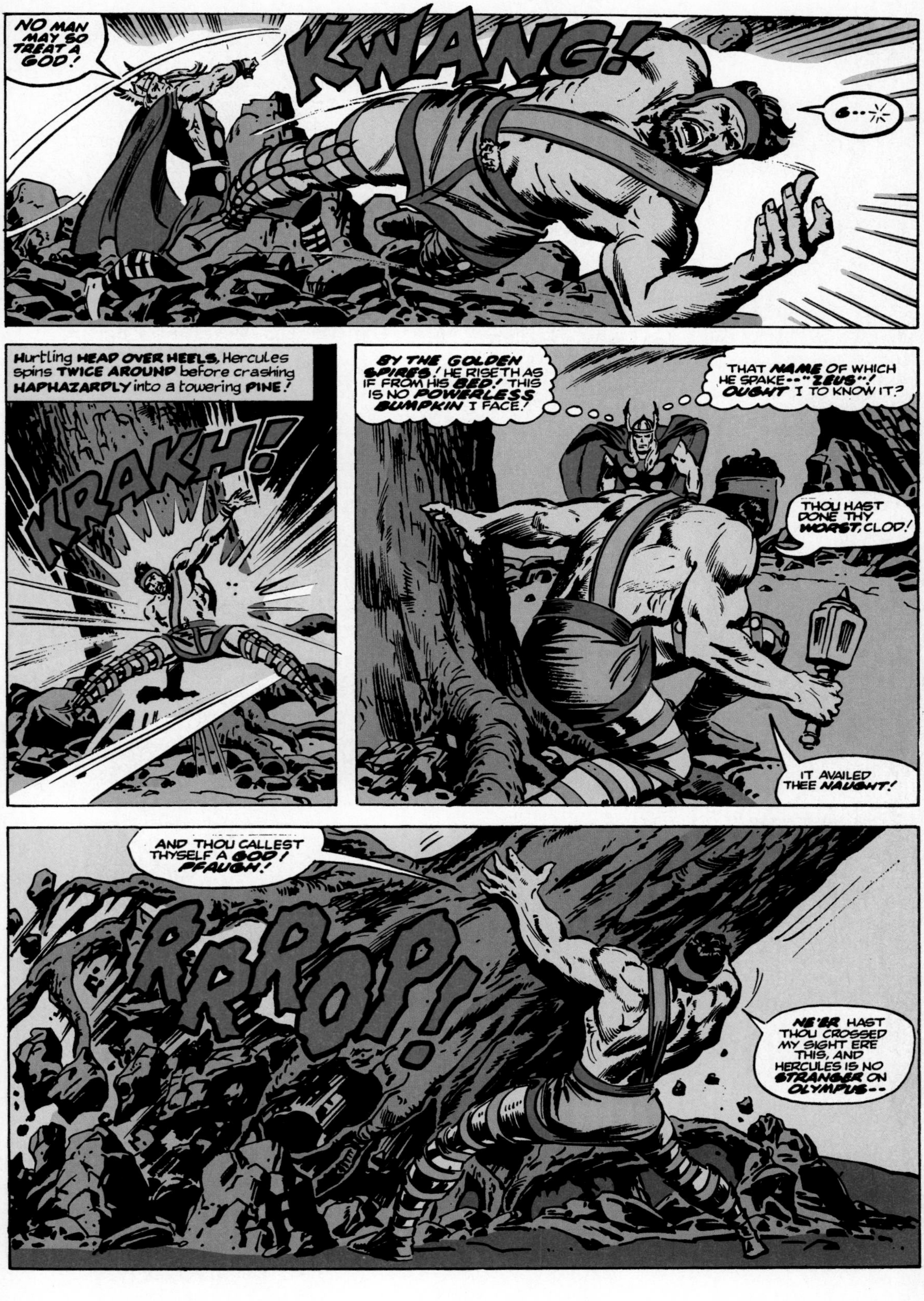
NO MAN MAY SO TREAT A GOD!
KWANG!
G..
Hurtling HEAD OVER HEELS, Hercules spins TWICE AROUND before crashing HAPHAZARDLY into a towering PINE!
KRAKH!
BY THE GOLDEN SPIRES! HE RISETH AS IF FROM HIS BED! THIS IS NO POWERLESS BUMPKIN I FACE!
THAT NAME OF WHICH HE SPAKE--"ZEUS"! OUGHT I TO KNOW IT?
THOU HAST DONE THY WORST, CLOD!
IT AVAILED THEE NAUGHT!
AND THOU CALLEST THYSELF A GOD! PFAUGH!
RRROP!
NE'ER HAST THOU CROSSED MY SIGHT ERE THIS, AND HERCULES IS NO STRANGER ON OLYMPUS--

AS THOU MUST NOW *COMPREHEND!*

BRAKKK!

But even as the massive Tree thunders toward Thor's *HEAD,* he swings *MJOLNIR* before him-- to *SPLIT* the great Trunk into *SHARDS!*

BY CHRONES! PERHAPS ALL THOU SAYEST BE *TRUE!*

IN SUCH CASE, THOU MUST EVEN MORE *CERTAINLY PERISH!*

The pine seems to *EXPLODE,* so violent is the impact--

--but when the *SPLINTERS* settle, the *THUNDER GOD STILL STANDS!*

FOR *OLYMPUS!*

FOR *ASGARD!*

22

From the surrounding **HILLSIDES**, clustered among the barren **TIMBER**, the Greeks and the Vikings survey this clash of titans transfixed with **HORROR**!

Neither their **CURRENT** war nor their **GENERATIONS** of wars can match the **SINGLE SUPERNATURAL STRUGGLE** taking place **HERE AND NOW**!

For nearly an **HOUR**, their heroes rend the **AIR** and **EARTH**, attempting to destroy **EACH OTHER** --and then, a **RINGING VOICE** is heard once more!

HOLD, HERCULES!

'TIS **CERTAIN** NOW WE **ARE** BOTH GODS-- YEA, AND **ABLE** ONES, AT THAT! **NEITHER** SHALL TASTE THE CUP OF TRIUMPH **TODAY!**

YET THERE **MUST** BE AN **ENDING!**

IF IT BE **AGREED**, I SAY WE MEET **AGAIN, ONE WEEK HENCE**, WHEN OUR **FELLOW** GODS MAY DO BATTLE AT OUR **SIDES**--

--THUS TO DETERMINE THE **TRUE** WORTH OF EACH REALM!

MEANTIMES OUR PEOPLE SHALL REFRAIN FROM **THEIR** CONFLICT! **AGREED?**

AGREED! GET YE **HENCE**, MEN OF THE ISLE--

--YET REST ASSURED THAT IN **SEVEN SHORT DAYS**, YOUR HONOR SHALL REMAIN **UNTARNISHED** --AS SHALL THAT OF HIGH **OLYMPUS!**

GO!

It's a **SOMBER** Thor who returns from Midgard as the sun reaches its **ZENITH**...

OTHER GODS! ANOTHER **ASGARD!** MY **MIND** DOTH REEL AND SHAKE AS MY **BODY** NE'ER DID!

ODIN MUST BE **TOLD**-- AND **QUICKLY!**

AH... **THOR!**

HAIL, NOBLE **SIRE!** THY SCION BRINGETH TIDINGS OF **IMPORT MOST DIRE!**

ENTER THE **PRESENCE IMPERIAL,** MY SON! SPEAK, I **PRAY** THEE!

FATHER, I HAVE MET AN IMMORTAL **NOT OF ASGARD,** WHO DID TELL OF A **SECOND** REALM FILLED WITH **OTHERS** OF HIS ILK!

WE HAVE AGREED TO A **MATCH,** HIS **OLYMPUS** 'GAINST **ASGARD**--

ON WHOSE AUTHORITY, GODLING?

BY WHAT **RIGHT** DIDST THOU COMMIT SUCH AN ACT?

EH?

NOBLE SIRE, I-- THE **BRAGGART** HERCULES DID **ATTACK** ME! AS A TRUE **WARRIOR** OF THE REALM, I SAW NO OTHER **COURSE!**

SURELY, WE **SHALL** FIGHT! OUR **HONOR**--

BAH! THERE WILL BE **NO BATTLE!**

THIS IS **MINE** AFFAIR, FATHER! 'TIS **I** WHO HAVE SWORN THE OATH!

THOR! I HAVE **SPOKEN!**

WE SHALL **SEE!**

AND HE WALKETH AWAY, **UNRESTRAINED!**

NE'ER HATH IT BEEN **DIFFERENT**, AND NE'ER **SHALL** IT! THE **TRUE-BORN** SON OF ODIN DOTH WHATE'ER HE MAY **PLEASE**, AND THE ALL-FATHER DOTH BLUSTER AND BELLOW **ONLY**--

--WHILE **LOKI**, THE **CHANGELING** SON, HATH BUT TO **THINK** OF THAT WHICH PLEASETH **HIM**, AND **CENSURE** DOTH FOLLOW LIKE **NIGHT** TO THE **DAY!**

AND **YET**... IN **THIS** INSTANCE, SAID INJUSTICE MAY PROVE TO BE A **BOON**...!

Without another moment's **HESITATION**, the Prince of Evil makes **FIVE MYSTIC PASSES**--

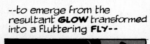

--to emerge from the resultant **GLOW** transformed into a fluttering **FLY**--

--indistinguishable from all **OTHERS**, save for a rather **SINISTER** sound to his **BUZZ**--

--which **RISES**, then **FALLS**, as the tiny creature skitters off toward the dark of the **ABYSS!**

Far to the **SOUTH**, in a land of **SUNNIER CLIMES** and **SOFTER LIFE**, rises the crest of **MOUNT OLYMPUS**, looking down upon the **AEGEAN SEA** from behind its crown of clouds.

There, in an **AMPHITHEATRE** far above the reach of **MAN**, a **SIMILAR** scene is now occurring -- **SIMILAR**, but **NOT** the **SAME** ...!

SO. IT'S **WAR** THOU DESIREST, MY SON?

AYE, ZEUS! THIS ILL-BRED NORTHMAN MUST **NOT** BE ALLOWED HIS **ARROGANCE** AND **LIFE TOGETHER**!

'TIS NOT FOR ONE SUCH AS **HERCULES** TO SPEAK OF ILL-**BREEDING**, WITH HIS MOTHER A **MORTAL** -- eh, ATHENE?

STILL, I PRAY HIS ENTREATY BE MET WITH **SUCCESS**, FOR **ARES**, GOD OF **WAR**, HATH AWAKENED TO PEACE **TOO MANY MORNINGS** IN RECENT YEARS!

SAY BUT THE **WORD**, MY FATHER, AND ASGARD SHALL TROUBLE US **NO LONGER!**

DOTH IT TROUBLE US -- OR **THEE**, HERCULES --

-- THIS REALM OF WHICH NO **OTHER** OLYMPIAN HATH E'ER **HEARD?**

SPOKEN LIKE THE MASTER I DID **MARRY**, SUPREME ONE! LET THIS **UNFORTUNATE** RESULT OF **EARLIER ESCAPADES** RETURN TO THE MORTAL WORLD **UNFULFILLED** --

-- THAT THY **PRESENT** UNION WITH **ME** MAY CONTINUE TO **PROSPER!**

SCHEMING FEMALE! THY HATRED FOR HERCULES BE **WELL-KNOWN** AND **OFT-NOTED**, HERA!

NOBLE ZEUS SHOULD **DECIDE** THE ISSUE ON ITS **MERITS ALONE** --MERITS WHICH, TO **ME**, APPEAR **MORE** THAN **SUBSTANTIAL!**

BUT WHERE BE THE **PROFIT** IN CONFLICT, ARES? WE HAVE **OTHER**, **BETTER** CONCERNS!

APOLLO DOTH NOT LIE! THIS IS **NOT** THE WAY OF PROUD **OLYMPUS!**

ARTEMIS STANDETH **AGAINST!**

AS DOTH **HERMES!**

HEPHAESTUS, SIRE! WE WISH TO **ADVANCE** THE ESTATE OF MAN, NOT **RETARD** IT!

I AM **SORRY**, MY SON! MY WILL AND **FATE** BE **ONE AND THE SAME**, AND THE SIGNS MOST **CLEARLY** POINT TOWARD **PEACE** AT THIS TIME!

With an ugly **SCOWL**, Hercules **TURNS AWAY.**

There, matters might falter to an INCONCLUSIVE END...

...except for a FLY high above.

In the few seconds since its ARRIVAL, it has heard and understood ALL! Now, SWIFTLY and UNSEEN, it drops to vast hall's FLOOR--

--and blossoms with a NEWER form EQUALLY ILLUSORY!

THOR!

AXE, BUFFOON! I COULD NOT BEAR TO WAIT THE WEEK--

--ERE STRIKING THINE UGLY FACE AGAIN!

P'TOK!

THOU DIDST TAKE HIM UNAWARES, FROM BEHIND!

WHAT OF IT, DECREPIT ONE? I BUT ACCORD HIM THE RESPECT I WOULD GIVE ANY OLYMPIAN!

HOLD THY TONGUE, ASGARDIAN--SO I MIGHT RIP IT FROM THINE INSOLENT MOUTH!

SAY ON, HERCULES! THOU AND I SHALL---

HA-HA-HA-HA-HA! FAREWELL, FOOLS!

BY HADES! HE DOTH VANISH!

28

HE BE *GONE*-- BUT THE *INSULTS* LINGER, VILE AND *VICIOUS!* NOW, NOBLE FATHER, WE *MUST* MEET THIS THREAT!

WE SHALL ACCEPT NO *LESS*, ZEUS!

EVEN *I* AM OBLIGED TO *CONCUR*, HUSBAND! WHATE'ER MY THOUGHTS OF THINE *OFFSPRING*, THIS *ASGARDIAN* IS *WORSE!*

I NEED NO *CONVINCING*, HERA! BY MY SOLEMN *DECREE*--

LET THERE BE--

--WAR!

29

CHAPTER TWO

WHEN GODS COLLIDE!

The plain is GRAY and GLIMMERING GHOSTLY in the vast ABYSS. From its NORTHERN REACHES, THOR sits atop his charger and chafes to BEGIN!

BEHIND him, his three closest COMPANIONS IN COMBAT ready their weapons--

--dashing FANDRAL--

--voluminous VOLSTAGG--

--and HOGUN THE GRIM!

Behind THEM, brave BALDER'S noble figure marks the leading edge of the Asgardian WARRIOR BRIGADES, though his heart is HEAVY at what he knows must come!

And OTHER gods, many now FORGOTTEN, simply STAND and WAIT...

...such as the enigmatic TYR, whose appearance, 'tis said, means battle at its MOST GLORIOUS!

THIS, thinks Thor, is an omen most WONDROUS!

But the OLYMPIANS, for THEIR part, are NO LESS well-represented. There is NOTHING more terrible than gods of PEACE when roused to ANGER, and their TWIN CHIEFTAINS, HERCULES and ARES have NEVER been known to FAIL!

Now, ARES is READY! Now he BELLOWS FORTH his ORDERS!

Now, the SOUTHERNERS begin to roll FORWARD--

--AND THE BATTLE IS JOINED!

ONWARD, ASGARDIANS! WE'LL SHOW THEM WHAT IT MEANS TO MOCK OUR GLORY--

--AYE, AND WE'LL SHOW THE ALL-FATHER, AS WELL!

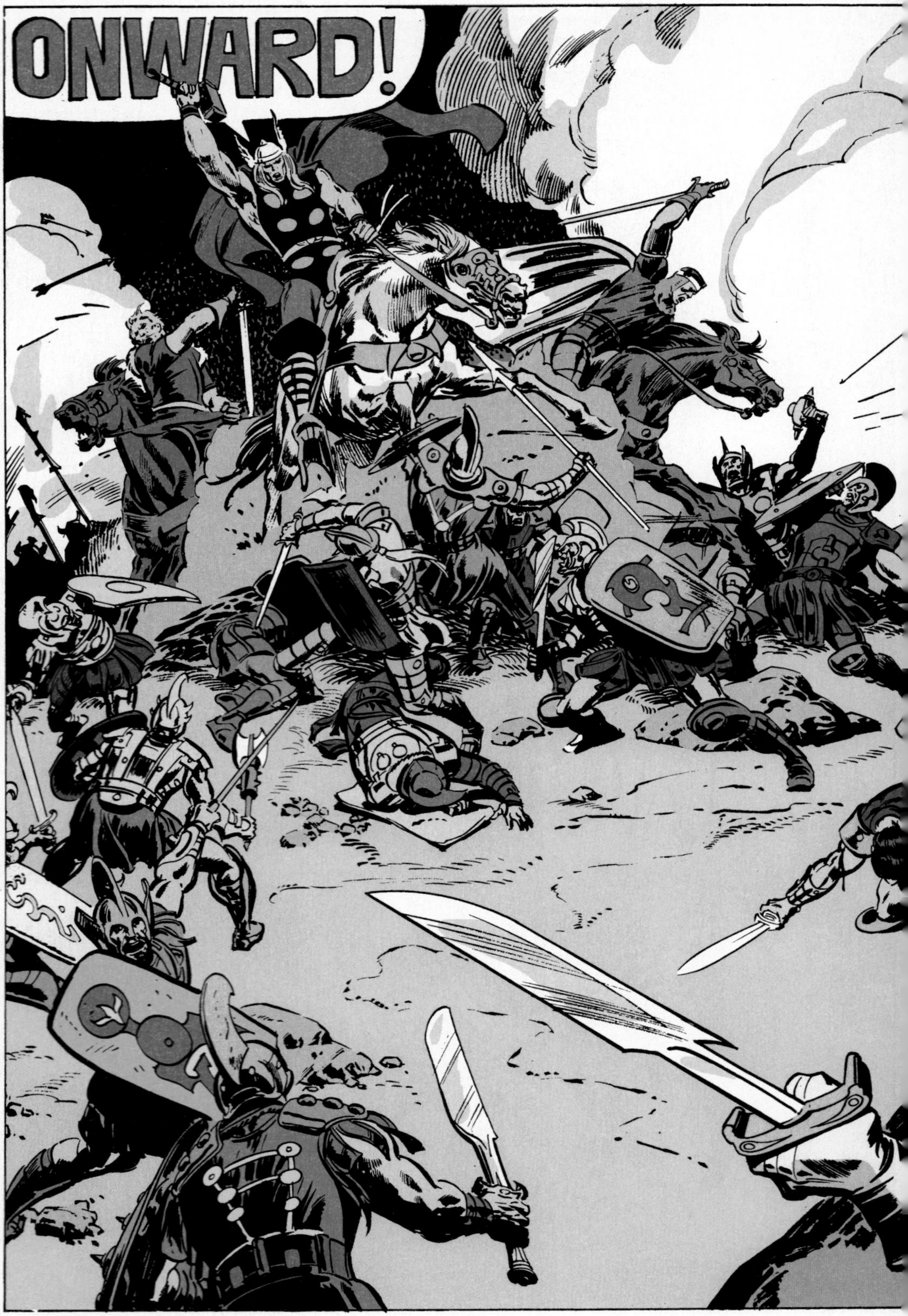
ONWARD!

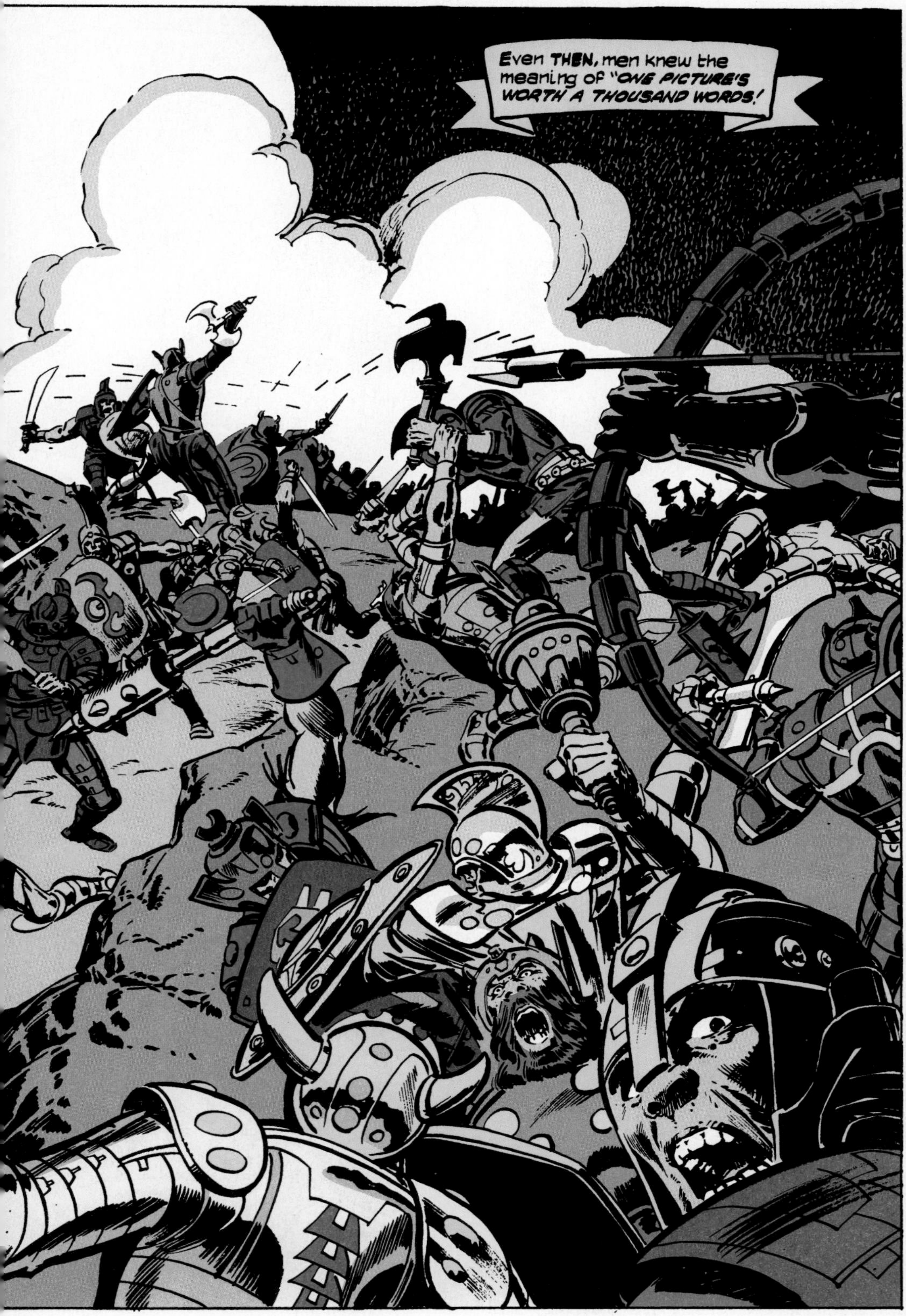
Even THEN, men knew the meaning of "ONE PICTURE'S WORTH A THOUSAND WORDS!

But words shall add to the TEXTURE!

THERE RIDETH AN *UNWARY VICTIM*, RIPE TO FEEL HIS *BRAINS* BURST BENEATH THE HARD-DRIVEN *BROAD-AXE OF ARES!*

NAY, CHURL! THOU DOST BOAST A BREATH *TOO SOON!*

ZOUNDS! HE DID HURL HIS *HORSE* INTO THE PATH OF *MINE!*

I STAND FOR *PEACE*, OLYMPIAN, BUT I'LL NOT LIE DOWN FOR *DEATH!*

I KNOW THY VISAGE *NOT* --

-- BUT THOU ART SURELY THE *GOD OF WAR!*

BAH! THOU COULDST BE ONE OF MY MILK-SOP ALLIES!

BY THE THREE-HEADED *SERPENT OF THRACE!* THESE *SOUTHERNERS* BE *ENDLESS!*

AYE, HOGUN! LOVELY, EH?

OH, THAT MY *STALLION'S PRANCING* SHOULD NOT DISTRACT MY *AIM* SO!

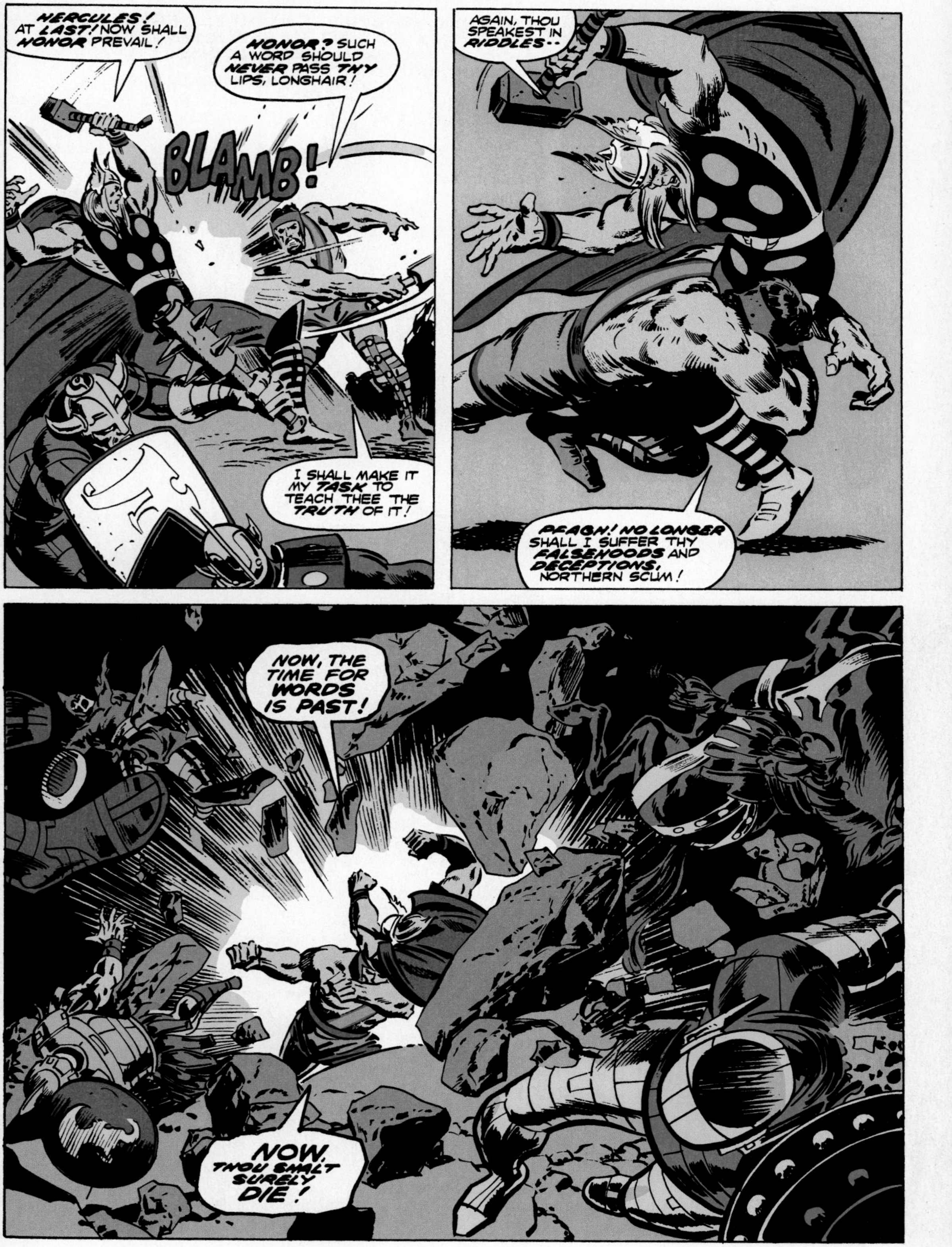
HERCULES! AT LAST! NOW SHALL HONOR PREVAIL!
HONOR? SUCH A WORD SHOULD NEVER PASS THY LIPS, LONGHAIR!
BLAMB!
I SHALL MAKE IT MY TASK TO TEACH THEE THE TRUTH OF IT!
AGAIN, THOU SPEAKEST IN RIDDLES--
PFAGH! NO LONGER SHALL I SUFFER THY FALSEHOODS AND DECEPTIONS, NORTHERN SCUM!
NOW, THE TIME FOR WORDS IS PAST!
NOW, THOU SHALT SURELY DIE!

On **ALL FRONTS**, many battles take their **TOLL**, piling **BODY** over **BODY** like **CORD WOOD** in the **AUTUMN**! **STILL**, the battles do not **SLOW**!

Upon a **storm-swept HILL**, a figure closely wrapped against the deadly **CHILL** is waiting... watching...

...never moving, until a **SECOND** figure, **SIMILARLY** swaddled, steps slowly from the swarming mists.

They do not **SPEAK**.

They do not **AID** their **FELLOWS**. Or even render them **FURTHER NOTICE**.

In actual **FACT**, it would appear that they do **NOTHING**...

...and yet, **ONE LOOK** is **LIKEWISE** worth a thousand words.

In that look, the battle hangs **SUSPENDED**--

--MEASURED and IMMEASURABLE 'gainst the **STAR-VAULT** all around.

There is more at **STAKE** here than the lives of mere **IMMORTALS**.

They **LOOK AWAY**. They **PART**.

The battle **GOES ON**.

Fire breaks out near misdirected **FLAME-ARROWS**, spilling **RED SHADOWS** where the **SUN** threw **NONE**! **STILL**, the slaughter **CONTINUES**...

...into the **EVENING**, and all of the following **DAY**...

...until, at the time of the sun's **SECOND SETTING**, the fury of it **ENDS**.

A **HORN** is heard, raised in **TRIUMPH**...

...an **ASGARDIAN** horn.

Here and there, across the **HORIZON**, bent figures loom in still and lonely splendor. These are the **SURVIVORS**.

The **HORIZON** IS the **OTHERS**.

Then, **FAINTLY** at first, but swiftly growing **LOUDER**, the rush of **MIGHTY WINGS** fills the empty, whistling skies. Down from the **OUTER WORLDS**, the **VALKYRIES** come riding--

--sent forth by **ODIN** to gather up all those who fell. Their task is **TREMENDOUS**.

Tonight, the halls of **VALHALLA** will **FLOW** with **MEAD**!

THERE, BUT FOR THE GRACE OF THE *ALL-FATHER*, GO WE...

...BUT I AM REMINDED THAT *ONE DAY*, WE ALL SHALL FOLLOW YON WARRIOR-MAIDS TO THE LANDS BEYOND *LIGHT* AND *DARKNESS!*

THAT DAY SHALL BE *RAGNAROK*, WHEN ALL OF *CREATION* SHALL BE SWEPT AWAY!

THE *MIDGARD SERPENT* SHALL RISE FROM THE SEAS, TO SPREAD *POISON* THROUGHOUT THE *UNIVERSE!* ODIN SHALL DIE, AND I, HIS *SON*, SHALL AVENGE HIM-- YET NOT BEFORE I, TOO, AM *TAINTED* WITH THE SERPENT'S VENOM!

THE GLORY OF THE *IMMORTALS* SHALL BE AS THE *LEAVES OF WINTER*, CRUMBLING INTO THE *PAST!*

OR SO IT IS *FORETOLD!*

TODAY WAS *NOT* THAT DAY, MY COMRADES-- BUT IT WAS *NEAR ENOUGH* FOR ME!

YEA, WE HAVE *TRIUMPHED*, BUT I *WONDER* NOW, IF THE *CAUSE* WAS WORTH THIS *COST!*

CHAPTER THREE

THE SPOILS OF WAR!

...AND *SO,* MY SON, THOU HAST REACHED THE GOAL TOWARD WHICH THOU DIDST *ASPIRE!*

BAH! E'EN *NOW,* OUR FATHER HATH STOLEN A *MARCH* ON THEE, THUNDER GOD!

THAT I *HAVE,* NOBLE ODIN! PERHAPS, IN *THIS* INSTANCE, THE *SON* HATH PROVEN WISER THAN THE *LIEGE!*

OLD MAY HE BE, BUT *NONE* HATH BETTER CLAIM TO THE *MANTLE OF POWER* HE YET *LIGHTLY* DOTH WEAR!

SILENCE, LOKI!

THY BROTHER'S *SMOOTH TONGUE* DOTH HOPE TO HIDE HIS *GUILT* IN THE *GOADING* OF THINE ENEMIES TO THEIR *DEATHS!* 'TWAS *ME* WHO DID FORCE THE *OLYMPIANS'* HAND IN THE END!

HOW IS IT--

--THAT I DO *KNOW* OF THIS? *GREAT* ARE THE POWERS OF ODIN, MY SON, AND *MYSTERIOUS* HIS *MANNER!* SHOULDST THOU PROVE THYSELF ONE DAY *WORTHY,* MAYHAP I SHALL *EXPLAIN!*

IN THE *INTERIM* ...

...I DO *RECOG-NIZE* THY VICTORY, AND THE *VALOR* WITH WHICH IT WAS *WON!*

AND THAT IS *ALL?* WILT THOU NOT PROCLAIM THY *PLEASURE* AT THIS *PERPETUATION* OF OUR GLORY?

MY SON...

...I HAVE *SPOKEN!*

THEN-- *SO BE IT!* I DO KNOW THAT WHAT HATH OCCURRED WAS TO THE *GOOD*, FOR ASGARD AND FOR MYSELF!

SHOULDST *THOU* PROVE THYSELF ONE DAY LESS *HIDEBOUND*, MAYHAP THOU WILL GRANT *ME* AND MY *COMRADES* THE HONORS DUE US!

LEAVE ME, THOR! LEAVE ME, ERE THOU DOST FORGET THYSELF *ENTIRE*--

--AND *I* FORGET *MYSELF!*

It would not *DO* to laugh in the *ALL-FATHER'S* face, but *NOT* to do so requires *ALL* of Thor's *STRENGTH*. The prophesies of *RAGNAROK* are *FAR AWAY*; the prophesies of the *PRINCE* becoming *KING* much *NEARER*. It could *EVEN BE* that the time is *CLOSE TO HAND!*

AFTER ALL, Odin had *STOPPED* with the *ORDERING* of the world. He has never *ENLARGED* the Asgardians' domains.

But as the *PEOPLE* cheer his *COMING*, THOR begins to realize that that is just what *HE'S* done.

And *ODIN* must realize it too.

COME, MY FRIENDS! LET US SEE WHAT IT IS WE HAVE *WON* WITH OUR TRIALS!

BIFROST CAN CONDUCT US TO THE FRINGES OF *MIDGARD* ONCE MORE--

--AND MY *CHARIOT* can carry us to the *SOUTHERN FIELDS!*

Never, in *ALL THE EONS*, have the heavens shone forth in such *SPLENDOR!* Even the *HE-GOATS* sense the euphoria emanating from the golden craft they draw--

--and *RACE* that much more *SWIFTLY* down the star-dappled winds, to see what waits *AHEAD!*

What *WAITS* is *GREECE*, a *GOLDEN* LAND...

...*DAZZLING* to slit-eyes grown hard against the endless northern *CHILL!*

Here, the women are *SOFT*...

...the men *HANDSOME* and TAN.

Here, a land of *UNDREAMT PLEASURES* waits for the word of *THOR THE MIGHTY!*

GOOD FOLK OF THE GRECIAN ISLES! I DO COME BEFORE THEE THIS DAY--

I SAY, GOOD FOLK OF THE GRECIAN ISLES!

HOW PASSING *STRANGE!* THEY DO SEEM *INDISPOSED* TO PAY ME *HEED!* I'LL HAVE NONE OF *THIS!*

WE--

STAND OUT OF MY *WAY,* BUFFOON! THIS IS A *PUBLIC* THOROUGHFARE!

ONE WOULD THINK *BARBARIANS* WOULD LEARN OUR *WAYS* ERE ENTERING GLORIOUS *ATHENS!*

ODIN'S BLOOD! THE *INSOLENCE* OF THE MAN!

MAYHAP, THESE FOLK MAY NOT YET *KNOW* THE GODS THEY MUST NOW WORSHIP--

--BUT SUCH INSUFFERABLE ARROGANCE MUST BE PUT ARIGHT *AT ONCE!* I SHALL SHOW THEM THE POWER OF *THOR!*

CHURN, HEAVENS! SWIRL--

--CLOUDS?

NAUGHT TRANSPIRETH!

MY POWER HATH *FLED!*

BRAGI! THOR HATH *RETURNED!* AND DIDST THOU SPY THE *THUNDER* IN HIS STRIDE?

HE DOTH ENTER THE *ODIN-KEEP!* THIS DOTH BODE *ILL!*

AH, *THOR!* RETURNED SO *SOON* FROM THY REWARDS?

FATHER, I SHALL HAVE A *RECKONING!* YEA, NO MATTER FROM *WHOM* IT MUST BE *TAKEN!* I HAVE SUFFERED A MOST *CRUEL* AND *UNJUST WRONG!*

42

EVEN THE *ALL-FATHER* HATH NO RIGHT TO STEAL AWAY THAT WHICH I HAVE WON WITH MINE *OWN HANDS!*

I QUITE *AGREE,* MY SON!

OH, INFAMOUS *BLACK-GUARD!* I SHALL BROOK NO *LIES--!*

HOLD THY TONGUE, STRIPLING!

NAY! I--

HOLD IT, I SAY! DIS-OBEY ME IN THIS INSTANCE AT THINE EXTREME *PERIL,* THOR!

DOST THOU *UNDERSTAND?*

DOST THOU *UNDERSTAND??*

AYE!

THEN SPEAK *NO MORE,* 'TIL I HAVE ONCE AGAIN GRANTED MY *PERMISSION!* ODIN YET RULETH IN ASGARD, AND THOU SHALT *NEVER AGAIN FORGET THAT!*

PREVIOUSLY, I HAVE *PERMITTED* THEE THY WILL, FOR REASONS OF *MINE OWN!* 'TWAS MY DESIRE THAT THOU MIGHT'ST *LEARN* SOMETHING, AND NOW WE SHALL DISCOVER IF THOU *HAST!*

THOR, WE BE IMMORTALS OF THE *NORTH!* THOU KNOWEST *ONLY TOO WELL* THAT WE SUSTAIN THE *VIKINGS--*

--YET IN A *VERY REAL* SENSE, THE *VIKINGS* LIKEWISE SUSTAIN *US!*

GODS BELIEVE IN *MEN,* AND *MEN* BELIEVE IN *GODS!* THEIR *OWN* GODS! 'TWAS *EVER* THUS!

GREECE CANNOT BE "WON" BY SUCH AS US! IT DOTH EXIST FOR THE *OLYMPIANS, BECAUSE* OF THE *OLYMPIANS!*

I DIDST MEET WITH *ZEUS* HIMSELF DURING THY WAR! 'TWAS AGREED THAT THOUGH IT BE *PAINFUL* TO US *BOTH,* THERE WAS A *LESSON* BOTH LANDS NEED LEARN!

THEY TOO, BELIEVED *THEY CONQUERED!* AND THEY TOO DISCOVERED THAT EVEN *TOTAL CONQUEST* AVAILETH THEM *NAUGHT!* WHILE MEN OF OUR LANDS BELIEVE WE EXIST, OUR POWER AND OUR LIVES ARE BEYOND THE *OLYMPIANS* REACH!

LIKEWISE, *THEY* CANNOT END BY *OUR* DEVICES!

THERE IS *MORE* TO THE RULING OF REALM THAN THY *NOT MEAD* E'ER IMAGINED, MY SON! WOULDST THOU NOT *AGREE*?

Thor says not a *WORD*--but he must *STALK AWAY*--

--before the *FURY* in his booming *HEART* bursts forth in *RINGING ROARS*!

I WAS *DECEIVED! DECEIVED!* HE DID ALLOW ME TO PAINT MYSELF THE *FOOL*, ALL THE WHILE CONVINCING ME THAT *HE* WAS RIPE FOR MOTLEY!

I THOUGHT MYSELF SO *RIGHTEOUS*-- SO *DARING*!

THOR! OH, THOR!

EH--? THE *NORN QUEEN*!

THIS IS *NOT SO*!

WHAT WILT THOU, SORCERESS? I HAVE *NO TIME* FOR ANY TALES *TODAY*!

COME--*SIT!* I KNOW OF THY *TROUBLED SOUL*, AS, IN TRUTH, I KNOW *ALL*!

THIS DAY, THOU HAST COME TO KNOW THY *FIRST LIMITATIONS!* NAUGHT COULD BE *WORSE* FOR THE SON OF *ODIN*!

YET BE OF *STOUT HEART*!

IN *TIME TO COME*, THE VIKINGS SHALL TRAVEL TO *ALL ENDS OF THE EARTH*, CARRYING *WITH* THEM THE TALES OF *THY POWER AND GLORY!*

IN *TIME TO COME*, ALL PEOPLES WILL COME TO KNOW THEE, AND *THEN*--

--THOU SHALT WALK WITH *FULL POWER, WHEREVER THOU WILT*, IN THE COMPANY OF MEN WHOSE *VISIONS* I NOW *INVOKE!*

THEY SHALL BE CALLED--

AVENGERS!

THIS IS MY *PROPHESY!* THOU *KNOWEST* THAT I AM *NEVER* IN *ERROR!*

SO LET NOT THY HEART BE *HARDENED!*

GO *FORTH* ONCE MORE, SECURE THAT THOU HAST LOST *NAUGHT* IN THY WARS--

--SAVE *IGNORANCE!*

AYE, MILADY!

AYE!

There is nothing more to SAY...

...except to HIMSELF.

I am YOUNG, YET! Her CONJURINGS, more than AUGHT ELSE, have caused me to realize HOW YOUNG!

And AS SUCH, I cannot be EXPECTED to understand ALL!

BUT THOUGH THERE MUST be MANY TRIALS REMAINING, of which I have NO NOTION, I shall NOT meet them as I did THIS LAST!

I am YOUNG, but I grow OLDER! AGE will bring WISDOM with it! IN THIS, AT LEAST, I need have NO DOUBT—

—FOR WHEN ALL is said and done—

—I am THE SON OF ODIN! THE GOD OF THUNDER!

THOR, THE MIGHTY!

FINIS

46

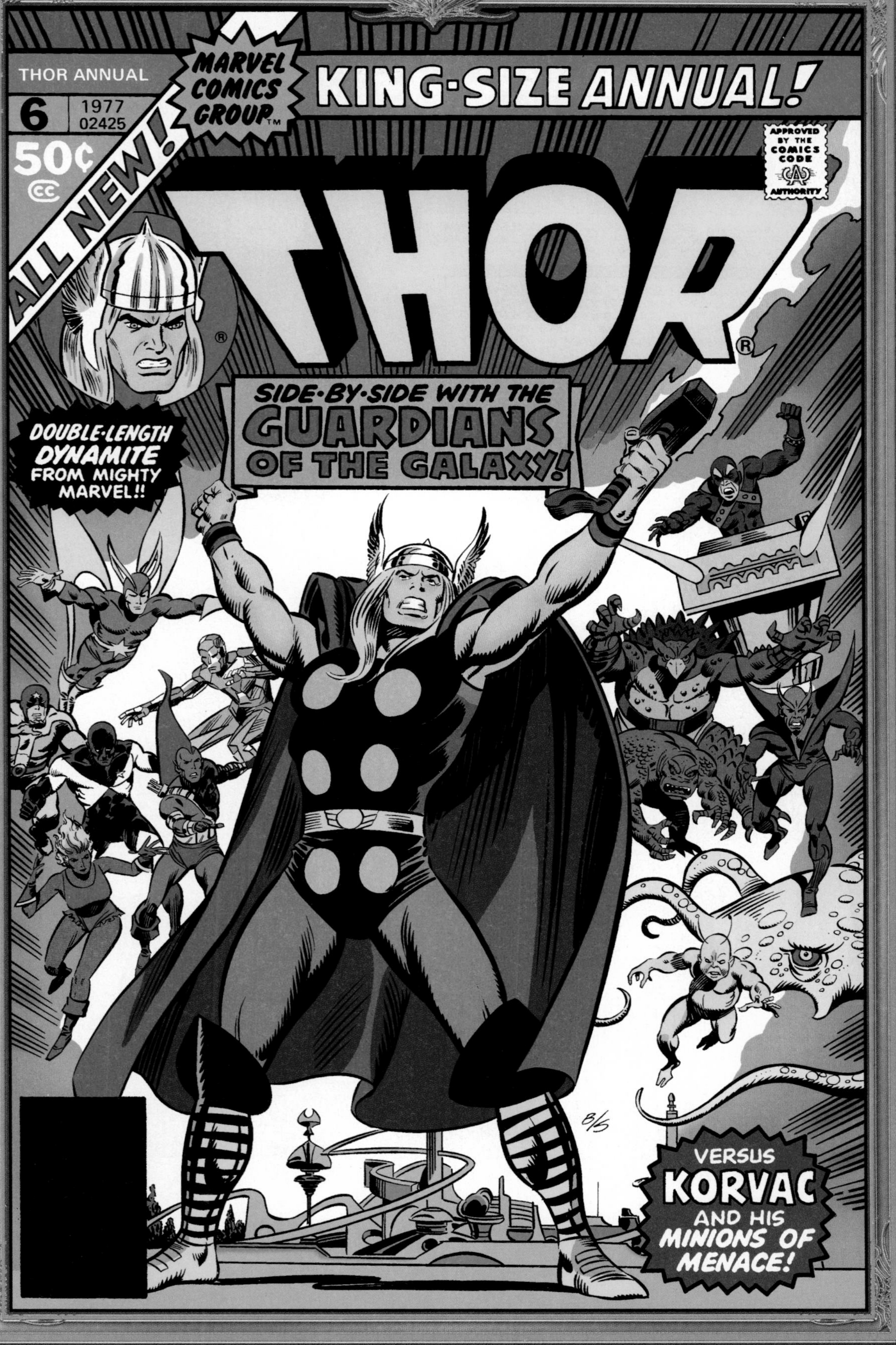
THOR ANNUAL
6
1977
02425
50¢
CC
ALL NEW!
MARVEL COMICS GROUP
KING-SIZE ANNUAL!
APPROVED BY THE COMICS CODE AUTHORITY
THOR
SIDE-BY-SIDE WITH THE
GUARDIANS
OF THE GALAXY!
DOUBLE-LENGTH DYNAMITE FROM MIGHTY MARVEL!!
VERSUS
KORVAC
AND HIS
MINIONS OF MENACE!

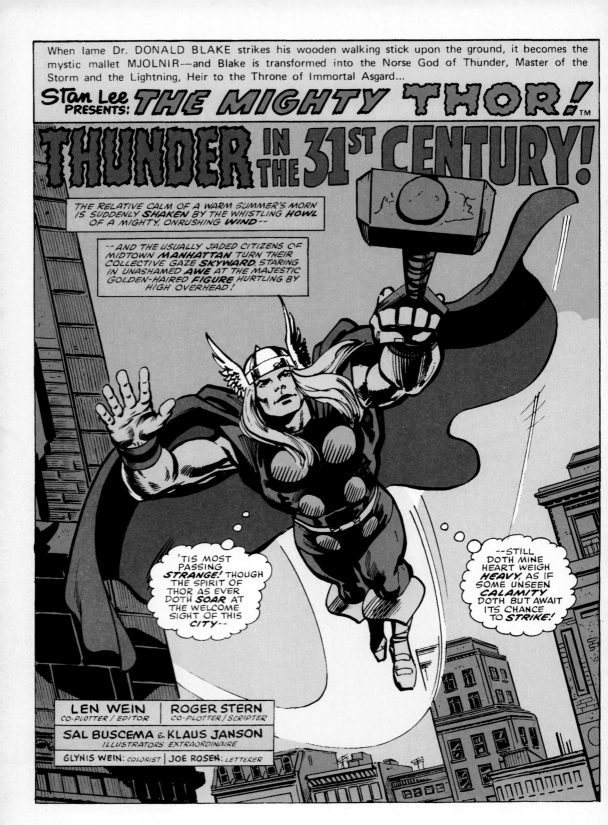

When lame Dr. DONALD BLAKE strikes his wooden walking stick upon the ground, it becomes the mystic mallet MJOLNIR—and Blake is transformed into the Norse God of Thunder, Master of the Storm and the Lightning, Heir to the Throne of Immortal Asgard...

Stan Lee PRESENTS: THE MIGHTY THOR! ™

THUNDER IN THE 31ST CENTURY!

THE RELATIVE CALM OF A WARM SUMMER'S MORN IS SUDDENLY SHAKEN BY THE WHISTLING HOWL OF A MIGHTY, ONRUSHING WIND--

--AND THE USUALLY JADED CITIZENS OF MIDTOWN MANHATTAN TURN THEIR COLLECTIVE GAZE SKYWARD, STARING IN UNASHAMED AWE AT THE MAJESTIC GOLDEN-HAIRED FIGURE HURTLING BY HIGH OVERHEAD!

'TIS MOST PASSING STRANGE! THOUGH THE SPIRIT OF THOR AS EVER DOTH SOAR AT THE WELCOME SIGHT OF THIS CITY--

--STILL DOTH MINE HEART WEIGH HEAVY, AS IF SOME UNSEEN CALAMITY DOTH BUT AWAIT ITS CHANCE TO STRIKE!

LEN WEIN CO-PLOTTER / EDITOR | ROGER STERN CO-PLOTTER / SCRIPTER

SAL BUSCEMA & KLAUS JANSON ILLUSTRATORS EXTRAORDINAIRE

GLYNIS WEIN: COLORIST | JOE ROSEN: LETTERER

48

BY ODIN! METHINKS MY FEARS HATH TOO SOON BORNE *FRUIT!* THE AUTHORITIES DOTH LAY *SIEGE* TO YONDER BUILDING!

...AND I CAN FAIRLY TASTE THE *FEAR* IN THE AIR!

ROXXON NUCLEONICS

CAREFUL, MEN-- WE DON'T WANT TO *PROVOKE* THEM--!

CLEARLY, MINE AID BE *NEEDED* HERE!

CAPTAIN-- *LOOK!*

JOHNSON, I *TOLD* YOU NOT TO... *HUH?*

WELL, IT'S ABOUT *TIME!*

HOW MAY THOR *ASSIST* THEE, OFFICER?

GOLDILOCKS, YOU GOTTA BE *KIDDING!* WE'VE GOT A HALF-DOZEN *TERRORISTS* BOTTLED UP IN THERE WITH AN *ACTIVE NUCLEAR REACTOR!*

WE DON'T GET 'EM OUT *FAST*-- AND WE CAN KISS THIS CITY *GOOD-BYE!*

THEN I PRAY THEE, GOOD SIR-- CALL THY MEN *ASIDE!*

THE *GOD OF THUNDER* SHALL ATTEND TO THIS--

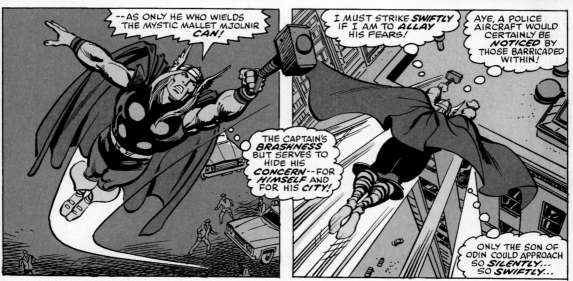

--AS ONLY HE WHO WIELDS THE MYSTIC MALLET MJOLNIR *CAN!*

THE CAPTAIN'S *BRASHNESS* BUT SERVES TO HIDE HIS *CONCERN*--FOR *HIMSELF* AND FOR HIS *CITY!*

I MUST STRIKE *SWIFTLY* IF I AM TO *ALLAY* HIS FEARS!

AYE, A POLICE AIRCRAFT WOULD CERTAINLY BE *NOTICED* BY THOSE BARRICADED WITHIN!

ONLY THE SON OF ODIN COULD APPROACH SO *SILENTLY*... SO *SWIFTLY*...

...AND THUS STRIKE WITH TOTAL SURPRISE!!

KRA-KOOM!

HOLY--!?!

IT'S WHAT'S-HIS-NAME--!!

THAT THUNDER GUY!!

THAT DOES IT, MAN! WE WARNED THOSE FOOLS ABOUT RUSHING US!

THE BLOOD WILL BE ON THEIR HANDS NOW!

WE DIE-- FOR THE CAUSE!!

THOR DOTH SAY THEE NAY, FOOLISH ONE! SO LONG AS MIGHTY MJOLNIR BE MINE TO COMMAND--

--THERE SHALL BE NO USELESS DEATH HERE THIS DAY!

"NOT EVEN THINE OWN!"

THRANG!

NO.

NOW LAY DOWN THINE ARMS, KNAVES! THOU SHALT THREATEN THIS FAIR CITY NO LONGER!

NO! WE'VE COME TOO FAR-- RISKED TOO MUCH! THE COPS'LL NEVER KNOW THAT REACTOR IS HARMLESS NOW--

--IF YOU'RE NOT ALIVE TO TELL THEM!!

WASTE 'IM, GUYS!!

BLAM!

BLAM!

BLAM!

POW!

CHURLS! HOWEVER NOBLE MIGHT BE THY CAUSE, THOU DOST DEMEAN IT BY THY COWARDLY ACTIONS!

SPOW!

SPWEE

SPOW!

50

VERILY, I SHALL **PERMIT** THY MINDLESS VIOLENCE **NO LONGER!!**

THROOM!

AND THE **SHOCKWAVE** GENERATED BY THE MIGHTY URU HAMMER COULD BE **RIVALED** ONLY BY THE POUNDING **FISTS** OF A CERTAIN **GREEN GOLIATH!**

I-IT'S **HOPELESS!** WE JUST CAN'T **FIGHT** HIM-- HE'S TOO **POWERFUL!**

AYE-- AND GIVE **THANKS**, THOU CRAVEN VARLETS, THAT THE SON OF ODIN DOTH **RESPECT** LIFE MORE THAN **THEE**...

...OR THOU WOULDST SIT AT THE LEFT HAND OF THE DEATH-GODDESS **HELA** ERE THIS BATTLE BE **DONE!**

Y-YOU JUST DON'T **UNDERSTAND**... HOW **COULD** YOU?

HOW COULD A **GOD** EVER **BEGIN** TO KNOW THE **HARDSHIP** -- THE **INJUSTICE** WE FACE EVERY DAY?

AND TO **AVENGE** THE INJUSTICES DONE THEE, THOU WOULDST SNUFF OUT THE **LIVES OF 10 MILLION PEOPLE?**

IF THY **CAUSE** COMES BEFORE EVEN **LIFE ITSELF**, THEN WHERE, PRITHEE, IS **ITS** JUSTICE?

NO-- **WAIT!** LOOK-- OVER **THERE!**

"SOMETHIN'S **HAPPENIN'** TO THE **REACTOR!** IT'S STARTIN' TO **GLOW** LIKE IT WAS ON **FIRE!**"

WHAT--?!? BY ASGARD, IF THIS BE **THY** DOING, KNAVE...

N-NO! YA GOTTA **BELIEVE** ME! IT'S THE **REACTOR** ITSELF--!

A STRAY **SHOT** MUST'VE **HIT** IT! IT'S **OVERLOADING!**

IT'S GONNA **BLOW!!**

THEN PRAY THERE DOTH BE SOME WAY TO **STOP** IT, KNAVE--

--OR SURELY **HELA** SHALL CLAIM US **ALL!!**

BY THE NORN! WHAT **WIZARDRY** IS THIS?

THE **GLOWING** COMES NOT FROM **WITHIN** THE REACTOR, BUT FROM **WITHOUT!**

STILL MUST I ATTEMPT TO...

THE SENTENCE GOES **UNFINISHED.** FOR SUDDENLY, THE AIR FAIRLY **CRACKLES** WITH ELDRITCH ENERGIES UNLEASHED-- THE ACRID STENCH OF **OZONE** FILLS THE CHAMBER, AND THEN...

SWEET **HEAVEN--** **NO!!**

I DIDN'T **KNOW** IT WOULD BE LIKE **THIS**-- NOT LIKE **THIS!!**

THAKOOOM!

AND WHEN THE **POLICE** BURST IN, MOMENTS LATER...

WELL, WHADDAYA **KNOW**? LOOKS LIKE THAT NUCLEAR FIRECRACKER DIDN'T GO BOOM **AFTER ALL**-- NOW, **DID** IT?

THERE'S THE **TERRORISTS,** ALL LAID OUT NICE AND **NEAT!**

BUT WHERE'S THAT BLASTED LONG-HAIRED **AVENGER** GONE TO?

C-CAPTAIN?

"I--AH--THINK I KNOW THE **ANSWER** TO THAT, SIR...

"...AND I **DON'T** THINK YOU'RE GOING TO **LIKE** IT!"

AND EVEN AS THE STUPIFIED POLICE CAPTAIN STARES AT THE SMOLDERING *HOLE* IN THE LABORATORY FLOOR IN SLACK-JAWED *WONDER*, THE MIGHTY THOR BLINKS BACK INTO *REALITY*...

...ALBEIT, A DRASTICALLY *DIFFERENT* REALITY BY FAR!

X MINUS

301

HEIMDALL'S *EYES!* WH-WHERE AM I?

EH? WHAT'S *THIS?*

MY *TIME PROBE* WASN'T SUPPOSED TO PICK UP *PASSENGERS!*

AY? I SEE THEE IN THE *SHADOWS!* WHAT MANNER OF BEING *ART* THOU?

I MIGHT WELL ASK THE SAME OF *YOU*-- BUT MY *DATA-BANKS* WILL SUPPLY THE ANSWER MUCH *FASTER!*

AND INSTANTS *LATER*...

WHAT *NONSENSE* IS THIS? THERE MUST BE A *CIRCUIT MALFUNCTION* SOME-WHERE!

SUBJECT IDENTIFICATION...
NAME: THOR...
DESIGNATION: GOD OF THUNDER...
AGE: DOES NOT COMPUTE...
DANGER!...*DANGER!*...

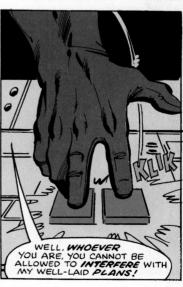

KLIK

WELL, *WHOEVER* YOU ARE, YOU CANNOT BE ALLOWED TO *INTERFERE* WITH MY WELL-LAID *PLANS!*

WHAT--? THOU DOST ATTACK WITHOUT *CAUSE*-- WITHOUT *PROVOCATION*?

SPAKT!

WHOEVER THOU ART, JACKAL-- THOU HAST SHOWN THY *TRUE COLORS*...

...BUT NOT *ALL* THY FEARSOME *FIRE-BOLTS* CAN MATCH THE *FURY* OF MINE OWN ENCHANTED *HAMMER*!

SHRAKT!

I WANT *ANSWERS*, KNAVE, AND I SHALL *HAVE* THEM OR...

OR *NOTHING*!

AS *IMPOSSIBLE* AS IT *SEEMS*, IT APPEARS MY DATA-BANKS HAVE IDENTIFIED YOU *CORRECTLY*!

BUT *YOUR* LEGENDARY POWER MATTERS *LITTLE*--AGAINST POWER SUCH AS *THIS*!

KLIK!

BY ASGARD'S GLEAMING *SPIRES*! ONCE AGAIN, I...*FADE*!

BUT *WHITHER* AM I TO BE TRANSPORTED *THIS* TIME?

THE *ANSWER* TO THAT IS AT ONCE *OBVIOUS*...AND *UNBELIEVABLE*!

OD'S BLOOD! I AM *LOST*... IN THE VOID OF *DEEP SPACE*!

HIS WARRIOR'S BLOOD *POUNDING* BEHIND HIS TIGHTLY-CLENCHED *EYES*, THE ASGARDIAN AVENGER STRUGGLES TO MAINTAIN HIS *CONSCIOUSNESS*--

--IN HOPES OF FINDING SOME *RESPITE*, SOME *REFUGE*!

BUT IT IS A MOST *FUTILE* HOPE INDEED.

WITHIN MOMENTS, HE FEELS THE FRIGID DARKNESS *RUSHING IN* ON HIM...

...AND EVERYTHING SWIFTLY FADES TO *BLACK*!

BILLIONS OF KILOMETERS AWAY, FIVE INTREPID ADVENTURERS SEND THEIR NEW STARSHIP-- THE *FREEDOM'S LADY*--HURTLING THRU THE OUTERMOST REACHES OF THE *MILKY WAY.*

THEY ARE THE LAST OF THEIR *KIND,* THESE FIVE: *CHARLIE-27,* THE JOVIAN MILITIAMAN... *MARTINEX,* THE CRYSTAL MAN OF PLUTO... *NIKKI,* THE FLAME-TRESSED MERCURIAN... *YONDU,* LAST OF THE ALPHA CENTAURI WEAPONS-MASTERS... AND *MAJOR VANCE ASTRO,* EARTH'S THOUSAND-YEAR-OLD SPACEMAN. TOGETHER THEY *PATROL* THIS SWIRLING PINWHEEL OF STARS--SELF-APPOINTED *PROTECTORS* OF LIFE AND LIBERTY!

CHAPTER TWO ▶ AND THEY SHALL BE GUARDIANS OF THE GALAXY™

JUST *LOOK* AT THAT KID! EVERY TIME I *SEE* HER, I FEEL LIKE I'M *BACK...*

AW, EYES *RIGHT,* ASTRO! YOU'RE JUST A FEW CENTURIES TOO *OLD* TO BE THINKING ABOUT *THAT* LITTLE LADY!

YOU'RE DOING *VERY WELL,* NIKKI! NOW BRING THE ENGINES UP TO *FULL.*

ATTA *GIRL,* SQUIRT! MARTY AND I'LL MAKE A HOTSHOT *PILOT* OUTTA YOU *YET!*

LISTEN, I'LL SETTLE FOR BEING A *WARM*SHOT! FLYING A FOUR-MAN SPACE YACHT IS *ONE* THING--

--BUT RIDING HERD ON *THIS* BATTLE WAGON IS SOMETHING *ELSE!*

AND OUTSIDE THE SHIP, A **SIXTH** GUARDIAN-- PERHAPS **PREFERRING** THE **SOLITUDE** OF SPACE--**PACES** THEIR FLIGHT.

THIS IS **STARHAWK**, THE **ENIGMATIC** ARCTURIAN **MUTANT**-- HEIR TO ALL THE POWER AND KNOWLEDGE OF AN ANCIENT **STAR-SPANNING** CIVILIZATION.

HE IS, SIMPLY, THE **"ONE WHO KNOWS!"**

BUT EVEN THE ALL-KNOWING STARHAWK IS **UNPREPARED** FOR THE SIZZLING **POWER BEAM** THAT SUDDENLY **STRIKES OUT** AT THE SHIP--

--CREATING **HAVOC** WITHIN HER!

NIKKI! FEED **MORE POWER** TO THE STARBOARD STABILIZERS-- **QUICKLY!!**

I- I'M **TRYING**-- BUT THERE'S NO **RESPONSE!**

NO WONDER-- **LOOK!**

"OUR INBOARD RELAY BANK HAS **BROKEN LOOSE!**"

BR **EEEEE**

IF THAT THING SHOULD TOPPLE **OVER**, WE COULD BE STUCK HERE FOR **DAYS!**

GOTTA STOP IT NOW!!

FOR VANCE ASTRO, THOUGHT QUITE **LITERALLY** BECOMES ACTION, AS A BOLT OF **PURE PSYCHO-KINETIC FORCE** LANCES OUT FROM HIS FOREHEAD--

--TO **HALT** THE FALLING MECHANISM IN ITS **TRACKS!**

GOOD MOVE, VANCE!

I CAN TAKE IT FROM HERE!

NO, CHARLIE-- **WAIT!** LOOK OUT FOR THE--

"--HIGH VOLTAGE CABLES!"

OBOY.

ZZZZZTT

CHARLIE! DON'T MOVE!

AND SO SAYING, YONDU SENDS A SOUND-SENSITIVE SHAFT OF *LIVING YAKA METAL* FLYING ACROSS THE CABIN.

THE FINNED GUARDIAN WHISTLES A *SINGLE* PIERCING NOTE, AND THE ARROW BEGINS TO *RESPOND*--

--*SPEARING* THE DEADLY ELECTRO-CABLES, *WRAPPING* THEM UP--

--AND TYING THEM *OFF*, SAFELY *OUT* OF THE JOVIAN'S WAY!

THANKS FOR THE *ASSIST*, YON! BEING *ELECTROCUTED* WOULD'VE *RUINED* MY WHOLE DAY!

AND SHORTLY...

THAT'S *IT*, CHARLIE! A LITTLE TO THE *LEFT* NOW-- *THERE!*

A SPOT OF *WELDING*, AND SHE'LL BE GOOD AS *NEW*.

BOY, WE'RE BECOMING A REGULAR LITTLE *TEAM*, AREN'T WE?

HEY, SPEAKING OF *TEAMS*, WHERE'S *STARHAWK* BEEN DURING ALL OF THIS?

DON'T TELL ME BLUE BOY'S *ABANDONED* US AGAIN? *

*AS HE DID-- MORE OR LESS-- IN MARVEL PRESENTS #10.-- LEN.

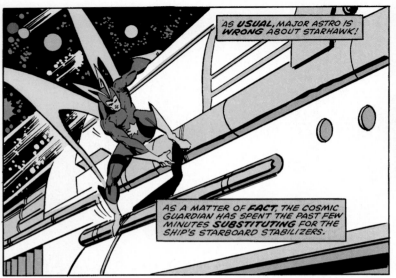

AS *USUAL*, MAJOR ASTRO IS *WRONG* ABOUT STARHAWK!

AS A MATTER OF *FACT*, THE COSMIC GUARDIAN HAS SPENT THE PAST FEW MINUTES *SUBSTITUTING* FOR THE SHIP'S STARBOARD STABILIZERS.

THE CRISIS NOW *OVER*, THE ONE-WHO-KNOWS STEPS UPON A CERTAIN SECTION OF THE OUTER HULL --

-- ACTIVATING THE STARCRAFT'S *TELEPORTATION* UNITS.

GUARDIANS! WE ARE *NEEDED!*

WELL! IT'S VERY *NICE* OF YOU TO *HONOR* US WITH YOUR *PRESENCE!*

JUST WHAT THE DEVIL *HAPPENED* OUT THERE?

SIMPLY *PUT*, MAJOR, WE INTERSECTED A POWER BEAM OF INCREDIBLE INTENSITY! HAD WE BEEN ANYWHERE NEAR ITS *FOCAL POINT*, WE WOULD HAVE BEEN COMPLETELY *DISINTEGRATED!*

SOMEONE, MY FRIENDS, IS PLAYING WITH *DEADLY* FORCES.

THEN I SUPPOSE IT'S UP TO *US* TO PLAY *SPACE COPS* AGAIN!

MARTY--?

I *READ* YOU, VANCE! WE'LL *FOLLOW* THAT BEAM RIGHT TO ITS *SOURCE!*

AND SO, WITH SHIP'S COMPUTERS *LOCKED* ONTO THE BEAM, THE MIGHTY STARSHIP TURNS ABOUT AND HEADS FOR THE AWESOME ENERGY TRAIL'S *POINT OF ORIGIN.*

BUT *AT* THAT POINT, THEIR SEARCH DOES NOT GO *UNNOTICED...*

SSSIR! SSSOMEONE *COMESSS!*

BLAST! THESE PETTY ANNOYANCES MUST *CEASE!*

I'VE ACCOMPLISHED *TOO MUCH* HERE! I WON'T *TOLERATE* ANY SNOOPERS INTERFERING WITH MY *POWER-SIPHON BEAM!*

KLIK!

AND WITH THE MEREST FLICK OF A *SWITCH,* DEEP SPACE SUDDENLY BECOMES *CROWDED* WITH ALL MANNER OF *ROCKY DEBRIS--*

--ALL OF IT *RUSHING* TOWARDS FREEDOM'S LADY AT *NEAR-LIGHT SPEED!*

MARTY! WHAT--?

METEOR STORM! BUT I'VE NEVER SEEN ONE *LIKE* IT!

HANG ON! PREPARE FOR *EVASIVE ACTION!*

HIS HANDS *FLYING* ACROSS THE CONTROLS, THE PLUVIAN SCIENCE OFFICER THROWS THE FREEDOM'S LADY INTO A *DESPERATE* PORT TURN--

--ONE NO STARSHIP WAS EVER *MEANT* TO PERFORM!

WOW! I KNEW WE WERE ON A *SHAKEDOWN* CRUISE, BUT THIS IS *RIDICULOUS!*

TO BE *SURE!* WE ESCAPED WITHOUT DAMAGE BY *CHANCE* MORE THAN ANYTHING ELSE.

UNFORTUNATELY, WE ARE NOW SEVERAL MILLION KILOMETERS *OFF COURSE.*

ODD! I CAN'T GET *OVER* THE *SUDDENNESS* OF THAT METEOR STORM!

THAT STORM WAS NO *ACCIDENT,* MARTINEX. IT WAS *DIRECTED* AT US!

WHAT? ARE YOU *SURE?*

I AM *ALWAYS* SURE-- AND SHIP'S SENSORS *CONFIRM* IT, YONDU.

OBVIOUSLY, *SOMEONE* DOES NOT WANT US TO *INVESTIGATE* THAT BEAM.

"I SUGGEST WE APPROACH THE *SOURCE-POINT* VIA A MORE *ROUND-ABOUT* ROUTE. *I* SHALL LEAD THE WAY."

AND SOON, THE MYSTERIOUS ARCTURIAN IS HURTLING THRU THE VOID, AS IF TO CLEAR A *PATH* FOR THE GIANT STARSHIP, HIS *SOLAR SAILS* FILLING WITH THE COLD STELLAR *WINDS.*

UNTIL...

WHAT? AN ICE-ENCRUSTED *HUMANOID?* WHAT *MANNER* OF GRISLY WARNING IS *THIS?*

INCREDIBLE! THIS BEING STILL *LIVES!*

BUT I SENSE THAT HE WILL *YET* PERISH IF HE DOES NOT REACH A FRIENDLY ENVIRONMENT-- AND *SWIFTLY!!*

IMPRESSED BY THE URGENT **CONDITION** OF HIS FIND, STARHAWK RACES **BACK** TO THE HAVEN OF THE WAITING STARSHIP...

...WHERE, SOON...

BOY, YOU SURE CAN **PICK** 'EM, 'HAWK!

THIS IS NO TIME TO **JOKE**, NIKKI! BY ALL **RIGHTS**, THIS MAN SHOULD BE **DEAD!**

AMAZING! I'D ALMOST SWEAR--!

I **MYSELF** AM PUZZLED, MARTINEX. THE VERY **MOISTURE** OF HIS BODY SEEMS TO HAVE FROZEN ABOUT HIM LIKE A **SHEATH.**

CONSIDER THIS **TABLEAU.** OVER A **THOUSAND** YEARS PAST, A GROUP THEN CALLED THE **AVENGERS** WITNESSED THE RESURRECTION OF **CAPTAIN AMERICA** -- A HERO OUT OF HIS **TIME.**

NOW, HISTORY REPEATS ITSELF!

WAIT-A-MINUTE! I- I **RECOGNIZE** THIS GUY FROM PICTURES I SAW AS A **BOY!** HE'S ONE OF THE GREATEST **HEROES** OF MY **CENTURY!**

"THIS IS **THOR** -- THE **GOD OF THUNDER!**"

AYE... 'TIS... TRUE.

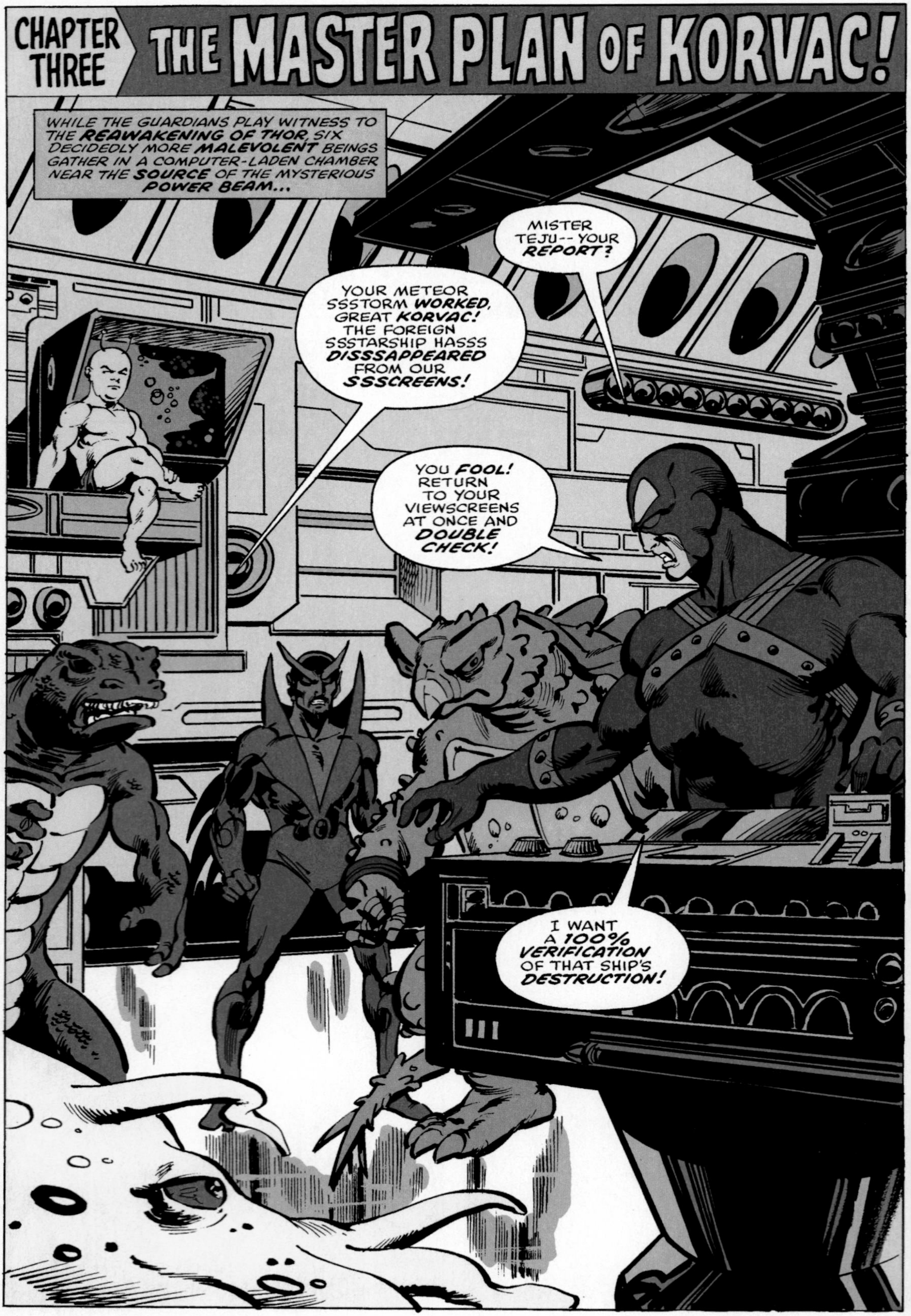
CHAPTER THREE
THE MASTER PLAN OF KORVAC!
WHILE THE GUARDIANS PLAY WITNESS TO THE REAWAKENING OF THOR, SIX DECIDEDLY MORE MALEVOLENT BEINGS GATHER IN A COMPUTER-LADEN CHAMBER NEAR THE SOURCE OF THE MYSTERIOUS POWER BEAM...
MISTER TEJU-- YOUR REPORT?
YOUR METEOR SSSTORM WORKED, GREAT KORVAC! THE FOREIGN SSSTARSHIP HASSS DISSSAPPEARED FROM OUR SSSCREENS!
YOU FOOL! RETURN TO YOUR VIEWSCREENS AT ONCE AND DOUBLE CHECK!
I WANT A 100% VERIFICATION OF THAT SHIP'S DESTRUCTION!

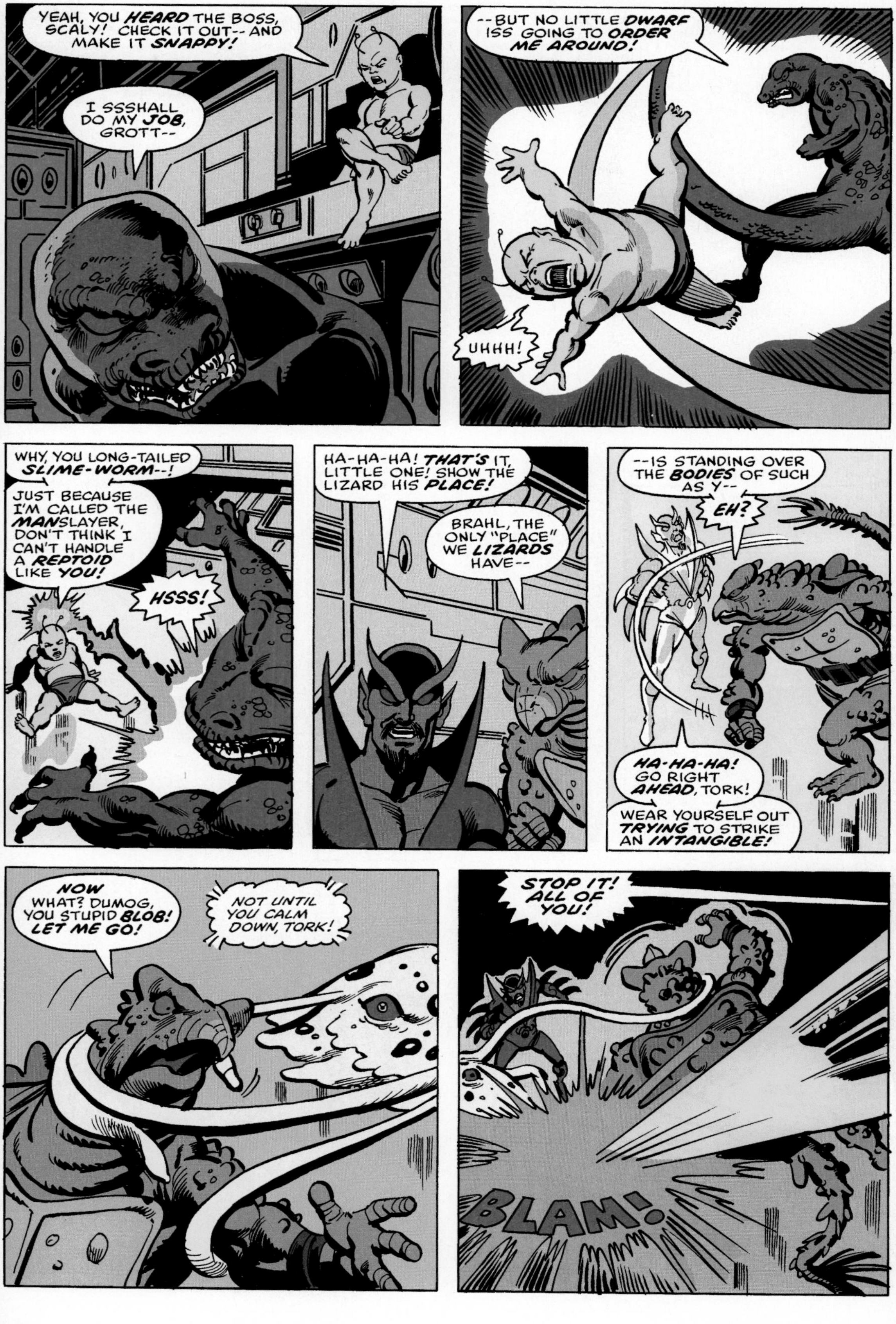
YEAH, YOU HEARD THE BOSS, SCALY! CHECK IT OUT-- AND MAKE IT SNAPPY!
I SSSHALL DO MY JOB, GROTT--
--BUT NO LITTLE DWARF ISS GOING TO ORDER ME AROUND!
UHHH!
WHY, YOU LONG-TAILED SLIME-WORM--!
JUST BECAUSE I'M CALLED THE MANSLAYER, DON'T THINK I CAN'T HANDLE A REPTOID LIKE YOU!
HSSS!
HA-HA-HA! THAT'S IT, LITTLE ONE! SHOW THE LIZARD HIS PLACE!
BRAHL, THE ONLY "PLACE" WE LIZARDS HAVE--
--IS STANDING OVER THE BODIES OF SUCH AS Y--
EH?
HA-HA-HA! GO RIGHT AHEAD, TORK!
WEAR YOURSELF OUT TRYING TO STRIKE AN INTANGIBLE!
NOW WHAT? DUMOG, YOU STUPID BLOB! LET ME GO!
NOT UNTIL YOU CALM DOWN, TORK!
STOP IT! ALL OF YOU!
BLAM!

I SHALL BROOK **NO DISSENSION** IN THE RANKS! YOU WILL ALL **CALM** YOURSELVES--

--OR YOU SHALL FACE THE FULL, UNFETTERED FURY OF **KORVAC!**

SILENCE FALLS LIKE A **CURTAIN** OVER THE CHAMBER. FOR ONE CHILLING MOMENT, NONE OF THE FIVE UNDERLINGS **DARE** TO SPEAK, BUT THEN...

MEANING NO **DISRESPECT,** SIR -- BUT WE **ARE** STILL IN THE **DARK** AS TO THE EXACT **NATURE** OF YOUR PROJECT.

IF YOU COULD JUST **EXPLAIN...**

VERY WELL, **DUMOG**-- YOU SHALL **HAVE** YOUR EXPLANATION!

MY RISE TO **POWER** BEGAN SOME EIGHT YEARS AGO. I WAS JUST A **COMPUTER-TECHNO** THEN.

"MY SUPERIORS HAD **CONSTANTLY** REFUSED TO RECOGNIZE THE SCOPE OF MY **ABILITIES.** THUS, WHEN THE **BADOON** INVADED THE SOLAR SYSTEM, I GLADLY BECAME A **COLLABORATOR.**

"SOON I WAS **IN CHARGE** OF ANALYTICAL SYSTEMS FOR **ENTIRE PLANETS!**

"UNFORTUNATELY, THE BADOON WERE PARTICULARLY **HARSH** TASKMASTERS. THE DAY CAME WHEN I **COLLAPSED** AT MY CONSOLE FROM **SHEER EXHAUSTION.**

"AS **PUNISHMENT,** THEY **ALTERED** MY CENTRAL NERVOUS SYSTEM AND **GRAFTED** MY BODY ONTO A **SPECIAL SYSTEMS MODULE.**

"IN SHORT, I BECAME A **LIVING** COMPUTER!

"BUT THE BADOON DID THEIR JOB **TOO** WELL. WITH MY HYPER-FAST **CALCULATING** ABILITIES, I WAS ABLE TO DEVELOP THE MEANS TO **OVERCOME** MY MASTERS.

"DOUBTLESS, I COULD HAVE **CONQUERED** THE ENTIRE **BADOON BROTHERHOOD**, HAD I NOT BEEN DRAWN THRU TIME BY THE **COSMIC GAMESMAN** KNOWN AS THE **GRANDMASTER**, TO BATTLE THE 20TH CENTURY SORCERER, **DR. STRANGE!** *"

* GIANT-SIZE DEFENDERS #3 -- LEN.

"THE MAGICIAN PROBABLY THOUGHT HIS USE OF COMMON **FISTICUFFS** TOOK ME BY **SURPRISE**-- BUT ACTUALLY, I HAD **ANTICIPATED** HIS MOVE AND **ALLOWED** HIM TO BEAT ME!"

"WHILE I SUPPOSEDLY LAID **BROKEN**, MY SENSORS WERE ANALYSING AND **SYNTHESIZING** A PORTION OF THE **GRANDMASTER'S** ENERGIES!"

"THUS, IN MY SO-CALLED **DEFEAT**, I GAINED MUCH **MORE** THAN I COULD **EVER** HAVE THRU **VICTORY.**

"UPON MY **RETURN** TO THE 31ST CENTURY, I UTILIZED MY NEWFOUND ABILITIES TO **TELEPORT** MYSELF TO THIS ONCE-DESOLATE **PLANETOID**--

"--WHERE, WITH ALL THE NEW **KNOWLEDGE** AT MY DISPOSAL, I WAS ABLE TO TRANSFORM **BARREN ROCK** INTO A TECHNOLOGICAL **WONDERLAND** UNLIKE ANY IN KNOWN SPACE.

"I **IMMEDIATELY** STARTED SENDING **PROBES** OUT THRU TIME AND SPACE, TO RECOVER **LONG-LOST** DEVICES AND ARTIFACTS--

"--AS WELL AS TO RECRUIT **YOU**, MY LIEUTENANTS-- FOR WHAT IS AN **EMPIRE** WITHOUT A LOYAL **HOME GUARD?**"

AN... *EMPIRE?*

INDEED! FOR SOON, THIS ENTIRE *GALAXY* SHALL BE MINE TO *RULE!!*

AND ON THAT DAY, I SHALL HAVE MY *REVENGE* UPON *ALL* WHO DARED DENY ME *POWER!*

HERE, I HAVE BUILT A TRUE *PARADISE!* HERE, THE ELITE OF A THOUSAND, *THOUSAND* WORLDS SHALL FLOCK--

--AND *ALL* SHALL PAY *HOMAGE* TO THE GLORY OF *KORVAC!*

"EVEN NOW, THE BEAM OF MY *POWER-SIPHON* STREAKS THRU THE HEAVENS, BOUND FOR *SOL*, THE INSIGNIFICANT LITTLE *STAR-SUN* OF MY WRETCHED HOMEWORLD *EARTH!*

"AND WHEN IT *STRIKES*, THE SUN WILL GO *NOVA!*

"THEN THE *SIPHON* WILL LEAP INTO OPERATION, *DRAWING* THE POWER OF THE *EXPLODING STAR* BACK ALONG THE BEAM TO FULLY *ENERGIZE* MY DEVICES."

THE PITIFUL LITTLE SOLAR SYSTEM THAT ONCE *IGNORED* ME WILL PROVIDE ME WITH POWER FOR *UNTOLD MILLENIA!*

X MINUS 200

AND THIS POWER BECOMES *MINE* IN JUST *TWO HOURS!* THAT IS WHY THERE MUST BE *NO INTERFERENCE!*

AND *THAT* IS WHY I WANT--!

SSSIRE! THE SSSHIP--

66

"--IT RETURNSSS!"

SO *THIS* IS YOUR BASIC *20th CENTURY HERO*, EH?

THERE'S NOTHING BASIC ABOUT *THOR*, NIKKI--

HE'S AN ACTUAL *ASGARDIAN IMMORTAL!*

REALLY, MAJOR! YOU DON'T ACTUALLY *BELIEVE* THIS BEING IS A *LIVING GOD?!*

WELL, MARTY, I...

MY LORD, I BEG YOU TO *FORGIVE* MY FRIEND. HE CANNOT SEE THE SPIRIT OF *ANTHOS* WITHIN YOU AS *I* CAN.

PLEASE--ACCEPT MY BOW IN *OFFERING.*

WHOA! YONDU WOULD *NEVER* GIVE UP HIS BOW *UNLESS...*

ARISE, GOOD SIR! THOR DOTH SEEK NEITHER ADORATION *NOR* OFFERING-- THOUGH IN TRUTH, THY *GIFT* DOES ME GREAT *HONOR.*

FOR BY THY *VISAGE*, THOU WOULDST BE ONE OF THE FABLED *GUARDIANS OF THE GALAXY--*

--WHO ONCE DID FIGHT AT THE SIDE OF *CAPTAIN AMERICA* AND THE BESTIAL *THING!* *

BUT BY *THAT* RECKONING, I AM IN THE *FAR FUTURE!*

DON'T LET IT *WORRY* YA, MUSCLES! THE 31ST CENTURY CAN BE FUN-- *IF* YOU HAVE THE *PROPER COMPANY!*

HEY, SHOW A LITTLE *CLASS*, SQUIRT! IT'S NOT *POLITE* TO VAMP A *THUNDER GOD!*

CHARLIE, YOU-- *YOU LUMMOX! PUT ME DOWN!*

* *MARVEL TWO-IN-ONE #5--LEN.*

DON'T MIND *THEM*, THOR--THEY'RE *ALWAYS* LIKE THAT!

I'M *MAJOR VANCE ASTRO*-- WELCOME ABOARD THE *FREEDOM'S LADY!*

THE HONOR BE *MINE*, MAJOR!

CAPTAIN AMERICA DID SPEAK *MOST HIGHLY* OF THE GUARDIANS IN HIS *AVENGERS REPORT.*

WELL, THEN IT'S *OUR* TURN TO BE *HONORED!*

OF COURSE, WE'VE HAD A COUPLE OF *ADDITIONS* SINCE WE MET CAP. THE *SOMBER* TYPE OVER THERE IN THE BLUE IS *STARHAWK*, AND THE LITTLE *LADY* IS *NIKKI!*

MY SOLEMNITY IS NOT WITHOUT *REASON*, MAJOR, WE *ALL* FACE A MOST DEADLY *FOE!*

I'LL *GET* YOU FOR THAT, CHUNKY!

AW, *STOW* IT!

AND ONCE STARHAWK HAS INFORMED THOR OF THEIR ENCOUNTER WITH THE *MYSTERIOUS BEAM...*

--THUS IT IS *EVIDENT* TO ME THAT WHOEVER *BROUGHT* YOU TO THIS ERA IS *ALSO* BEHIND THE *MACHINATIONS* OF THE *BEAM.*

BUT IF OUR "FOE" IS THROWING AROUND *THAT* KIND OF ENERGY, WHAT IS HE HOPING TO *ACCOMPLISH?*

WHAT? IS IT NOT *ENOW* THAT HE HATH *PROVEN* HIS VILLAINY THRICE OVER?

BY MY *TROTH*, HE *MUST BE STOPPED!*

FIRED BY THE RESOLVE OF THE THUNDER GOD, THE *GUARDIANS* SOON HAVE THEIR STAR-SHIP *HURTLING* THRU THE VOID, HEADED FOR THE POWER BEAM'S *SOURCE* ONCE MORE.

WHILE IN THE *LAIR* OF KORVAC...

EVEN *NOW* THE VESSEL DRAWSSS *NEAR!* WHAT SSSHOULD I DO?

FOOL! DO YOU HAVE TO BE TOLD *EVERYTHING?* *ACTIVATE* THE DEFENSE DRONES!

AT KORVAC'S COMMAND, THREE DECEPTIVELY SMALL SHIPS *BURST FREE* OF THE PLANET'S ATMOSPHERE AND *RUSH* TO MEET THE APPROACHING CRAFT...

BEFORE ANY OF THE GUARDIANS CAN *REACT*, THEIR SHIP IS *BESET* BY THE THREE MINIATURES -- EACH ONE *BLASTING* AWAY WITH THE FIREPOWER OF A *FULL-SCALE STARSHIP!*

WITHIN MOMENTS, THE LADY'S *FORCE-SCREENS* BEGIN TO *BUCKLE.*

AW, *NO!* NOT *AGAIN!* WE JUST *LOST* ONE SHIP* -- WE *CAN'T* LET THE LADY FALL, *TOO!*

AND WE *WON'T*, VANCE -- *CONTROL* YOURSELF!

SHOW THOR TO THE *TELEPORTER* WHILE I ENGAGE THE *AUTO-PILOT PROGRAM.*

*THE STARSHIP "CAPTAIN AMERICA" IN MARVEL PRESENTS #10 -- LEN.

SIX SPACE TRAVELERS AND ONE ASGARDIAN *GOD* STEP UPON THE GLOWING PLATE, AND EVEN AS THEIR *MOLECULAR STRUCTURES* ARE REDUCED TO *ELECTRO-MAGNETIC IMPULSES* --

-- THE MIGHTY STARSHIP *RETREATS* TO A SAFER, MORE *DISTANT* ORBIT, ITS *AUTOMATIC SENSORS* AWAITING THE SIGNAL TO *RETURN* --

-- WHILE *SEVEN FIGURES* MATERIALIZE ALMOST *INSTANTANEOUSLY* ON THE PLANET'S *SURFACE.*

I- I WASN'T EXPECTING *ANYTHING* LIKE *THIS!* THE PLACE IS LIKE SOMETHING OUT OF *LOST HORIZON!*

DO NOT MAKE YOURSELVES *TOO* COMFORTABLE, MY FRIENDS -- OR THIS WORLD COULD EASILY BECOME YOUR *FINAL RESTING PLACE!*

WHAT?

CHAPTER FOUR

THIS BATTLEGROUND PARADISE!

BRIGANDS! WE HAVE NO QUARREL WITH *THEE!* STAND *ASIDE* OR--!

WAIT, THOR! THESE BEINGS ARE MERE *UNDERLINGS!*

IT IS THEIR *MASTER*--THIS *KORVAC*--WE MUST *FIND!*

WELL, WHAT'RE YOU *WAITING* FOR? *GO* ON AND *GET* THIS KORVAC GUY!

WE CAN HANDLE *THESE* CLOWNS!

AND WITHOUT HESITATION, TWO *MIGHTY* FIGURES TAKE TO THE SKIES...

THE *POWER BEAM* SEEMS TO *EMANATE* FROM THAT SPRAWLING STRUCTURE *AHEAD.*

THEN 'TIS *THERE* WE SHALL *STRIKE!*

WHILE *BELOW...*

WELL, CHARLIE-- THANKS A *LOT!* YOU JUST SENT AWAY OUR TWO *STRONGEST* FIGHTERS!

AW-- THESE GUYS WILL BE NO *TROUBLE!*

THINK *SO,* DO YA?

LET'S GO, CREW-- *ATTACK!!*

SSSTUPID MAMMAL! DO YOU THINK YOUR **BULK** CAN SSSAVE YOU FROM MY SSSLASHING TAIL?

WHUP!

DROP BACK, CHARLIE-- AND WE SHALL SEE IF HIS TAIL IS ANY **DEFENSE** AGAINST MY **YAKA** ARROWS!

I THINK **NOT**, MY FRIEND--

--NOT WHILE **DUMOG** IS AROUND!

AAGGH! MY LEG!

YA **FELT** THAT, HUH, DIAMOND JIM?

NOW YOU KNOW **WHY** THEY CALL GROTT... THE **MANSLAYER!**

HOLD STILL, **GNAT!**

NOT ON YOUR LIFE, **UGLY!**

LITTLE FOOL! SOONER OR LATER, TORK SHALL **GET** YOU! YOUR **PUNY WEAPON** BARELY **STINGS** ME!

INTERESTING-- **MOST** INTERESTING!

DO YOU REALIZE THAT YOUR **PSYCHE-BLASTS** ARE VERY **SIMILAR** TO THOSE OF MY LITTLE FRIEND **GROTT**?

YOU-- YOU'RE **IN-TANGIBLE!**

WHEN I **WISH** TO BE-- **YES!**

BUT EVEN AS THE GUARDIANS BATTLE *DESPERATELY* AGAINST KORVAC'S *MINIONS*, THOR AND STARHAWK REACH THEIR *GOAL*...

BLACKGUARD! THOR HATH *RETURNED* -- FOR *VENGEANCE!*

WHAT?! YOU?

I...AM *IMPRESSED.* BUT NOT EVEN YOU AND YOUR FRIEND *CAN STOP* MY PLANS *NOW!*

LOOK *ABOVE* YOU, THUNDER GOD!

BOOM

WHEN THAT *TIME-CLOCK* REACHES *ZERO,* THE EARTH'S SUN WILL GO *NOVA-*

--AND THEN, ALL THE *POWER* THUS GENERATED SHALL BE MINE!

WHAT? THOU WOULDST *DOOM* THE ENTIRE *SOLAR SYSTEM?*

FIEND! NOT EVEN THE TRAGIC *GALACTUS* WAS SO *CALLOUS!*

INDEED! YOU MUST BE--

FA MP

--STOPPED?

BY THE ALL-FATHER! WE HAVE BEEN *RETURNED* TO OUR *POINT OF ENTRY!*

HIS *TELEPORTATION ABILITIES* BETRAY AN *UNPARALLELED* TECHNOLOGY!

WE *MUST* STOP HIM!

AYE... IF WE *CAN.*

WELL, BACK SO *SOON*? *HA-HA-HA!* WE CAN FIX *THAT!*

AND ONCE AGAIN...

FA MP

HE-- HE *TOYS* WITH US-- AS WOULD A *CAT* WITH A *MOUSE!*

BUT NOT FOR *LONG!* HIS OWN *DEVICE* HAS *BETRAYED* HIM!

THERE-- THAT BANK OF *MACHINERY* TO HIS *LEFT!* ITS *INDICATOR LIGHT* HAS *GLOWED* EACH TIME WE WERE *TELEPORTED!*

THEN *STAND THEE ASIDE,* STARHAWK--

--FOR BY THE *GOLDEN GATES* OF ASGARD, YON DEVICE WILL BEDEVIL US NO MORE!

WHA--?

SPLANG

FOOL! DO YOU THINK *THAT* WILL *SAVE YOU?* TELEPORTATION IS BUT *ONE* OF THE *MANY WEAPONS* AT MY *DISPOSAL!*

THEN *UNLEASH* THY *WORST,* JACKAL! WE SHALL FACE IT *ALL LIKE WARRIORS BORN!*

AND WE SHALL NOT *STOP* UNTIL YOU ARE *DEFEATED!*

74

WELL, THEN-- LET'S SEE HOW YOU *FARE* AGAINST THE *IMPENETRABLE BARRIER* OF MY *STASIS FIELD!*

DEMON! I'LL--!

NO, THOR-- *WAIT!* BRUTE STRENGTH IS *USELESS* AGAINST SUCH A *FIELD!*

BUT *NOT SO* THE *POWER* OF A *LIVING STAR!*

I AM THE *LIGHT* AND THE *GIVER OF LIGHT*-- AND NO MERE *ENERGY FIELD* CAN LONG STAND THE *FULL FURY* OF MY POWER!

NO! KORVAC SHALL *NOT* BE STOPPED! I'VE COME *TOO FAR!* YOU SHALL *INTRUDE* UPON MY *WONDERWORLD* NO *FURTHER!*

I WILL NOT *LET* YOU DE-STROY THIS *PARADISE!*

KLAK

NAY, SIRRAH! 'TIS NOT A *PARADISE* THAT IS BUILT ON THE *BODIES* OF *INNOCENT BEINGS!*

THERE IS BUT *ONE WORD* FOR SUCH AN *ACT* AS THINE-- *MADNESS!*

THOU ART AS *MAD* AS THE *TERRORISTS* OF YORE-- SPEAKING OF LIBERTY, BUT DEALING IN *DEATH!*

YOU *MISJUDGE* ME, THUNDER GOD! COULD A *MADMAN* DEVISE *THIS?*

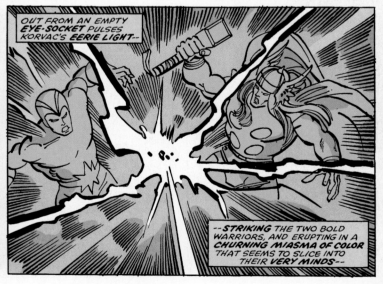

OUT FROM AN EMPTY *EYE-SOCKET* PULSES KORVAC'S *EERIE LIGHT*--

--*STRIKING* THE TWO BOLD *WARRIORS*, AND ERUPTING IN A *CHURNING MIASMA OF COLOR* THAT SEEMS TO SLICE INTO THEIR *VERY MINDS*--

--WITH **STARTLING** RESULTS.

IF YOU'RE SO **EAGER** TO **FIGHT**, THEN YOU SHALL FIGHT **EACH OTHER!**

MY **NEURAL BEAM** WILL KEEP YOU BATTLING UNTIL YOU **BOTH DROP!**

THOR... I ...MUST FIGHT...

BY MY TROTH-- MY **LIMBS** WILL NOT **OBEY!**

I ...FEEL **COMPELLED** TO... **KILL STARHAWK!**

BUT AS THE TWO **TITANS** RUSH AT ONE ANOTHER, THE **GUARDIANS** FIND THEMSELVES ON THE **LOSING END** OF ANOTHER **BATTLE**...

UHH!

FORGET IT, GEM! ANOTHER FEW **BLASTS**, AND YOU'VE **HAD IT!**

HE'S **RIGHT!** IT'S JUST A MATTER OF **TIME** BEFORE HE **SHATTERS** MY **CRYSTALLINE** BODY.

BUT IF I **MUST FALL**--

--I'LL TAKE A FEW OF THEM WITH ME!

A BLAST OF EXTREME **CRYOGENIC** FORCE SURGES OUT FROM THE **PLUVIAN'S** HAND--

--INSTANTLY **FREEZING** THE **BLOB** INTO A SOLID MASS.

MARTINEX, YOU HAVE SHOWN ME THE **PATH** TO **VICTORY!**

WE MUST **SWITCH** OUR **OPPONENTS!**

WHAT'S **THIS?** THAT **ARROW**-- IT'S **VIBRATIONS** ARE DISRUPTING MY BODY!

I- I'M **LOSING CONTROL**--

--BECOMING... SOLID...

THUD!

THANKS, YON! THAT'S **TWO** DOWN!

ALL RIGHT, *MISTER*--

--LET'S SEE IF YOUR *HEAD* IS AS HARD AS YOUR *TAIL!*

HSSSS!

CHARLIE-- SEE TO *NIKKI!*

WILL DO, *BOSS!*

YOU'RE *SLOWING DOWN,* GAMIN-- *GOOD!*

IT WILL BE OVER *SOON* NOW!

YOU'RE RIGHT ABOUT *THAT,* PAL--

FRAK

--BUT *NOT* THE WAY YOU *THINK!*

KA-

BLAM

AND *NOW,* GROTT--!

YOU THINK YOU'VE *GOT* ME, *DON'T* YOU?

IN A WORD... *YES!*

YOU'RE NOT GOING TO GIVE *ME* ANY TROUBLE!

LISTEN, YOU *JERKS*-- I WAS GOING *EASY* ON *DIAMOND BOY* THERE! I ALMOST *TOTALLED* THE *HULK* ONCE*--

((♡)) ((♡))

--JUST LIKE I'M GONNA *CREAM YOU!*

**GIANT-SIZE DEFENDERS* #3 --LEN.

I'VE NEVER *HEARD* OF THIS *HULK,* JUNIOR--

--SO PARDON *ME* IF I DON'T *QUAKE* IN *FEAR!*

BRRTTTZZZ

OH NO.

77

MY ANTENNA!

SHE *SNICKED OFF* MY ANTENNA!

IT'LL TAKE ME A *YEAR* TO GROW 'EM *BACK!*

YAAAAHHH!

BOY, THEY JUST DON'T MAKE *MANSLAYERS* LIKE THEY *USED TO!*

WELL, NOW THAT THE *GOON SQUAD* IS TAKEN *OUT*-- LET'S GO FIND *THOR* AND *STARHAWK!*

SOUNDS ALL RIGHT BY *ME*, VANCE-- BUT I REALLY THINK THAT *THOSE TWO* CAN TAKE CARE OF *THEMSELVES.*

MAYBE *SO*, BUT I'LL FEEL A LOT *BETTER* ONCE I KNOW JUST WHAT THEY'RE *FIGHTING!*

PERHAPS *NOT*, MAJOR!

THOR...WE *MUST*...FIGHT...THIS *COMPULSION!* TIME IS...*RUNNING OUT!*

I...*KNOW*, MY FRIEND, BUT...'TIS AS IF...THE *WARRIOR MADNESS* WAS...UPON ME!

THOUGH I...*STRUGGLE* WITH ALL MY MIGHT...I CAN...DO NAUGHT BUT...*LESSEN* THE FORCE...OF MY *BLOWS.*

THEN...WE MUST FIGHT IN *EARNEST*...INCREASE THE FORCE OF BATTLE...UNTIL WE *DESTROY* THIS *CITADEL!*

NAY...'TWOULD MEAN THY *DEATH!*

MY LIFE...MEANS *LITTLE.* WE MUST...*STOP KORVAC!*

THEN, MAY ODIN FORGIVE ME...

HAVE AT THEE!

THE VERY *AIR* OF THE CHAMBER SEEMS TO *THROB* WITH THE FURY OF THEIR *CONFLICT.* NEVER BEFORE HAS THERE BEEN SUCH A *CONFRONTATION*--

--A BATTLE BETWEEN MAN-LIKE *GOD* AND GOD-LIKE *MAN*, WITH NO QUARTER GIVEN, NO HOLDS *BARRED!*

IT IS TRULY A BATTLE *OUT OF TIME*-- A STRUGGLE OF *MYTHOS* VERSUS *SUPER SCIENCE*-- WITH THE EXISTENCE OF A *SOLAR SYSTEM* HANGING IN THE *BALANCE!*

FRAM

THOOM

THIS IS THE STUFF OF WHICH *LEGENDS* ARE MADE--

--THE SORT OF *BATTLE* WHICH LITERALLY *BRINGS DOWN THE HOUSE!*

NO! IT--IT IS NOT *POSSIBLE!*

MY LABS WERE BUILT TO WITH-STAND THE *MIGHTIEST* OF *EARTHQUAKES!*

IT *CAN'T* END THIS WAY! IT *MUSTN'T!*

HAVE TO FALL BACK ON MY *EMER-GENCY RE-SOURCES*--

--TELEPORT AWAY...

FAMP

KA-BLAM!

AND WITH KORVAC'S *DEPARTURE*--

THE SPELL IS *LIFTED!*

STARHAWK-- ART THOU--?

I...WILL BE *FINE,* THOR!

QUICKLY, WE MUST *STOP* KORVAC'S *POWER BEAM!*

HERE--*HERE* IS THE CENTRAL CONSOLE!

BUT THE CONTROLS ARE *JAMMED*--THE *NOVA-CYCLE* IS *BEGINNING!*

THEN THERE BE *NO TIME* TO *SPARE!*

THIS INFERNAL DEVICE MUST CEASE TO BE!

KLA-BLAM!

FOR A MOMENT, THE TWO STAND IN *SOLEMN SILENCE*. DESTRUCTION OF THE SOLAR SYSTEM HAS BEEN *AVERTED*--

--WITH *LESS* THAN A *MINUTE* TO SPARE.

WE MUST *QUIT* THIS PLACE AT *ONCE!*

NO, MY FRIEND-- NOT "*WE*"!

YOU BELONG TO *ANOTHER TIME*-- ANOTHER *PLACE*.

FARE YOU *WELL*, THOR! WE SHALL MEET *AGAIN*.

AND, *OUTSIDE* THE STRUCTURE...

I *THINK* WE FOUND 'EM!

GOOD LORD! THAT PLACE IS READY TO--

"--COLLAPSE!"

BLA- THOOM!

THE BATTLE IS *WON*, GUARDIANS! THE *THREAT* OF KORVAC IS *ENDED*.

BUT--*THOR*-- WHERE'S THOR?

THOR HAS BEEN *RETURNED* TO HIS *OWN ERA.*

I CAN *ASSURE* YOU, IT WAS FOR THE *BEST*--ON MY WORD AS *ONE-WHO-KNOWS!*

YEAH? GEE, I WISH WE'D HAD A *CHANCE* TO SAY GOOD-BYE.

TO *THINK* THAT A *GOD* WALKED AMONG US--!

WELL, HE WAS *OKAY*-- BUT I'M NOT GONNA LOSE ANY *SLEEP* OVER HIM!

AND, BACK IN THE TWENTIETH CENTURY...

I CAN'T GET *OVER* IT! IT'S AS IF SOME *GIANT* SCOOPED HIM UP AND CARRIED HIM *OFF!*

WELL, COME *AWAY* FROM THERE, YOU *TWO!*

WE'VE WASTED *ENOUGH* TIME HERE. AND I'LL NEED YOUR *HELP* FILING THE *BLASTED* REPORTS!

BUT NO SOONER DO THE OFFICERS *CROSS THE ROOM, THAN...*

FAMP

ALL RIGHT, I GIVE UP! HOW'D YA DO IT?

HOW DID YOU MANAGE TO MAKE YOURSELF *AND* THAT REACTOR *VANISH* FOR THE BETTER PART OF *TEN HOURS?*

CAPTAIN--

--IF I *TOLD* THEE, THOU WOULDST NOT *BELIEVE* ME!

OUT INTO THE NIGHT STRIDES THE *GOD OF THUNDER*-- AND FOR A LONG TIME, HE STARES OFF INTO THE STAR-FLECKED *FIRMAMENT,* HIS HEART *AGLOW* WITH MEMORIES OF COMRADES *YET TO COME...*

FARE THEE *WELL,* GUARDIANS--

AYE...FARE THEE WELL.

FIN

THOR
MARVEL COMICS GROUP
APPROVED BY THE COMICS CODE AUTHORITY
35¢
267
JAN
02450
THE MIGHTY
THOR
©1977 MARVEL COMICS GROUP
BY ODIN! I MUST STOP THE DEADLY MISSILE PLUNGING TOWARDS ME--
--ERE IT DESTROYS THE UNITED NATIONS!
THE THUNDER GOD RETURNS TO EARTH-- TO FIND CHAOS AWAITING HIM THERE!
TO MIDGARD..AND MAYHEM!

When lame Dr. DONALD BLAKE strikes his wooden walking stick upon the ground, it becomes the mystic mallet MJOLNIR—and Blake is transformed into the Norse God of Thunder, Master of the Storm and the Lightning, Heir to the Throne of Immortal Asgard...

STAN LEE PRESENTS: THE MIGHTY THOR!™

LEN WEIN ✶ **WALT SIMONSON & TONY DeZUNIGA** ✶ **GLYNIS WEIN** ✶ **JOE ROSEN**
WRITER/EDITOR ✶ ARTISTS / ILLUSTRATORS ✶ COLORIST ✶ LETTERER

ONCE MORE, TO MIDGARD!

VERILY, THERE IS GREAT **REJOICING** IN IMMORTAL ASGARD THIS DAY. THE THREAT OF THE DREADFUL **DESTROYER** AT LAST IS **ENDED**, ALMIGHTY **ODIN** ONCE MORE SITS THE GOLDEN THRONE--

--AND **THOU**, O TRUE BELIEVER, ART HEREBY INVITED TO PARTAKE IN THE **FESTIVITIES**!

THE RECONSTRUCTION CERTAINLY GOES **SWIFTLY**, MY FATHER!

AYE, THUNDER GOD-- **MORE** SWIFTLY THAN EVEN **I** HAD E'ER ANTICIPATED!

THE NOBLE **BALDER** DOTH TAKE HIS TASK MOST **SERIOUSLY**!

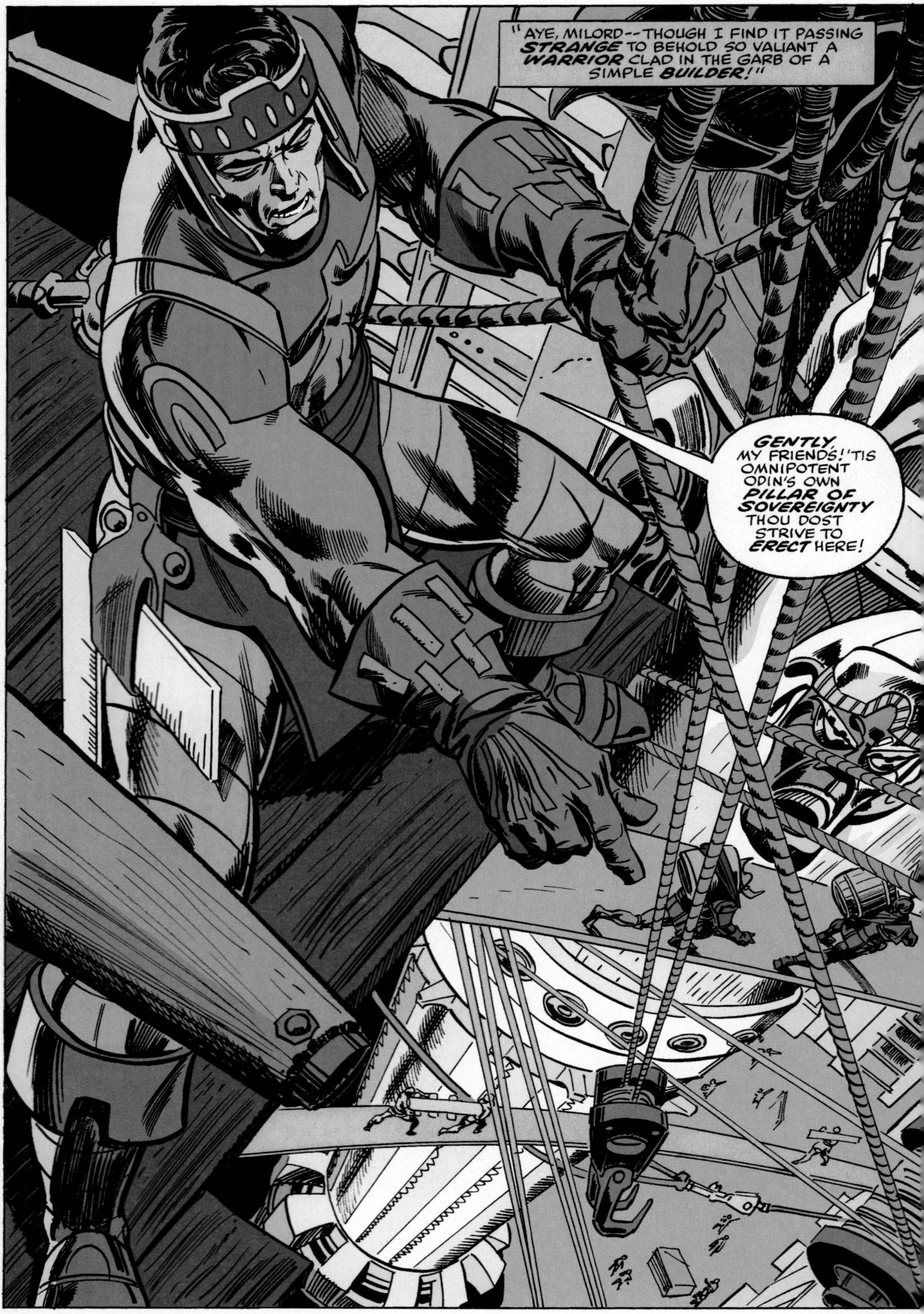
"AYE, MILORD--THOUGH I FIND IT PASSING STRANGE TO BEHOLD SO VALIANT A WARRIOR CLAD IN THE GARB OF A SIMPLE BUILDER!"
GENTLY, MY FRIENDS! 'TIS OMNIPOTENT ODIN'S OWN PILLAR OF SOVEREIGNTY THOU DOST STRIVE TO ERECT HERE!

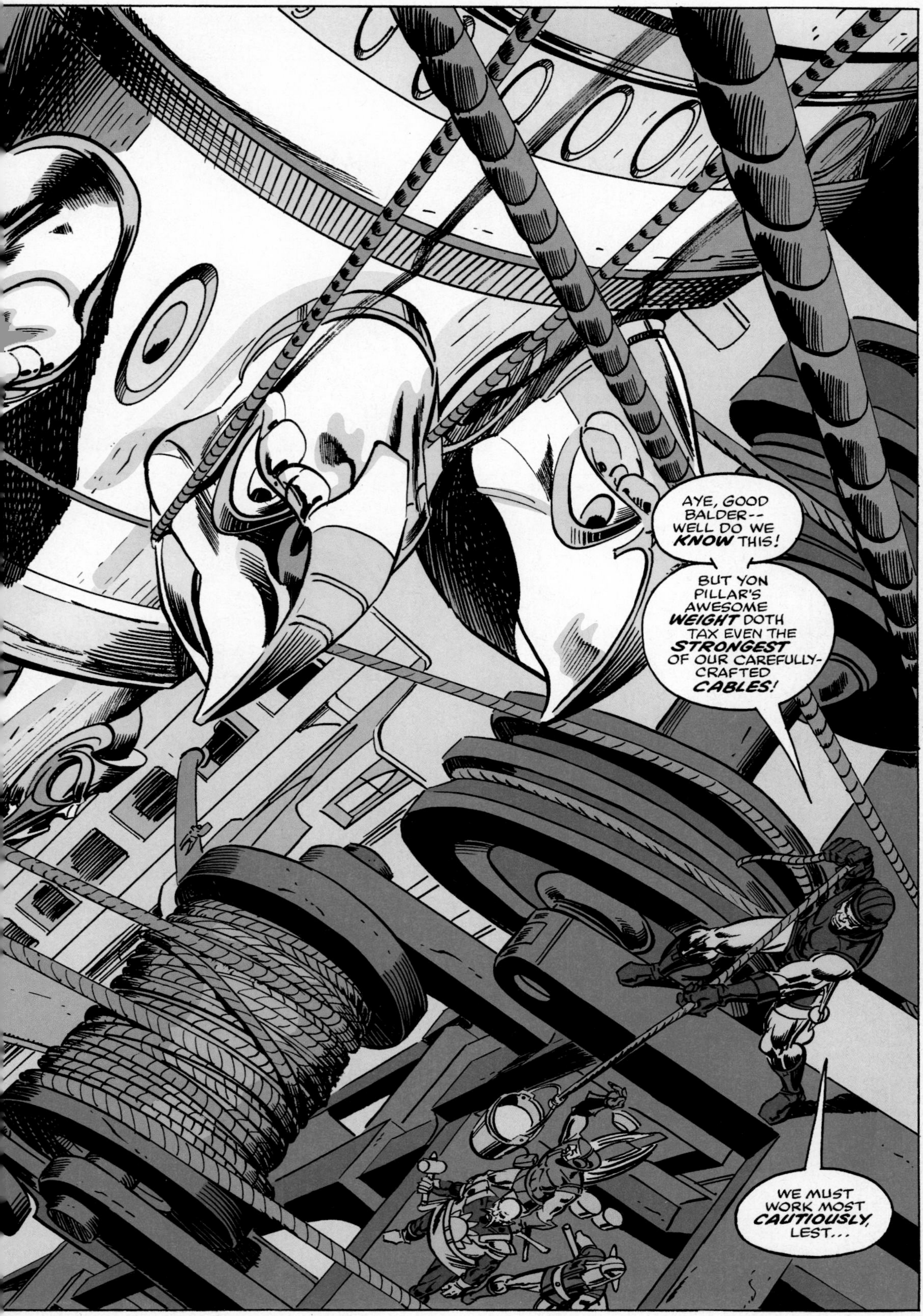
AYE, GOOD BALDER-- WELL DO WE KNOW THIS!
BUT YON PILLAR'S AWESOME WEIGHT DOTH TAX EVEN THE STRONGEST OF OUR CAREFULLY-CRAFTED CABLES!
WE MUST WORK MOST CAUTIOUSLY, LEST...

EH?

SHRAKKK

NAY! THE MASTER CABLE-- IT HATH BEGUN TO UNRAVEL--!

SWIFTLY, ALL-- WE MUST EASE THE STRAIN ERE...

BUT IT IS ALREADY FAR TOO LATE! FOR WITH A SCREAM LIKE A SOUL IN TORMENT, THE CABLE IS SUDDENLY SEVERED...

SKKKRANG!

...AND UNTOLD TONS OF ORNATE MARBLE ABRUPTLY TOPPLE TOWARDS THE PANIC-STRICKEN THRONG BELOW!

FLEE, GOOD COMRADES!

FLEE FOR THY LIVES!!

BUT THEY CAN NE'ER FLEE SWIFTLY ENOUGH!

VERILY, THE DEATH-GODDESS HELA SHALL EMBRACE MANY NEW SUBJECTS THIS DAY...

"...LEST THE ENCHANTED MALLET MJOLNIR DOTH POSSESS POWER ENOW TO REVERSE THE TOWERING PILLAR'S PLUNGE!

SKA-THOOM!

"THANK THE FATES! MINE URU HAMMER HATH SET THE COLUMN UPRIGHT ONCE MORE..."

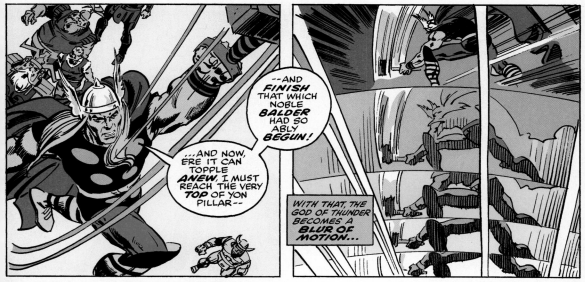

--AND *FINISH* THAT WHICH NOBLE *BALDER* HAD SO ABLY *BEGUN!*

...AND NOW, ERE IT CAN TOPPLE *ANEW,* I MUST REACH THE VERY *TOP* OF YON PILLAR--

WITH THAT, THE GOD OF THUNDER BECOMES A *BLUR OF MOTION...*

...AND WHEN, AT LAST, HE IS *THROUGH...*

WELL *DONE,* MY SON! THE PILLAR OF SOVEREIGNTY IS ONCE MORE *SECURE!*

'TIS NOTHING THAT *BALDER* WOULD NOT HAVE DONE, MILORD-- HAD THAT CABLE NOT BEEN *SUNDERED!*

NOW, IF THOU WOULDST *EXCUSE* ME, MY LIEGE-- I WOULD RETIRE TO MY *QUARTERS* FOR THE NONCE!

WHICH IS WHERE WE *REJOIN* THE SON OF ODIN A SHORT WHILE *LATER...*

THOU DOST SEEM *TROUBLED,* MILORD. DOES MY NEW ATTIRE *DISTURB* THEE?

NAY, MILADY SIF--'TIS MERELY THE THOUGHT OF THAT WHICH WE MUST NEXT *WITNESS!*

THE TIME HATH COME FOR MINE HALF-BROTHER *LOKI* TO BE *SENTENCED* FOR HIS MANY CRIMES AGAINST THE *REALM ETERNAL!**

AND THOUGH THE GOD OF MISCHIEF IS TRULY *EVIL INCARNATE,* STILL I CANNOT HELP BUT *PITY* HIM NOW!

AND *THAT,* NOBLE THOR, IS WHY I *LOVE* THEE SO.

*AS WITNESSED THESE SEVERAL ISSUES PAST. --LEN.

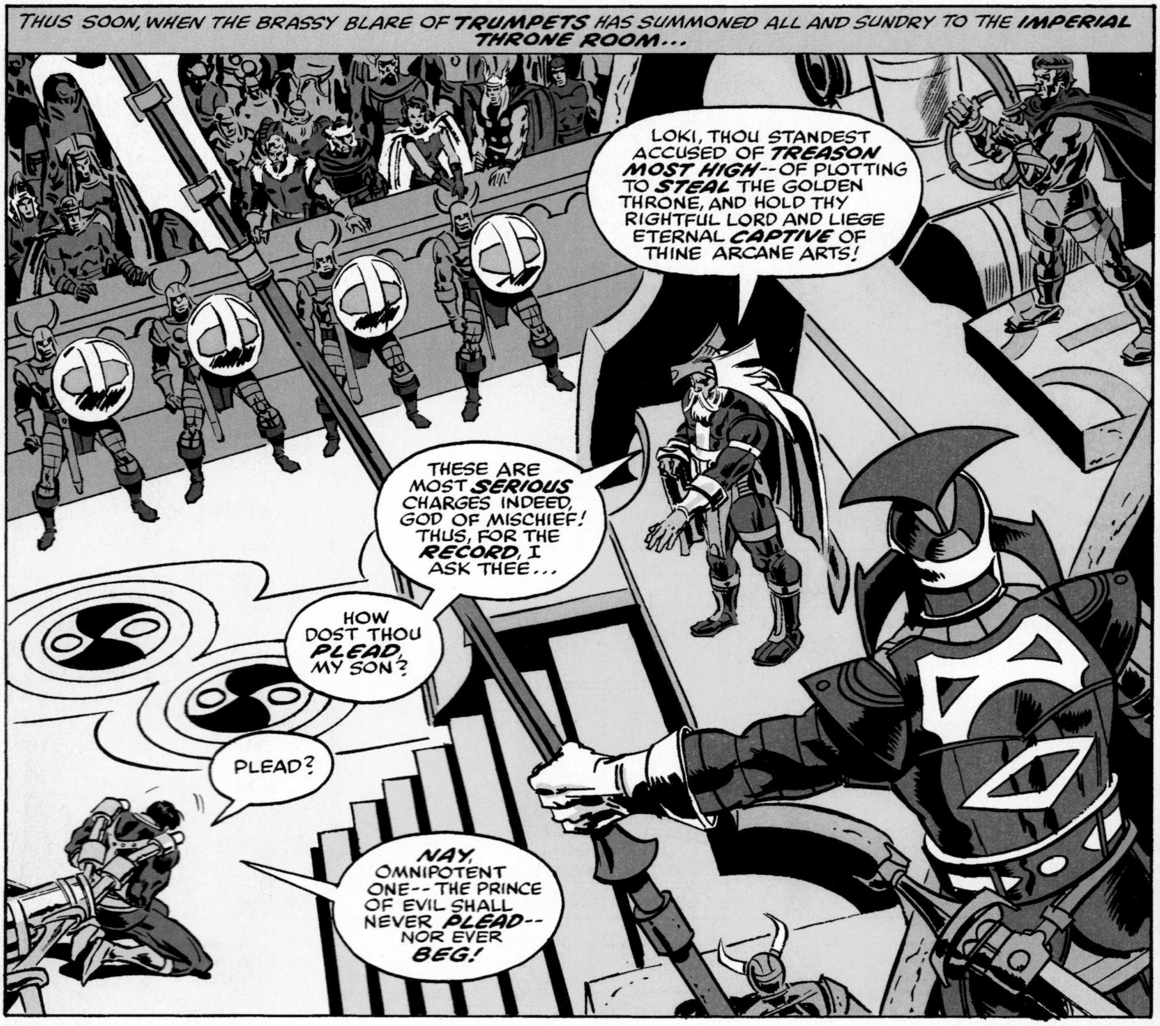
THUS SOON, WHEN THE BRASSY BLARE OF TRUMPETS HAS SUMMONED ALL AND SUNDRY TO THE IMPERIAL THRONE ROOM...
LOKI, THOU STANDEST ACCUSED OF TREASON MOST HIGH--OF PLOTTING TO STEAL THE GOLDEN THRONE, AND HOLD THY RIGHTFUL LORD AND LIEGE ETERNAL CAPTIVE OF THINE ARCANE ARTS!
THESE ARE MOST SERIOUS CHARGES INDEED, GOD OF MISCHIEF! THUS, FOR THE RECORD, I ASK THEE...
HOW DOST THOU PLEAD, MY SON?
PLEAD?
NAY, OMNIPOTENT ONE--THE PRINCE OF EVIL SHALL NEVER PLEAD--NOR EVER BEG!

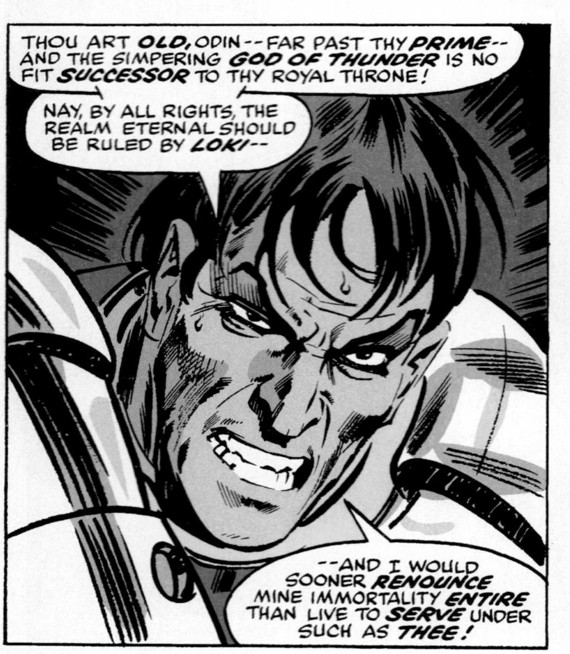
THOU ART OLD, ODIN--FAR PAST THY PRIME--AND THE SIMPERING GOD OF THUNDER IS NO FIT SUCCESSOR TO THY ROYAL THRONE!
NAY, BY ALL RIGHTS, THE REALM ETERNAL SHOULD BE RULED BY LOKI--
--AND I WOULD SOONER RENOUNCE MINE IMMORTALITY ENTIRE THAN LIVE TO SERVE UNDER SUCH AS THEE!

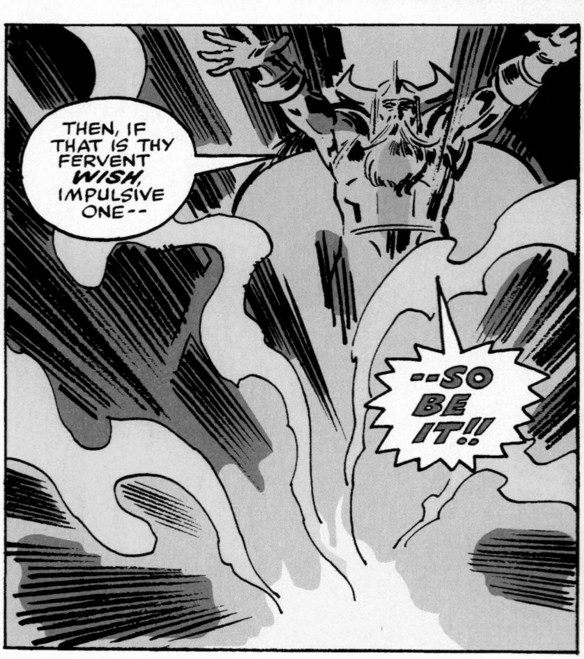
THEN, IF THAT IS THY FERVENT WISH, IMPULSIVE ONE--
--SO BE IT!!

AND THOSE POOR ALCOHOL-BESOTTED SOULS ON MAN-HATTAN'S LOWER EAST SIDE HARDLY *NOTICE* THE SUDDEN APPEARANCE OF ONE MORE ALMOST-MINDLESS *DERELICT* IN THEIR MIDST...

...A DERELICT WHO ONCE HAD ALL BUT *OWNED* THE *STARS!*

PERHAPS, WHEN THE GOD OF MISCHIEF HAS FINALLY LEARNED HIS *LESSON*, I WILL *RESTORE* TO HIM HIS *MEMORY*...AND HIS *GODHOOD!*

AYE... *PERHAPS.*

THOU ART *WISDOM IN-CARNATE*, MY *LIEGE.* LET THY WILL BE *DONE.*

NOW, BY THY *LEAVE*, MILORD-- I WOULD BID *FAREWELL* TO A *FRIEND.*

RECORDER, WE SHALL *MISS* THEE! TRULY, THOU ART A BEING *NOBLE* BEYOND MEASURE!

STATEMENT: MY WORK HERE IS *DONE!* I HAVE WITNESSED THE END OF THE *ODIN-QUEST* AS ORDERED BY MY RIGILLIAN *MASTERS*...

...AND NOW THE TIME HAS COME FOR ME TO RETURN *HOME!*

RESOLUTION: BUT I SHALL NEVER *FORGET* WHAT I HAVE SEEN AT YOUR *SIDE*, ASGARDIAN...

...AND A *PART* OF ME WILL ALWAYS BE *WITH* YOU!

AND WHEN THE RECORDER HAS FINALLY FADED FROM *VIEW*...

VERILY, LOKI'S EXILE TO MIDGARD HATH SET ME TO *THINKING*-- AND SET MINE HEART TO *STIRRING!*

METHINKS MAYHAP 'TIS TIME I *RETURNED* TO EARTH ONCE MORE--

--AND LET THE MORTAL *DR. DON BLAKE* TAKE UP HIS LIFE *ANEW!*

A *SPLENDID* IDEA, FRIEND THOR-- AND WITH THY THREE STAUNCH *COMPANIONS* BESIDE THEE, METHINKS THERE'LL BE *ADVENTURE* A'PLENTY AWAITING US!

EH? BUT I... AH... I...

NAY, GOOD WARRIORS--THOUGH THE *THUNDER GOD* IS BOUND FOR *MIDGARD*, THERE IS STILL WORK FOR *YE* IN THE *REALM ETERNAL!*

MAGRAT, SNAYKAR, AND KRODA ARE STILL *AT LARGE*--AND MUST NEEDS BE BROUGHT TO *JUSTICE!* I CHARGE YE THREE TO *FIND* THEM!

AS *EVER,* ALL-FATHER--THY WORD IS OUR *WILL!*

WE SHALL RETURN *WITH* THOSE THREE SCOUNDRELS--OR WE WILL RETURN *NOT AT ALL!*

THEN, AFTER THE WARRIORS THREE HAVE RELUCTANTLY *DEPARTED...*

IT IS *DONE!* THY COMRADES YET HAVE THEIR *PRIDE,* MY SON--WHILST *THOU* DOST HAVE THY *PRIVACY!*

AYE, FATHER--THOUGH FANDRAL, HOGUN AND VOLSTAGG ARE AS *BROTHERS* TO ME, STILL MUST I HAVE SOME TIME TO *MYSELF* NOW!

I *THANK* THEE... FOR *UNDERSTANDING!*

CANST *THOU* UNDERSTAND THAT, MILADY? THOUGH THE HEART OF *THOR* IS EVER *THINE,* THE SPIRIT OF *DON BLAKE* CRIES OUT FOR *RELEASE*--

--AND I MUST HEED ITS CALL *ALONE!*

THEN DO AS THOU *MUST,* BELOVED--AND KNOW THE LADY *SIF* SHALL COUNT THE DAYS TILL THY *RETURN!*

WHILE, AT THE VERY *EDGE* OF THE GOLDEN CITY, A FAREWELL QUITE *DIFFERENT*--YET DISTRESSINGLY *SIMILAR*--IS EVEN NOW TAKING PLACE...

ART THOU CERTAIN THOU MUST *GO,* KARNILLA?

THE *NORN QUEEN* NEEDS ANSWER TO *NO ONE,* BALDER!

IF THOU WOULDST *SEEK* ME, THOU KNOWEST WHERE TO *FIND* ME!

AYE, SORCERESS... THAT I *DO.*

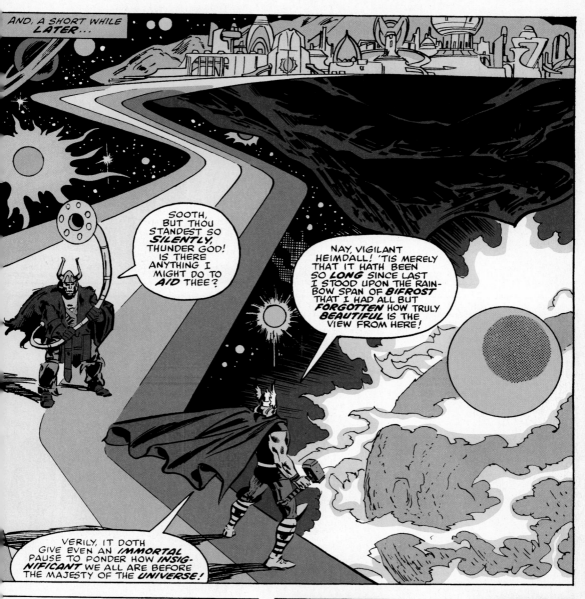

SOOTH, BUT THOU STANDEST SO *SILENTLY,* THUNDER GOD! IS THERE ANYTHING I MIGHT DO TO *AID* THEE?

NAY, VIGILANT HEIMDALL! 'TIS MERELY THAT IT HATH BEEN SO *LONG* SINCE LAST I STOOD UPON THE RAIN- BOW SPAN OF *BIFROST* THAT I HAD ALL BUT *FORGOTTEN* HOW TRULY *BEAUTIFUL* IS THE VIEW FROM HERE!

VERILY, IT DOTH GIVE EVEN AN *IMMORTAL* PAUSE TO PONDER HOW *INSIG-NIFICANT* WE ALL ARE BEFORE THE MAJESTY OF THE *UNIVERSE!*

YET THERE IS BEAUTY AND WONDER-MENT OF A WHOLLY *DIFFERENT* STRIPE AWAITING ME ON THE BRIGHT GREEN WORLD CALLED *EARTH!*

I NEED ONLY WHIRL MINE ENCHANTED HAMMER SWIFTLY *ABOUT* ME--

--AND THE FURIOUS *VORTEX* THUS CREATED SHALL SPEED ME TO MY SECOND *HOME!*

IN A TWINKLING, THE SON OF ODIN IS *GONE* FROM THE RAINBOW BRIDGE...

...AND INSTANTLY, ON THE BUSTLING STREETS OF *NEW YORK*, A GLAD-HEARTED *GOD* WALKS PROUDLY AMONG *MEN* ONCE MORE!

BY ODIN, 'TIS GOOD TO *STAND* AGAIN UPON THIS WORLD WHICH IS SO *DEAR* TO ME!

YET, THOUGH MY SPIRIT SOARS TO *BE* HERE, 'TIS NOT FOR THOR *ALONE* THAT I HAVE *RETURNED* TO HECTIC MIDGARD!

THUS, LET THE MYSTIC MJOLNIR LIFT ME *SKYWARD*--

--THAT I MIND FIND A PLACE OF GREATER *CONCEALMENT* IN WHICH TO EFFECT MINE ALMOST-FORGOTTEN *TRANSFORMATION!*

AND WHEN THE GOLDEN-HAIRED ASGARDIAN HAS *LANDED* IN A SHADOWED *ALLEYWAY...*

I HAVE BUT TO *STRIKE* MINE ENCHANTED MALLET *ONCE* UPON THE *GROUND*--

"--AND THE GOD OF THUNDER WILL CEASE TO *BE* FOR A TIME--"

--SO THAT THE LAME *DOCTOR DONALD BLAKE* CAN AT LONG LAST TASTE OF *LIFE* AGAIN!

IT'S BEEN SO *LONG*, I'D NEARLY FORGOTTEN HOW *ALIVE* THIS CITY FEELS!

BUT MY *OFFICE* IS JUST AROUND THIS *CORNER*, AND...

HUH?

NO--IT'S IMPOSSIBLE! I COULDN'T HAVE BEEN GONE *THAT* LONG!!

MY OLD **OFFICE BUILDING**-- IT'S BEEN **TORN DOWN**--!

AND THERE'S A **HIGH-RISE PARKING LOT** HERE IN ITS PLACE!!

SHORTLY, AS THE BEWILDERED PHYSICIAN SLUMPS DEJECTEDLY ON A NEARBY **PARK BENCH**...

A **YEAR**, THEY TELL ME... IT'S BEEN AN ENTIRE **YEAR** SINCE MY LEASE LAPSED AND THEY TORE THE **BUILDING** DOWN!

I WONDER-- HOW MUCH **ELSE** HAS CHANGED WHILE MY ASGARDIAN ALTER EGO WAS **GALAVANTING** ACROSS THE UNIVERSE?

IN SO MANY WAYS, I HARDLY **RECOGNIZE** THIS CITY ANYMORE! DO I REALLY STILL **BELONG** HERE?

FOR A TIME, THE MELANCHOLY DONALD BLAKE SITS IN SILENT **CONTEMPLATION**, AS THE HURRIED RUSH OF HUMANITY PASSES BY ALL BUT **UNNOTICED**...

BUT THEN, AT LAST--

NO! DON BLAKE IS NO **QUITTER!**

IF THINGS HAVE **CHANGED**, THEN I'LL JUST HAVE TO CHANGE **WITH** THEM--

"--AND I KNOW JUST THE PLACE TO **START**!"

THUS, SOON AFTER, AT MANHATTAN'S FAMOUS **TRINITY GENERAL HOSPITAL**...

JACOB, IT'S GOOD TO **SEE** YOU AGAIN, OLD FRIEND!

AND **YOU**, MY BOY! WHEN THEY TOLD ME THE EVER-ELUSIVE **DR. DONALD BLAKE** WAS HERE TO SEE ME, YOU COULD HAVE KNOCKED ME OVER WITH THE PROVERBIAL **FEATHER!**

HOW HAVE YOU BEEN **KEEPING** YOURSELF, MY BOY--

--AND, MORE IMPORTANTLY, **WHERE** HAVE YOU BEEN KEEPING YOURSELF?

I'M **FINE**, JACOB. I'VE--AH-- BEEN **OUT OF TOWN** FOR A WHILE.

93

SO *TELL* ME THEN, MY BOY-- WHAT BRINGS YOU *BACK*?

FRANKLY, JACOB-- I NEED YOUR *HELP*! WITH MY OLD OFFICES *DEMOLISHED*, AND MY OLD *PATIENTS* LONG SINCE SCATTERED TO MY *COLLEAGUES*, I'M LOOKING FOR *WORK* RIGHT NOW...

...AND I FIGURED IF *DOCTOR JACOB WALLABY*-- MY OLD COLLEGE *MENTOR*-- COULDN'T SUGGEST SOMETHING, *NOBODY* COULD!

DR. J. WALLABY
CHIEF OF STAFF

AND YOU'VE, OF COURSE, CONSIDERED OPENING A *NEW* PRACTICE *ELSEWHERE*, MY BOY?

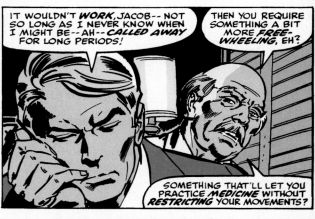

IT WOULDN'T *WORK*, JACOB-- NOT SO LONG AS I NEVER KNOW WHEN I MIGHT BE-- AH-- *CALLED AWAY* FOR LONG PERIODS!

THEN YOU REQUIRE SOMETHING A BIT MORE *FREE-WHEELING*, EH?

SOMETHING THAT'LL LET YOU PRACTICE *MEDICINE* WITHOUT *RESTRICTING* YOUR MOVEMENTS?

GRANTED, IT MAY SOUND *STRANGE*, JACOB-- BUT THAT'S *PRECISELY* WHAT I'M LOOKING FOR!

WELL, AS YOU MAY *KNOW*, MY BOY-- THIS HOSPITAL IS PARTIALLY FUNDED BY *STARK INTERNATIONAL*, TO ENABLE US TO STUDY VARIOUS NEW EXPERIMENTAL *SURGICAL TECHNIQUES*!

S. I. ALSO FUNDS A *PEOPLE'S FREE MEDICAL CLINIC* ON THE UPPER WEST SIDE...

...AND THEY'RE CONSTANTLY LOOKING FOR-- IF YOU'LL EXCUSE THE EXPRESSION-- *NEW BLOOD*!

IT DOESN'T *PAY* ANYTHING, BUT THE *OTHER* REWARDS ARE BEYOND CALCULATION! IF YOU CAN AFFORD THE *TIME*, IT'S SOMETHING YOU OUGHT TO LOOK *INTO*.

IT WOULD BE A SHAME TO SEE A *TALENT* LIKE YOURS GO TO *WASTE*!

THANK YOU, JACOB-- IT SOUNDS LIKE JUST THE THING I'M *LOOKING* FOR!

TO BE HONEST, I'VE NEVER QUITE UNDER-STOOD YOU, MY BOY! YOUR SKILL AS A SURGEON SURPASSES ANY OTHER I'VE EVER SEEN--

--YET I'VE ALWAYS HAD THE FEELING MERE MEDICINE WASN'T ENOUGH FOR YOU...AS IF THERE WAS SOME-THING INSIDE YOU THAT CRAVED MORE EXCITE-MENT, MORE ADVENTURE...

BELIEVE ME, JACOB-- I'VE HAD JUST ABOUT ALL THE EXCITEMENT I CAN STAND FOR A...

WHA--?

THWAMM!

WHAT'S GOING ON HERE?

THAT OVER-ENTHUSIASTIC INTERN DARED TO ATTACK ME, AND NOW HE HAS FELT THE FULL, UNFETTERED FURY OF-- DAMOCLES!

BUT IF YOU ALL WILL STAND PERFECTLY STILL WHILE WE TAKE THE MATERIAL WE HAVE COME FOR-- NONE OF THE REST OF YOU NEED BE HURT!

THAT *CANISTER*-- IT CONTAINS THE *SYNTHETIC COBALT* STARK LENT US TO AID IN OUR *CANCER RESEARCH!*

GREAT SCOTT--*NO!* THEY CAN'T BE ALLOWED TO *ESCAPE* WITH THAT!

MY BOY-- DON'T!!

NOW A *CRIPPLE* ATTEMPTS TO SUBDUE ME?

FOOL!!

HE'S *RIGHT*-- I *WAS* A FOOL! I'VE BEEN THE *THUNDER GOD* FOR SO LONG, I *FORGOT* MYSELF!

BROK!

CONSIDER YOURSELF *FORTUNATE* I LEAVE YOU YOUR *LIFE*, DOLT!

BUT DAMOCLES CAN AFFORD TO BE *GENEROUS* THIS DAY--

--FOR I HAVE GAINED THE *PRIZE* WHICH WILL SOON LAY THIS *CITY* AT MY *FEET!*

WE GOT THAT ATOMIC STUFF *LOCKED AWAY*, BOSS!

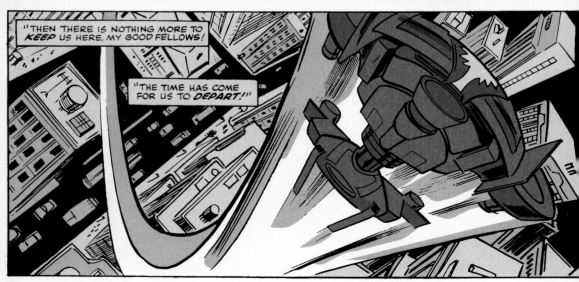

"THEN THERE IS NOTHING MORE TO *KEEP* US HERE, MY GOOD FELLOWS!"

"THE TIME HAS COME FOR US TO *DEPART!*"

MY BOY, ARE YOU **ALL RIGHT**?

I'M **FINE**, JACOB-- BUT THAT **DAMOCLES** CHARACTER IS **GETTING AWAY**!

I WANT TO **THANK** YOU FOR ALL YOUR **ADVICE**, OLD FRIEND-- BUT I'M AFRAID I HAVE TO **RUN**!

I'LL TALK TO YOU **SOON**, OKAY?

PLEASE, MY BOY, I DON'T KNOW **WHAT** YOU HAVE IN **MIND**-- BUT I BEG YOU NOT TO BE **FOOLISH**!

DON'T **WORRY**, JACOB-- I'LL TRY TO BE **CAREFUL**!

AND, MOMENTS LATER, IN A SECLUDED **ALLEYWAY** NEARBY, THE LAME PHYSICIAN STRIKES HIS GNARLED WALKING STICK **ONCE** UPON THE GROUND...

...AND A FURIOUS **GOD OF THUNDER** TAKES TO THE GRAY-STREAKED **SKIES** ONCE MORE!

VERILY, MIDGARD HATH CHANGED **LESS** THAN I HAD **HOPED**!

STILL DOTH **CRIME** AND **INJUSTICE** RUN RAMPANT THROUGH ITS **STREETS**--

--BUT SO LONG AS THE SON OF ODIN DOTH CALL THIS WORLD HIS **OWN**--

--**TREACHERY** SHALL **NEVER** TRIUMPH!!

BRAK-KOOM!

BY THE STARS-- **NO**! IT'S THE AVENGER THEY CALL **THOR**!

THE CURSED THUNDER GOD POSSESSES **POWER** ENOUGH TO **THWART** ALL MY CAREFULLY-LAID **SCHEMES**, UNLESS...

QUICKLY, MEN--**RELEASE** THE **DESTRUCT-DRONE**!!

BY THE BRISTLING BEARD OF **ODIN!** THE FIENDS HAVE LAUNCHED A FIERY **MISSILE** AT THE VERY **HEART** OF THIS FAIR CITY--

--AND IT DOTH STREAK TOWARDS THE TOWERING **UNITED NATIONS BUILDING** ITSELF!

IF I ATTEMPT TO **STOP** YON MISSILE, DAMOCLES WILL **ESCAPE**--

--BUT ONLY MINE ENCHANTED **MALLET** DOTH POSSESS THE OVERWHELMING **SPEED** REQUIRED TO **OVERTAKE** HIS DREADFUL WEAPON--

"--THOUGH I FEAR EVEN THE MYSTIC **MJOLNIR** MAY NOT REACH ITS TARGET **IN TIME!**"

DESPERATELY, AS IF POSSESSING A LIFE OF ITS **OWN**, THE THUNDER GOD'S WONDROUS WEAPON **PURSUES** ITS DEADLY QUARRY ACROSS THE ISLAND OF **MANHATTAN**...

...UNTIL, MERE **FEET** FROM THE WORLD FAMOUS MEETING HALL'S GLEAMING GLASS **FACADE**--

WHA-WHOOM!

--THE HURTLING HAMMER **STRIKES** HOME!

WHILE, WITHOUT HIS ENCHANTED MALLET TO SUSTAIN HIS **FLIGHT**, THE MIGHTY THOR PLUNGES **EARTHWARD**--

--EVEN AS HIS **SPIRIT** SOARS IN **TRIUMPH!**

PRAISE THE FATES! TRUSTY MJOLNIR STRUCK **TRUE!**

AND EVEN NOW, IT DOTH RETURN TO MINE *HAND* -- AS ALMIGHTY ODIN'S ENCHANTMENT HATH DECREED IT EVER *MUST!*

THUS DO I TAKE UP THE *PURSUIT* OF THE DIABOLICAL *DAMOCLES* ONCE MORE -- THOUGH HIS WELL-ARMED *AIRCRAFT* IS NOWHERE IN *SIGHT!*

AND AFTER AN AIRBORNE *SEARCH* OF THE ENTIRE CITY HAS PROVEN *FRUITLESS*...

IT APPEARS THE MAN CALLED DAMOCLES HATH *ESCAPED* ME FOR THE *NONCE* --

-- BUT, BY MY *TROTH*, WE SHALL MEET *AGAIN!*

AND EVEN AS THE THUNDER GOD PONDERS THE *PURPOSE* OF DAMOCLES' THEFT, IN THE HIDDEN LAIR OF THE MADMAN HIMSELF...

NOW THAT WE *GOT* THIS ATOMIC STUFF, BOSS -- WHADDA WE GONNA *DO* WITH IT?

IT'S REALLY QUITE *SIMPLE* MY FRIEND -- WE'RE GOING TO CONSTRUCT A *COBALT CANNON!*

AND THEN THE CITY OF NEW YORK SHALL BOW TO MY *DEMANDS* -- OR BE WIPED CLEAN OFF THE FACE OF THE *EARTH!!*

NEXT ISSUE: **DEATH, THY NAME IS BROTHER!**

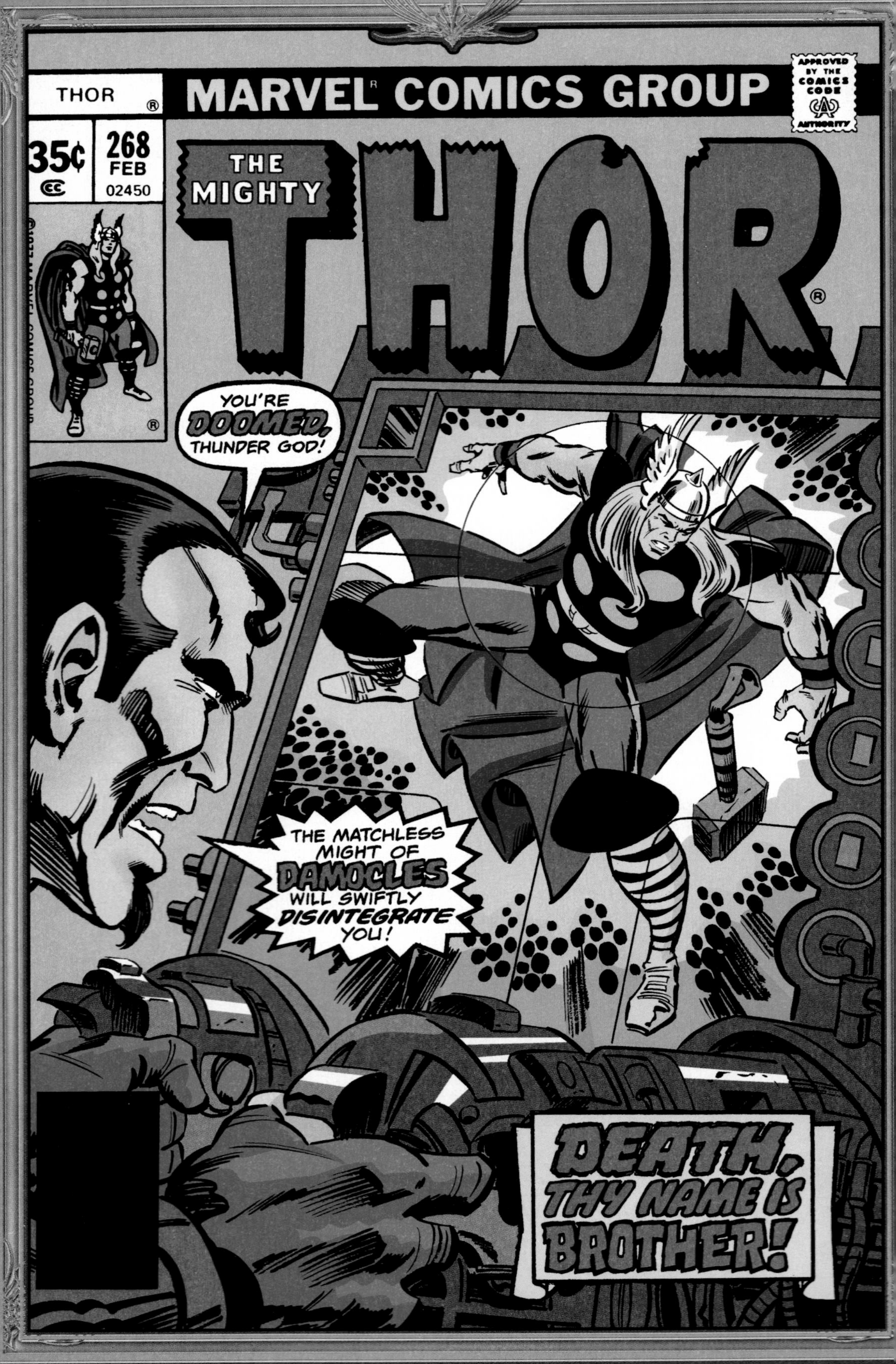
THOR
MARVEL COMICS GROUP
APPROVED BY THE COMICS CODE AUTHORITY
35¢
268
FEB
02450
THE MIGHTY
THOR
YOU'RE DOOMED, THUNDER GOD!
THE MATCHLESS MIGHT OF DAMOCLES WILL SWIFTLY DISINTEGRATE YOU!
DEATH, THY NAME IS BROTHER!

When lame Dr. DONALD BLAKE strikes his wooden walking stick upon the ground, it becomes the mystic mallet MJOLNIR—and Blake is transformed into the Norse God of Thunder, Master of the Storm and the Lightning, Heir to the Throne of Immortal Asgard...

Stan Lee PRESENTS: THE MIGHTY THOR! ™

LEN WEIN ✳ **WALT SIMONSON & TONY DeZUNIGA** ✳ **GLYNIS WEIN** ✳ **JOE ROSEN**
WRITER / EDITOR — ARTISTS / ILLUSTRATORS — COLORIST — LETTERER

DEATH, THY NAME IS BROTHER!

THE *RAIN* HAD BEGUN QUITE *SUDDENLY,* SENDING MANHATTAN'S MID-DAY PEDESTRIANS SCURRYING FOR *SHELTER,* THEIR JACKETS AND NEWSPAPERS HELD HIGH ABOVE THEIR *HEADS*--

--BUT THE LAME *DR. DONALD BLAKE* STROLLS THROUGH THE STORM *UNHURRIED,* ALMOST *REVELING* IN THE ICY SPRAY AGAINST HIS FACE, ALLOWING THE SHOWER TO WASH HIS TROUBLED MIND *CLEAN* ONCE MORE...

...AND HE HAS ALMOST *SUCCEEDED,* WHEN...

HEY-- YOUR NAME *DON BLAKE?*

WHAT--?!?

POLICE

SKREEECH!

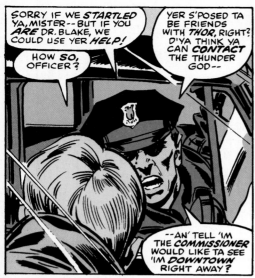

SORRY IF WE *STARTLED* YA, MISTER--BUT IF YOU *ARE* DR. BLAKE, WE COULD USE YER *HELP!*

HOW *SO,* OFFICER?

YER S'POSED TA BE FRIENDS WITH *THOR,* RIGHT? D'YA THINK YA CAN *CONTACT* THE THUNDER GOD--

--AN' TELL 'IM THE *COMMISSIONER* WOULD LIKE TA SEE 'IM *DOWNTOWN* RIGHT AWAY?

WELL, I'M NOT *PROMISING* ANYTHING, MIND YOU--

--BUT I'LL *SEE* WHAT I CAN *DO!*

AND FRANKLY, FRIEND, I CAN DO *PLENTY!*

AND SOON, IN A CONVENIENT *ALLEYWAY...*

BACK ON EARTH LESS THAN 24 *HOURS* AND NOTHING HAS REALLY *CHANGED...*

...A NEW *CRISIS* SEEMS TO REAR ITS HEAD EVERY OTHER *MINUTE...*

...AND ONLY THE *MYSTIC MALLET MJOLNIR* DOTH POSSESS *POWER* ENOW TO *COMBAT* THEM!

THOK!

THEN, AS THE ENCHANTED HAMMER CARRIES ITS HEROIC MASTER ACROSS THE *CITY...*

THE STORM IN THE SKY HATH *ABATED*--BUT THE STORM IN MY *HEART* ERUPTS *ANEW!*

WHATE'ER DARES *THREATEN* THIS CITY I HOLD *DEAR,* IT SHALL FACE THE SWIFT AND RIGHTEOUS WRATH OF--*THOR!*

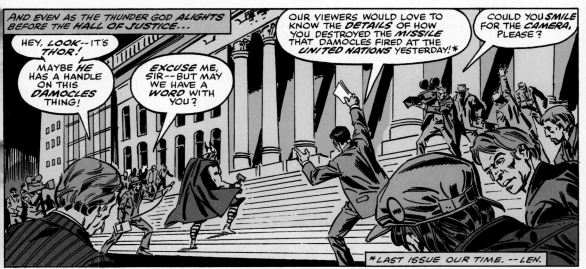

AND EVEN AS THE THUNDER GOD *ALIGHTS* BEFORE THE *HALL OF JUSTICE...*

HEY, *LOOK*--IT'S *THOR!*

MAYBE *HE* HAS A HANDLE ON THIS *DAMOCLES* THING!

EXCUSE ME, SIR--BUT MAY WE HAVE A *WORD* WITH YOU?

OUR VIEWERS WOULD LOVE TO KNOW THE *DETAILS* OF HOW YOU DESTROYED THE *MISSILE* THAT DAMOCLES FIRED AT THE *UNITED NATIONS* YESTERDAY!*

COULD *YOU SMILE* FOR THE *CAMERA,* PLEASE?

*LAST ISSUE OUR TIME. --LEN.

METHINKS THOU DOST MAKE *TOO MUCH* OF MINE ACTIONS, GOOD FELLOWS!

I MERELY DID MY *DUTY* AS I *SAW* IT--NOTHING *MORE!*

NOW, IF THOU WOULDST *EXCUSE* ME...?

HEY-- *WAIT!* YOU CAN'T JUST *WALK OFF* LIKE THAT! WE WANT SOME *ANSWERS!*

WELL, YOU'LL JUST HAFTA *WAIT* FOR 'EM, FRIEND!

GOLDILOCKS HAS GOT SOME-- *BUSINESS* NOW-- WITH THE *CHIEF!*

AND THUS, MOMENTS *LATER...*

THOU DIDST *CALL* AND THOR HATH *ANSWERED,* COMMISSIONER!

HOW MAY THE SON OF ODIN *SERVE* THEE?

WE APPRECIATE YOUR *RESPONDING* TO OUR INVITATION SO *QUICKLY,* THOR! WE MAY HAVE A *BREAKTHROUGH* ON THIS *DAMOCLES* CASE!

BY ODIN, THAT IS *JOYOUS* NEWS INDEED, MY FRIEND! SUCH *VILLAINY* MUST BE BROUGHT TO *TASK*-- AND *SWIFTLY!*

THEN PLEASE COME INTO MY *OFFICE,* THOR! I HAVE SOME- ONE THERE I'D LIKE YOU TO *MEET!*

...A MOST **NONDESCRIPT** SOMEONE INDEED!

F-FORGIVE MY **NERVOUSNESS**, THOR--BUT I'VE NEVER ACTUALLY **MET** A REAL LIVE **GOD** BEFORE!

Y-YOU LOOK MUCH **TALLER** THAN YOU DO ON **TELE-VISION!**

OH...UH... MY NAME IS **BENNETT BARLOW!**

PLEASE, MR. BARLOW--TIME IS **CRUCIAL** AT THE MOMENT! NOW THAT THOR IS **HERE**, AS YOU REQUESTED...

...WILL YOU KINDLY **DIVULGE** THE INFORMATION YOU CLAIM TO HAVE, REGARDING **DAMOCLES?**

AYE, MORTAL--IF THOU DOST **KNOW** THE EVIL ONE'S WHEREABOUTS, PRAY **SPEAK!**

ALL I KNOW ABOUT HIS **CURRENT** BUSINESS IS WHAT I READ IN THE **PAPER**, I'M AFRAID--BUT I **CAN** TELL YOU ALL ABOUT HIS **BACKGROUND!**

YOU SEE, THE MAN YOU CALL **DAMOCLES** IS ACTUALLY **ERIC BARLOW...**

FOR... ...UN ATTACK!

...MY **BROTHER!!**

THEN, BY THE BRISTLING BEARD OF ODIN-- **SAY ON**, MAN!

I WOULD KNOW MORE OF WHAT **CREATES** SUCH A MAN AS **DAMOCLES!**

"I DON'T KNOW, MAYBE ERIC WAS **ALWAYS** LIKE THIS--CONFUSED, **SEARCHING** FOR SOMETHING...

"...AND TAKING HIS **FRUSTRATIONS** OUT ON THE ONE WHO **LOVED** HIM MOST IN ALL THE WORLD...HIS LITTLE **BROTHER**...ME!

"I MEAN, NOBODY WAS PROUDER THAN **I** WAS, WHEN ERIC **GRADUATED** COLLEGE THE YEAR I **ENTERED...**

"HE'D MADE **HONORS** ALL THE WAY...THE **TOP** OF HIS **CLASS**...HE HAD THE WHOLE **WORLD** AT HIS FEET...

"...BUT SOMEHOW, THINGS JUST KEPT GETTING **WORSE!**

"ERIC DRIFTED FROM JOB TO JOB, STILL LOOKING FOR A **DIRECTION...**

"...WHILE I THOUGHT I'D *FOUND ONE!*

"WHEN THIS NATION'S COLLEGES SHOOK WITH *PROTEST*, I WAS RIGHT THERE ON THE *FRONT LINES...*

PEACE NOW!

PEACE NOW!

"...EVEN AS POOR *ERIC* FADED FURTHER INTO THE *BACKGROUND!*

"I WAS YOUR CLASSIC *COLLEGE REVOLUTIONARY*, EVEN TO MAJORING IN *PHYSICS*, SO I COULD LEARN TO BUILD MY OWN *NUCLEAR BOMB* IF NECESSARY...

"...WHILE MY *BROTHER* JUST STOOD BY, *WATCHING!*

"IRONICALLY, MY EDUCATION *PAID OFF* IN THE END, WHEN THE PROTESTS QUIETLY *DIED*, MY PHYSICS DEGREE GOT ME A JOB *TEACHING* AT CITY UNIVERSITY...

"A FEW YEARS BACK, I GOT *MARRIED*... AND ERIC WENT HIS SEPARATE *WAY!*

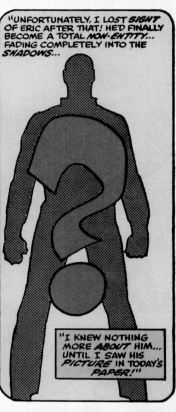

"UNFORTUNATELY, I LOST *SIGHT* OF ERIC AFTER THAT! HE'D FINALLY BECOME A TOTAL *NON-ENTITY...* FADING COMPLETELY INTO THE *SHADOWS...*

"I KNEW NOTHING MORE *ABOUT* HIM... UNTIL I SAW HIS *PICTURE* IN TODAY'S *PAPER!*"

A FASCINATING TALE *INDEED*, FRIEND BARLOW-- BUT 'TWILL TAKE MORE THAN *THAT* FOR US TO *FIND* THY BROTHER!

GEE, I...I DON'T KNOW WHAT *ELSE* I HAVE TO OFFER, EXCEPT...

WELL, I CAN SHOW YOU THE *HOUSE* WHERE WE BOTH *ROOMED* TOGETHER, IF THAT WOULD BE A *HELP.*

'TIS A PLACE TO *START*, MORTAL! WITH *LUCK*, 'TWILL BE *ENOUGH!*

I CERTAINLY *HOPE SO.*

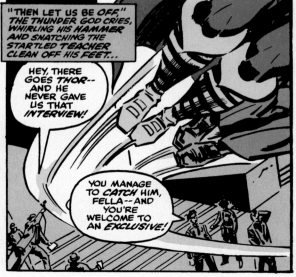

"THEN LET US BE *OFF*," THE THUNDER GOD CRIES, WHIRLING HIS *HAMMER* AND SNATCHING THE STARTLED *TEACHER* CLEAN OFF HIS FEET...

HEY, THERE GOES *THOR*-- AND HE NEVER GAVE US THAT *INTERVIEW!*

YOU MANAGE TO *CATCH* HIM, FELLA-- AND YOU'RE WELCOME TO AN *EXCLUSIVE!*

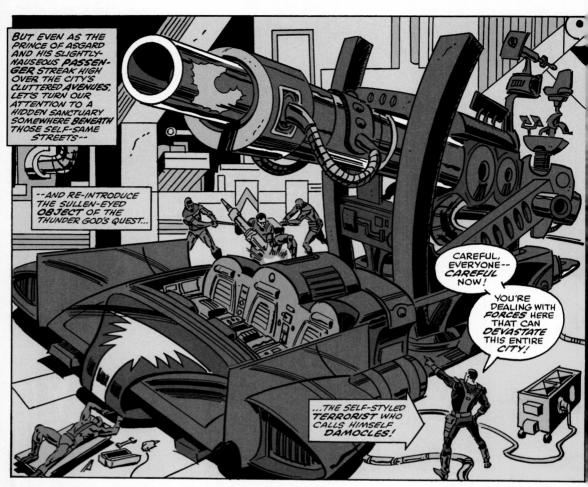

BUT EVEN AS THE PRINCE OF ASGARD AND HIS SLIGHTLY-NAUSEOUS *PASSENGER* STREAK HIGH OVER THE CITY'S CLUTTERED *AVENUES,* LET'S TURN OUR ATTENTION TO A HIDDEN SANCTUARY SOMEWHERE *BENEATH* THOSE SELF-SAME STREETS--

--AND RE-INTRODUCE THE SULLEN-EYED *OBJECT* OF THE THUNDER GOD'S QUEST...

CAREFUL, EVERYONE-- *CAREFUL* NOW!

YOU'RE DEALING WITH *FORCES* HERE THAT CAN *DEVASTATE* THIS ENTIRE *CITY!*

...THE SELF-STYLED *TERRORIST* WHO CALLS HIMSELF *DAMOCLES!*

AND SOON-- *SOON* --WHEN OUR WEAPON IS *FINISHED,* THE SIMPERING FOOLS WHO ABUSED AND IGNORED ME WILL *FEEL* THAT POWER!

LIKE THE *SWORD* WHICH DANGLED BY A THREAD OVER THE HEAD OF THE *ORIGINAL* DAMOCLES, THE THREAT OF MY *COBALT-CANNON* WILL HANG OVER THEIR HEADS--

--AND *BEND* THEM TO MY *WILL!!*

SOON, I SHALL BE *REPAID* FOR ALL THE *INDIGNITIES* I HAVE BEEN FORCED TO ENDURE... AYE, *SOON!*

BUT WHAT ABOUT *US,* BOSS? WHEN WILL *WE* BE REPAID?

WE GOT *INTO* THIS GIG BECAUSE YOU PROMISED US *BIG BUCKS,* REMEMBER?

EH?

106

YOU DARE TO QUESTION MY *JUDGMENT*, YOU SIMPLE-MINDED *FOOL*?

NOBODY DISPUTES THE WORD OF *DAMOCLES*-- WITHOUT *PAYING* FOR IT IN *FULL*!!

BWA-DOW!

IT TAKES DAMOCLES ONLY A *MOMENT* TO DRAW AND FIRE-- JUST LONG ENOUGH FOR *MORTAL FEAR* TO WELL UP IN HIS HENCHMEN'S THROATS!

BUT IT IS A FEAR THAT SEEMS *UNFOUNDED*, AS THE *CONCUSSION-SHELL* STRIKES ONLY A STACK OF EMPTY *OIL DRUMS*...

KWA·VA·VOOM!

...SENDING MEN AND METAL *SPRAYING* ACROSS THE ROOM!

AND WHEN THE SAVAGE TURMOIL HAS SETTLED INTO A SMOLDERING SEMBLANCE OF *ORDER* ONCE MORE...

YOU WOULD ALL DO WELL TO *REMEMBER* THIS LITTLE DEMONSTRATION, GENTLEMEN! *NEXT* TIME, I WILL NOT BE SO *LENIENT*!

I AM *MASTER* HERE-- COMPLETE AND *ABSOLUTE*-- AND HE WHO DARES TO DEFY MY WILL...*DIES*!!

WH-WHATEVER YOU *SAY*, BOSS!

YA AIN'T GONNA GET NO MORE ARGUMENT FROM *US*!

HIS FACE A COLD, GRIM *MASK*, THE MALEVOLENT DAMOCLES STRIDES INTO HIS PRIVATE *CHAMBERS*...

...WHERE, ONCE HE HAS *SEALED* THE DOOR *BEHIND HIM*...

I HELD THEM IN CHECK *THIS* TIME, BUT WHAT ABOUT *NEXT* TIME, OR THE TIME AFTER *THAT*?

I DON'T KNOW HOW MUCH *LONGER* I CAN *CONTROL* THEM! THINGS ARE DEFINITELY STARTING TO GET *OUT-OF-HAND*!

AND THOUGH THE CHAMBER IS UNCOMMONLY *WARM*, DAMOCLES SUDDENLY BEGINS TO *TREMBLE*.

WHILE, IN A MAXIMUM-SECURITY *PRISON,* SOMEWHERE UPSTATE...

I'VE GOT TO THINK THIS *THROUGH...* WORK OUT A PROPER *PLAN...*

NO PRISON HAS EVER HELD ME *BEFORE* -- AND THIS ONE WON'T BE AN *EXCEPTION!*

IF I COULD ONLY GET MY HANDS ON MY *OUTFIT,* I MIGHT... *EH?*

THE OUTSIDE *WALL* -- IT'S BEGUN TO *MELT* --!?!

GOT TO FIND *COVER* BEFORE IT...

...EXPLODES.

SKROOM!

AND BEFORE THE SHATTERED RUBBLE CAN *SETTLE...*

I HAVE *COME* FOR YOU, LITTLE MAN!

NO! STAY *AWAY* FROM ME --!!

Y-YOU'RE NOT *HUMAN!!*

BUT THE BESPECTACLED CONVICT'S TERRIFIED CRIES ARE *STIFLED,* AS HE IS SWEPT OFF THE GROUND BY AN INHUMANLY-POWERFUL *ARM,* AND...

KEEP *FIRING,* MEN! WE CAN'T LET THEM *ESCAPE!*

BLAM!

BLAM!

BUT THEY ARE ALREADY *GONE!*

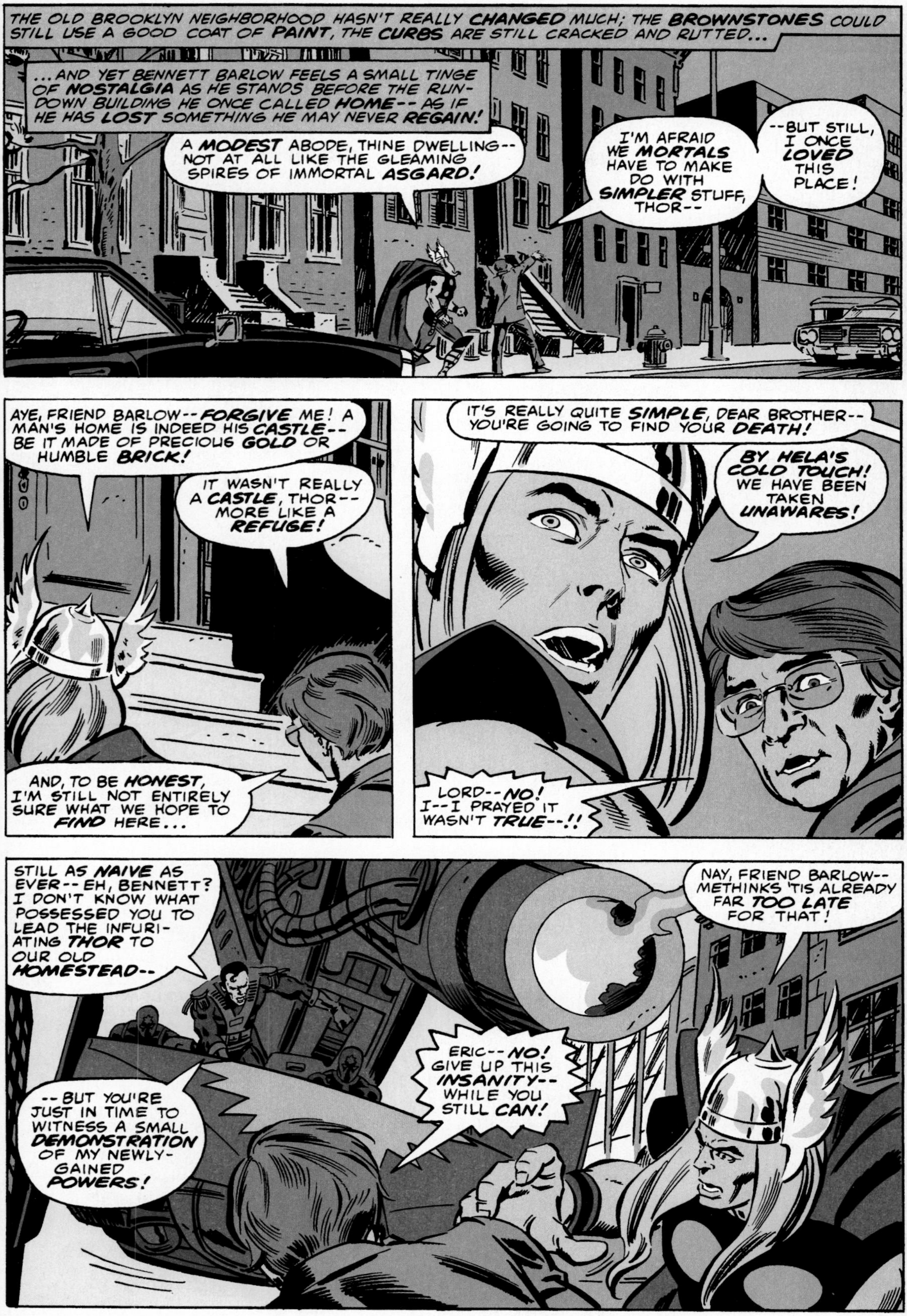

THE OLD BROOKLYN NEIGHBORHOOD HASN'T REALLY CHANGED MUCH; THE BROWNSTONES COULD STILL USE A GOOD COAT OF PAINT, THE CURBS ARE STILL CRACKED AND RUTTED...
...AND YET BENNETT BARLOW FEELS A SMALL TINGE OF NOSTALGIA AS HE STANDS BEFORE THE RUN-DOWN BUILDING HE ONCE CALLED HOME-- AS IF HE HAS LOST SOMETHING HE MAY NEVER REGAIN!
A MODEST ABODE, THINE DWELLING-- NOT AT ALL LIKE THE GLEAMING SPIRES OF IMMORTAL ASGARD!
I'M AFRAID WE MORTALS HAVE TO MAKE DO WITH SIMPLER STUFF, THOR--
--BUT STILL, I ONCE LOVED THIS PLACE!
AYE, FRIEND BARLOW--FORGIVE ME! A MAN'S HOME IS INDEED HIS CASTLE-- BE IT MADE OF PRECIOUS GOLD OR HUMBLE BRICK!
IT WASN'T REALLY A CASTLE, THOR-- MORE LIKE A REFUGE!
AND, TO BE HONEST, I'M STILL NOT ENTIRELY SURE WHAT WE HOPE TO FIND HERE...
IT'S REALLY QUITE SIMPLE, DEAR BROTHER-- YOU'RE GOING TO FIND YOUR DEATH!
BY HELA'S COLD TOUCH! WE HAVE BEEN TAKEN UNAWARES!
LORD--NO! I--I PRAYED IT WASN'T TRUE--!!
STILL AS NAIVE AS EVER-- EH, BENNETT? I DON'T KNOW WHAT POSSESSED YOU TO LEAD THE INFURIATING THOR TO OUR OLD HOMESTEAD--
NAY, FRIEND BARLOW-- METHINKS 'TIS ALREADY FAR TOO LATE FOR THAT!
ERIC--NO! GIVE UP THIS INSANITY-- WHILE YOU STILL CAN!
--BUT YOU'RE JUST IN TIME TO WITNESS A SMALL DEMONSTRATION OF MY NEWLY-GAINED POWERS!

GRINNING TRIUMPHANTLY, THE MAN CALLED DAMOCLES STABS A BUTTON ON THE CONTROL BOARD BEFORE HIM -- AND BRIGHT BLUE FIRE SWIFTLY ERUPTS FROM THE COBALT-CANON'S MAW...

ERIC -- NO!!

THOU DOST *ENTREAT* THY BROTHER IN *VAIN*, FRIEND BARLOW!

HE DOTH MEAN TO DISPOSE OF US *BOTH*!!

BUT, SIZZLING THROUGH THE SPACE WHERE BARLOW AND THUNDER GOD HAD STOOD SPLIT-SECONDS *BEFORE*, THE AWESOMELY- POWERFUL BEAM OF COBALT-ENERGY IN-STEAD STRIKES THE BROWNSTONE BUILDING WHERE THE BARLOW BROTHERS HAD ONCE LIVED --

WHA-WHOOM!

-- AND REDUCES IT TO AN IN-CINERATED *MEMORY*!!

SWEET HEAVEN -- THE *POWER* OF THAT DEVICE -- IT'S ALMOST *UNIMAG-INABLE*!

MY BROTHER OR NOT, ERIC HAS TO BE *STOPPED*!

AYE, FRIEND BARLOW -- AND 'TIS MY TASK TO *SEE* TO IT!

FOOL! SO LONG AS THE COBALT- CANNON IS *MINE*, THERE IS *NOTHING* THAT CAN STOP ME!

AT MY COMMAND -- FIRE!!

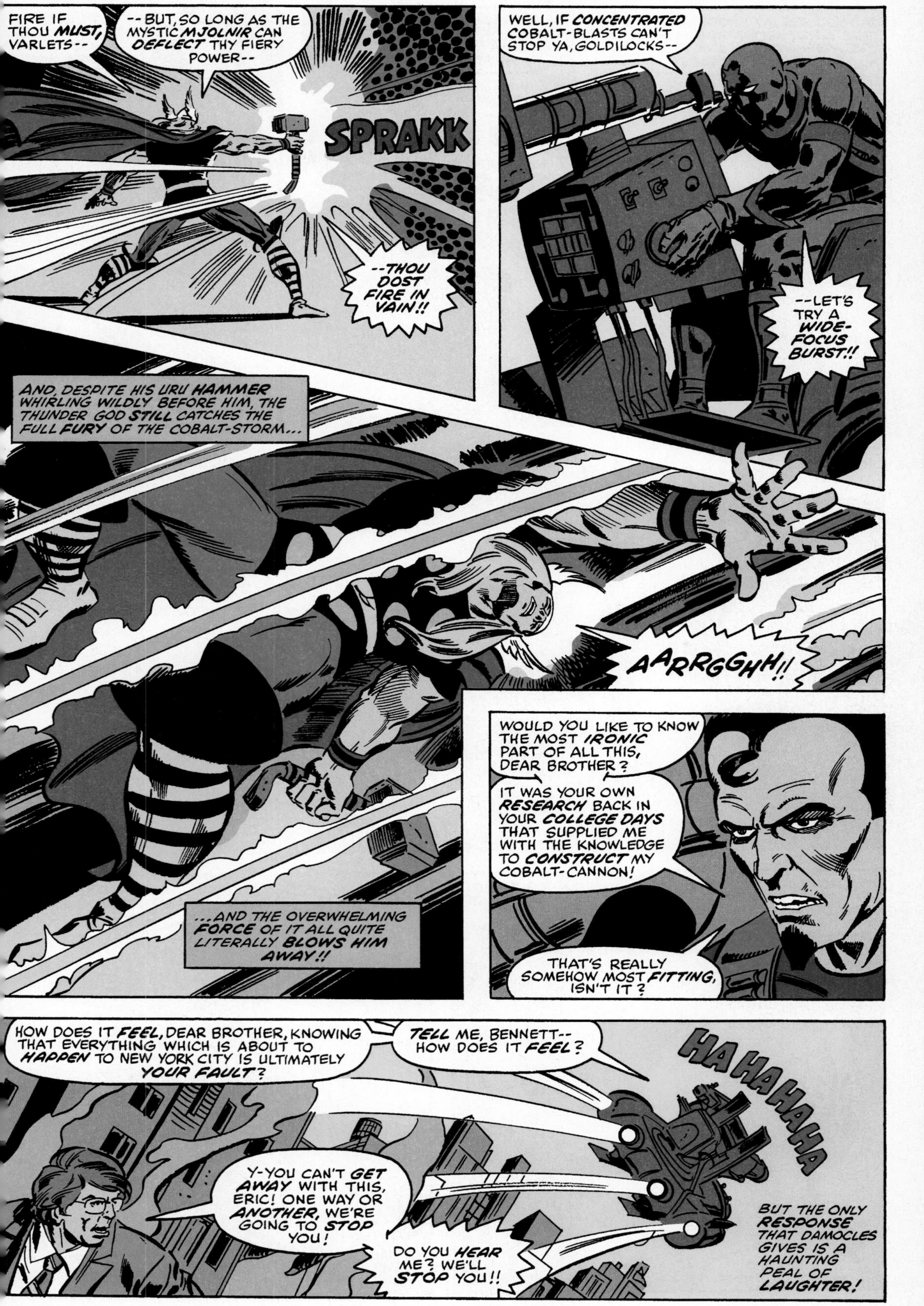

FIRE IF THOU MUST, VARLETS--
--BUT, SO LONG AS THE MYSTIC MJOLNIR CAN DEFLECT THY FIERY POWER--
SPRAKK
--THOU DOST FIRE IN VAIN!!
WELL, IF CONCENTRATED COBALT-BLASTS CAN'T STOP YA, GOLDILOCKS--
--LET'S TRY A WIDE-FOCUS BURST!!
AND, DESPITE HIS URU HAMMER WHIRLING WILDLY BEFORE HIM, THE THUNDER GOD STILL CATCHES THE FULL FURY OF THE COBALT-STORM...
AARRGGHH!!
...AND THE OVERWHELMING FORCE OF IT ALL QUITE LITERALLY BLOWS HIM AWAY!!
WOULD YOU LIKE TO KNOW THE MOST IRONIC PART OF ALL THIS, DEAR BROTHER?
IT WAS YOUR OWN RESEARCH BACK IN YOUR COLLEGE DAYS THAT SUPPLIED ME WITH THE KNOWLEDGE TO CONSTRUCT MY COBALT-CANNON!
THAT'S REALLY SOMEHOW MOST FITTING, ISN'T IT?
HOW DOES IT FEEL, DEAR BROTHER, KNOWING THAT EVERYTHING WHICH IS ABOUT TO HAPPEN TO NEW YORK CITY IS ULTIMATELY YOUR FAULT?
TELL ME, BENNETT-- HOW DOES IT FEEL?
HA HA HA HA HA
Y-YOU CAN'T GET AWAY WITH THIS, ERIC! ONE WAY OR ANOTHER, WE'RE GOING TO STOP YOU!
DO YOU HEAR ME? WE'LL STOP YOU!!
BUT THE ONLY RESPONSE THAT DAMOCLES GIVES IS A HAUNTING PEAL OF LAUGHTER!

DID YOU SEE MY BROTHER'S *FACE*? THAT *LOOK* ALONE WAS WORTH ALL THE *HUMILIATION* I'VE ENDURED OVER THE YEARS!

WELL, WHAT *NOW*, BOSS?

EH? WHAT DO YOU *MEAN*?

NOW THAT WE'VE PROVEN THIS GIZMO OF YOURS *WORKS*, DON'T YA THINK IT'S TIME WE WENT AFTER THE *MONEY*?

WELL, I HAD *PLANNED* TO...TO...

NO--PERHAPS YOU'RE *RIGHT*, MY FRIEND!

THIS CRUEL, UNCARING WORLD *OWES* US-- OWES US *GREATLY*--

--AND, AS OF *NOW*, WE BEGIN TO *COLLECT*.!!

BY ODIN... WHAT...?

Y-YOU WERE KNOCKED *UNCONSCIOUS* BY ERIC'S COBALT-CANNON, THAT'S ALL....JUST KNOCKED *UNCONSCIOUS*!

ANYONE *ELSE* WOULD HAVE BEEN COMPLETELY *INCINERATED*!

THE SON OF ODIN IS MADE OF *STERNER STUFF*, FRIEND BARLOW-- BUT *NO* MAN MAY STRIKE THE PRINCE OF ASGARD WITH *IMPUNITY*!

DIDST THOU *SEE* WHICH WAY THY VILLAINOUS BROTHER *FLED*?

H-HE HEADED *WEST*... I THINK.

THEN, WHITHER HE HATH *TRAVELED*, WE SHALL *FOLLOW*--

--TO PUT AN *END* TO HIS MADNESS *FOREVER*.!!

VERILY, HAD I BUT *KNOWN* HIS THEFT OF THAT SYNTHETIC COBALT * WOULD CAUSE SUCH *CHAOS,* I'D HAVE...

WHAT--?!?

DID YOU SAY... *SYN-THETIC* COBALT?

AYE, FRIEND BARLOW, BUT...

*LAST ISH, RIGHT? --LEN.

YOU DON'T *UNDERSTAND,* THOR-- SYNTHETIC COBALT IS *UNSTABLE!*

BY ODIN-- *NAY!*

UNLESS WE *FIND* ERIC BEFORE IT REACHES *CRITICAL MASS,* THAT CANNON WILL BECOME A *COBALT BOMB* WHICH CAN *ERADICATE NEW YORK!!*

THEN LET MINE ENCHANTED *HAMMER* STRAIN AS IT NE'ER HATH STRAINED *BEFORE!*

FOR HAVING ONCE BEEN *BATHED* IN THE RAYS OF THE COBALT-CANNON, MIGHTY MJOLNIR CAN NOW *TRACE* THAT SAVAGE POWER TO ITS *SOURCE!*

BUT EVEN AS THE GOD OF THUNDER AND HIS COMPANION HURTLE THROUGH THE HEAVENS, THAT AFOREMENTIONED *SAVAGE POWER* IS ONCE AGAIN AT *WORK...*

SKADA-WHOOM!

...REDUCING THE THICK STEEL *VAULT DOOR* OF A CERTAIN 47th STREET *JEWELRY EXCHANGE* TO SO MUCH *SCRAP METAL!*

QUICKLY, MEN-- *GET TO WORK!!*

YOU *GOT* IT, BOSS! THIS JOINT'LL BE STRIPPED *NAKED* BY THE THE TIME THE *COPS* GET HERE!

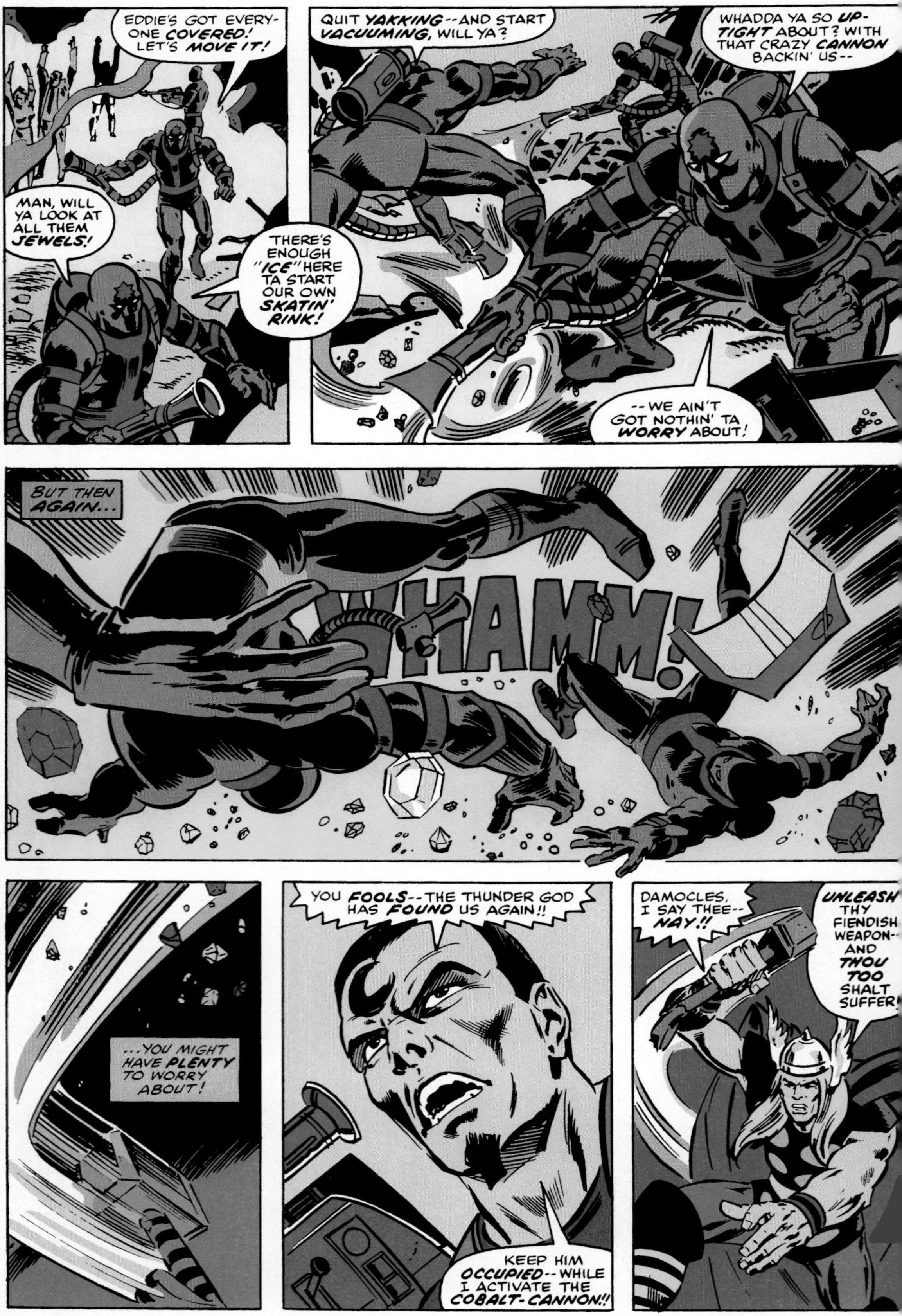
EDDIE'S GOT EVERY-ONE COVERED! LET'S MOVE IT!
MAN, WILL YA LOOK AT ALL THEM JEWELS!
THERE'S ENOUGH "ICE" HERE TA START OUR OWN SKATIN' RINK!
QUIT YAKKING--AND START VACUUMING, WILL YA?
WHADDA YA SO UP-TIGHT ABOUT? WITH THAT CRAZY CANNON BACKIN' US--
--WE AIN'T GOT NOTHIN' TA WORRY ABOUT!
BUT THEN AGAIN...
WHAMM!
...YOU MIGHT HAVE PLENTY TO WORRY ABOUT!
YOU FOOLS--THE THUNDER GOD HAS FOUND US AGAIN!!
KEEP HIM OCCUPIED--WHILE I ACTIVATE THE COBALT-CANNON!!
DAMOCLES, I SAY THEE--NAY!!
UNLEASH THY FIENDISH WEAPON--AND THOU TOO SHALT SUFFER!

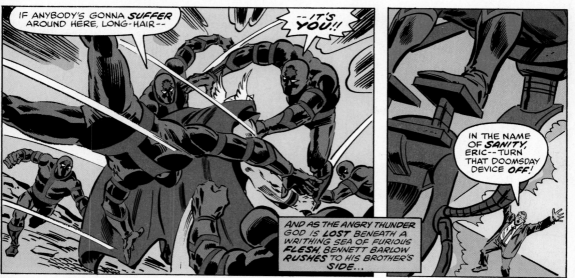

IF ANYBODY'S GONNA **SUFFER** AROUND HERE, LONG-HAIR--

--IT'S **YOU**!!

IN THE NAME OF **SANITY**, ERIC-- TURN THAT DOOMSDAY DEVICE **OFF**!

AND AS THE ANGRY THUNDER GOD IS **LOST** BENEATH A WRITHING SEA OF FURIOUS **FLESH**, BENNETT BARLOW **RUSHES** TO HIS BROTHER'S SIDE...

NOT UNTIL THE ANNOYING **THOR** IS FINALLY **DESTROYED**!

YOU **MANIAC**! YOU'RE GOING TO DESTROY US **ALL**!

THE COBALT YOU USED WAS **UNSTABLE**! LOOK AT THE **GLOW** AROUND YOUR CANNON! I'M TELLING YOU IT'S GOING TO **EXPLODE**!

NO.

IT ISN'T **POSSIBLE**--! NOT AFTER ALL MY **WORK**-- ALL MY **PLANNING**--!

THERE MUST BE SOMETHING I CAN **DO** BEFORE...

AYE, FANATIC ONE-- THERE IS **INDEED**!

HUH?

THOU CANST **SURRENDER** THYSELF, DAMOCLES--

--WHILST STILL THOU ART **ABLE**!!

THIS IS ALL **YOUR** FAULT, THOR! BUT BEFORE I'D GIVE UP **NOW**--

--I'LL SEE US ALL IN **HELL**!!

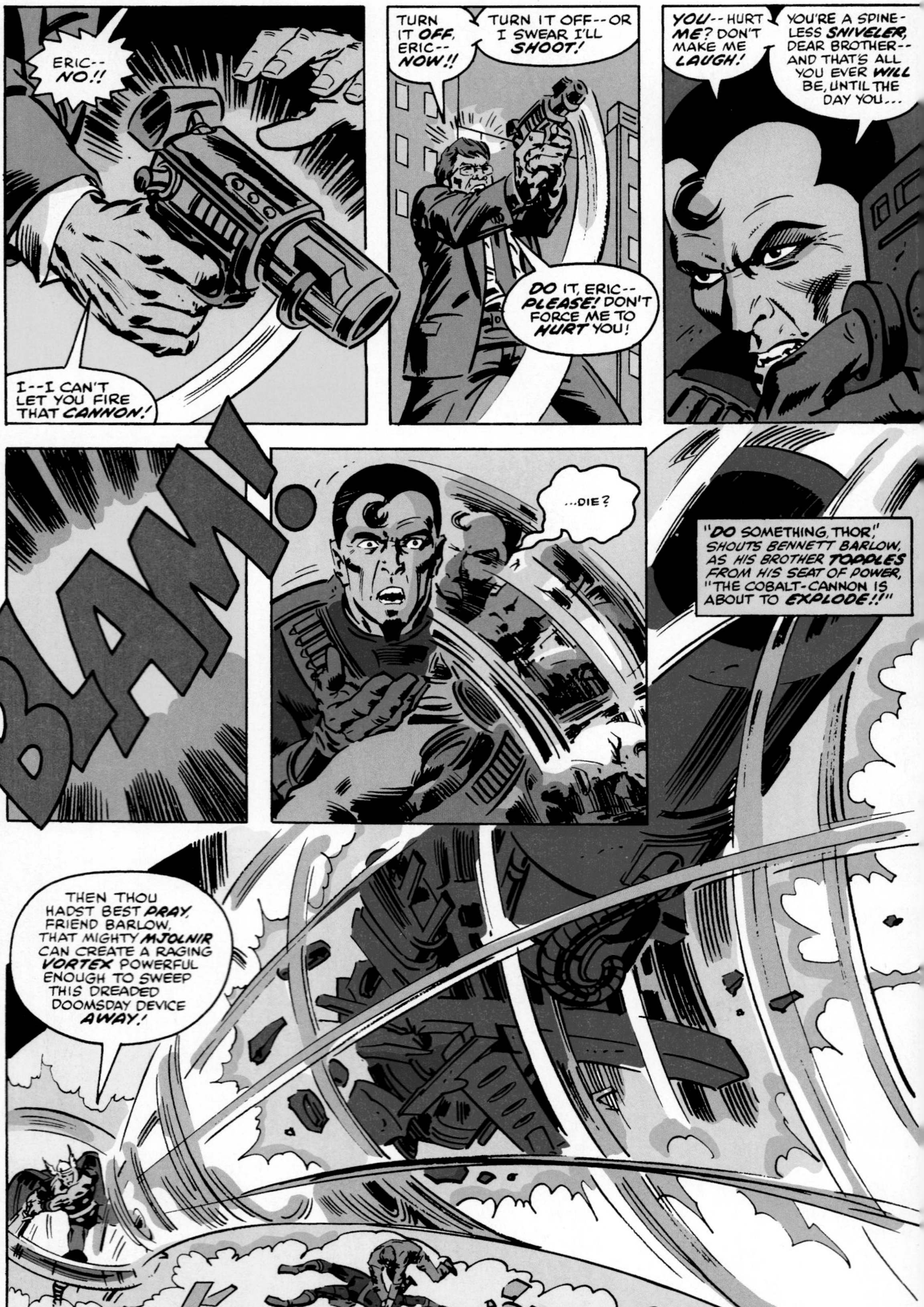
ERIC-- NO!!
I--I CAN'T LET YOU FIRE THAT CANNON!
TURN IT OFF, ERIC-- NOW!!
TURN IT OFF--OR I SWEAR I'LL SHOOT!
DO IT, ERIC-- PLEASE! DON'T FORCE ME TO HURT YOU!
YOU--HURT ME? DON'T MAKE ME LAUGH!
YOU'RE A SPINE-LESS SNIVELER, DEAR BROTHER-- AND THAT'S ALL YOU EVER WILL BE, UNTIL THE DAY YOU...
BLAM!
...DIE?
"DO SOMETHING, THOR," SHOUTS BENNETT BARLOW, AS HIS BROTHER TOPPLES FROM HIS SEAT OF POWER, "THE COBALT-CANNON IS ABOUT TO EXPLODE!!"
THEN THOU HADST BEST PRAY, FRIEND BARLOW, THAT MIGHTY MJOLNIR CAN CREATE A RAGING VORTEX POWERFUL ENOUGH TO SWEEP THIS DREADED DOOMSDAY DEVICE AWAY!

AND THE OVERWHELMING *SIGH OF RELIEF* THAT IS HEARD, AS THE VORTEX-TOSSED COBALT-CANNON ABRUPTLY *VANISHES*, IS FAR MORE *AUDIBLE* THAN THE MIND-SHATTERING *MEGA-BLAST* WHICH SIGNALS THE DEATH-DEALING WEAPON'S *DESTRUCTION*--

--FOR THERE IS, AFTER ALL, NO *SOUND* IN THE *FRIGID DEPTHS* OF *SPACE!*

'TIS *OVER,* FRIEND BARLOW!

AND, VERILY, THIS FAIR CITY DOTH OWE THEE A GREAT VOTE OF *THANKS!*

THOU HAST SAVED *LIVES BEYOND NUMBERING* THIS DAY-- THOUGH THOU HAST *LOST* A LIFE MOST *PRECIOUS* TO THEE IN THE PROCESS!

I SHALL LEAVE THEE ALONE WITH THY *GRIEF* NOW, BENNETT BARLOW--

--AYE, AND WITH THIS *THOUGHT* AS WELL!

THOUGH THY BROTHER LIVED IN *INFAMY*--TRULY DID HE DIE IN *GLORY!*

FOR HOW MANY *OTHER* MEN HAVE LEFT A *STAR* TO MARK THEIR *PASSING?*

NEXT ISSUE: A WALK ON THE WILD SIDE! BE HERE!

THOR
MARVEL® COMICS GROUP
APPROVED BY THE COMICS CODE AUTHORITY
35¢
CC
269
MAR
02450
©1977 MARVEL COMICS GROUP
THE MIGHTY
THOR®
THE STILT-MAN HATH RETURNED--AND MY HAMMER CANNOT STOP HIM!!
BUT HIS ROCKET-PODS MAY SOON SLAY ME!!
AND IF THAT ISN'T TROUBLE ENOUGH FOR OUR HERO--WAIT'LL YOU SEE STILTY'S NEW PARTNER!

When lame Dr. DONALD BLAKE strikes his wooden walking stick upon the ground, it becomes the mystic mallet MJOLNIR—and Blake is transformed into the Norse God of Thunder, Master of the Storm and the Lightning, Heir to the Throne of Immortal Asgard...

STAN LEE PRESENTS: THE MIGHTY THOR!™

LEN WEIN | WALT SIMONSON & TONY DeZUNIGA | GLYNIS WEIN: COLORIST
WRITER/EDITOR | ILLUSTRATORS/STORYTELLERS | JOE ROSEN: LETTERER

A WALK ON THE WILD SIDE!

NOW *HERE'S* SOMETHING YOU DON'T SEE EVERY DAY: A CLASSIC FIGURE OF NORSE MYTHOLOGY, *PERUSING* THE LOCAL TABLOIDS.

SURPRISED, FAITHFUL ONE? *ASTONISHED?* WELL, YOU *SHOULDN'T* BE!

AFTER ALL, EVEN A *THUNDER GOD* HAS TO KEEP TABS ON THINGS *SOMEHOW!*

DAILY BUGLE
SPIDER-MAN AND THE GREEN GOBLIN--
PARTNERS IN CRIME?

MAN, I'D NEVER'VE *BELIEVED* IT! OL' GOLDILOCKS *HIMSELF*-- STOPPIN'-- AT *MY* NEWSSTAND!

AND I WISH TO **THANK** THEE FOR THY **HOSPITALITY**, FRIEND NEWSDEALER. LACKING SUITABLE **COIN OF THE REALM**, I CANNOT **REPAY** THEE FOR THE USE OF THY...

EH?

HEY-- IT'S **THOR!**

OH, **WOW**-- IT'S REALLY **HIM!**

SOOTH, BUT I HAD **DREADED** THIS!

GEE, I HATE TO **BOTHER** YOU OR ANYTHING-- BUT CAN I HAVE YOUR **AUTOGRAPH**, MR. THOR?

IT WOULD REALLY MEAN A **LOT** TO ME!

YOU CAN SIGN THE PAGE RIGHT AFTER **BILLY CARTER**... AND COULD YOU MAKE IT OUT TO **SALLY JANE?**

AYE, CHILD--'TWILL BE MY **PLEASURE!**

WHEN YOU'RE **DONE**, COULD YOU LET LITTLE JIMMY TOUCH YOUR **HAMMER** MISTER?

HE'S A BIG **FAN** OF YOURS!

AH, THOR'S **OKAY**-- BUT HE'S NOT HALF AS NEAT AS **IRON MAN!**

AND SO IT GOES, UNTIL...

FORGIVE ME, GOOD CITIZENS-- BUT I FEAR I MUST TAKE MY **LEAVE** NOW!

THE CLARION CALL TO **DUTY** HATH BEEN **SOUNDED**--

--AND THE **SON OF ODIN**, AS EVER, MUST **ANSWER!**

THOUGH METHINKS THERE ARE TIMES I WOULD RATHER FACE AN **ARMY** OF MY FIERCEST **FOES** THAN A CROWD OF MY MOST ARDENT **ADMIRERS!**

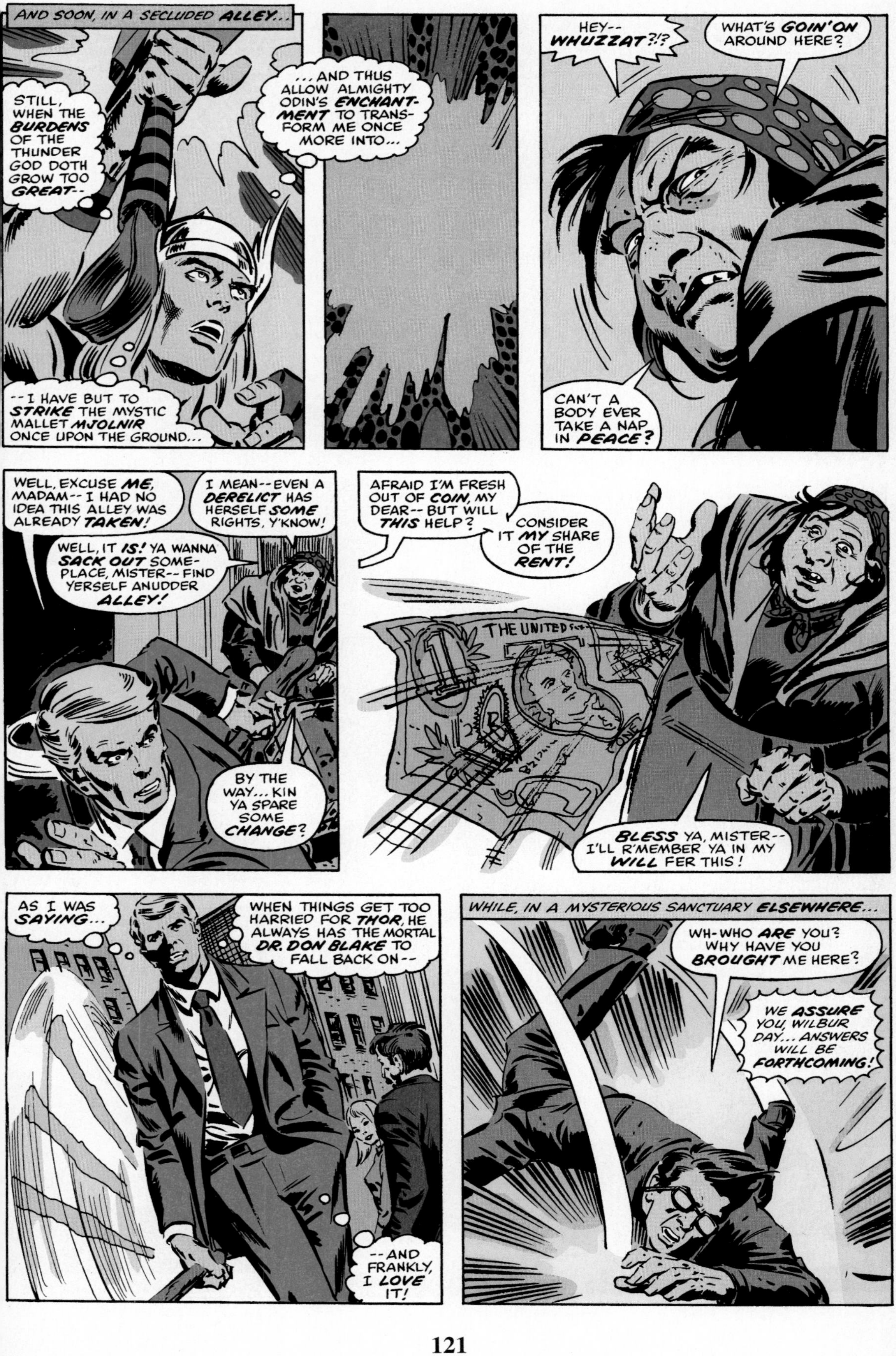
AND SOON, IN A SECLUDED ALLEY...
STILL, WHEN THE BURDENS OF THE THUNDER GOD DOTH GROW TOO GREAT--
--I HAVE BUT TO STRIKE THE MYSTIC MALLET MJOLNIR ONCE UPON THE GROUND...
...AND THUS ALLOW ALMIGHTY ODIN'S ENCHANTMENT TO TRANSFORM ME ONCE MORE INTO...
HEY-- WHUZZAT?!?
WHAT'S GOIN' ON AROUND HERE?
CAN'T A BODY EVER TAKE A NAP IN PEACE?
WELL, EXCUSE ME, MADAM-- I HAD NO IDEA THIS ALLEY WAS ALREADY TAKEN!
I MEAN--EVEN A DERELICT HAS HERSELF SOME RIGHTS, Y'KNOW!
WELL, IT IS! YA WANNA SACK OUT SOMEPLACE, MISTER-- FIND YERSELF ANUDDER ALLEY!
BY THE WAY... KIN YA SPARE SOME CHANGE?
AFRAID I'M FRESH OUT OF COIN, MY DEAR-- BUT WILL THIS HELP?
CONSIDER IT MY SHARE OF THE RENT!
THE UNITED
BLESS YA, MISTER-- I'LL R'MEMBER YA IN MY WILL FER THIS!
AS I WAS SAYING...
WHEN THINGS GET TOO HARRIED FOR THOR, HE ALWAYS HAS THE MORTAL DR. DON BLAKE TO FALL BACK ON--
--AND FRANKLY, I LOVE IT!
WHILE, IN A MYSTERIOUS SANCTUARY ELSEWHERE...
WH-WHO ARE YOU? WHY HAVE YOU BROUGHT ME HERE?
WE ASSURE YOU, WILBUR DAY... ANSWERS WILL BE FORTHCOMING!

*LAST ISH.--LEN.

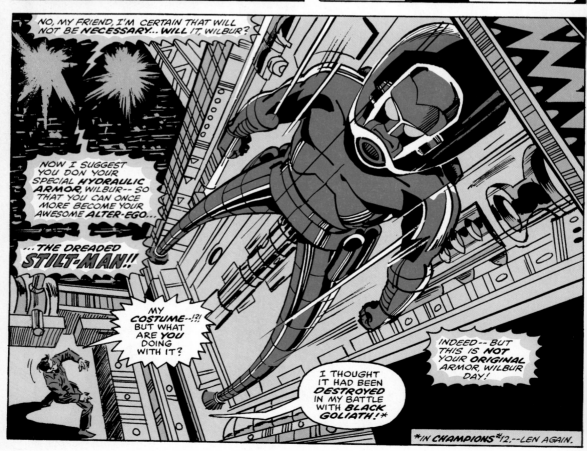

*IN CHAMPIONS #12.--LEN AGAIN.

122

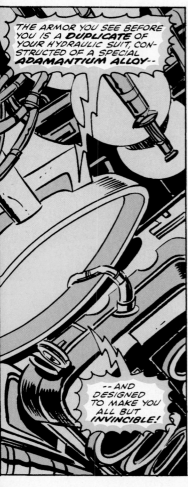

THE ARMOR YOU SEE BEFORE YOU IS A *DUPLICATE* OF YOUR *HYDRAULIC SUIT,* CONSTRUCTED OF A SPECIAL *ADAMANTIUM ALLOY*--

--AND DESIGNED TO MAKE YOU ALL BUT *INVINCIBLE!*

YOU'RE *RIGHT!* I'VE NEVER *FELT* SUCH A SENSE OF *ABSOLUTE POWER!*

WE NEVER *DOUBTED* THAT, STILT-MAN! NOW LISTEN *CLOSELY*-- AND I'LL EXPLAIN YOUR *ASSIGNMENT!*

AND IF YOU VALUE YOUR *LIFE,* LITTLE MAN--

OKAY, WHOEVER YOU ARE-- YOU WANT SOMETHING *DONE,* I'M YOUR *MAN!*

--YOU WILL NOT *FAIL!!*

AND WHEN THE STILT-MAN HAS BEEN GIVEN HIS *INSTRUCTIONS...*

WHAT YOU'RE PLANNING IS *BIZARRE,* TO SAY THE LEAST, MISTER--

--BUT IF *ANYONE* CAN PULL IT OFF, IT'S *ME!*

I'M *LEAVING* NOW! I WILL *RETURN* WHEN THE JOB IS *DONE!!*

AND THOUGH YOU WILL NOT *KNOW* IT, I WILL BE *WITH* YOU, LITTLE MAN--

--WAITING TO *SLAY* YOU AT THE FIRST SIGN OF *BETRAYAL!*

ELSEWHERE, SOON AFTER...

...SO THE FAT MAN SAYS, "THAT WAS NO *LADLE*, THAT WAS MY *KNIFE!*"

NOT *FUNNY*, FRED.

WHAT DO YA *WANT* FOR THESE PRICES, JOE-- *ABBOTT AND COSTELLO?*

YA THINK A LITTLE *PEACE AN' QUIET* WOULD BE TOO MUCH TO ASK?

SHEESH! EVERYBODY IS A *CRITIC!*

BLANG! BLANG!

HUH? HEY, YOU *EXPECTIN'* ANYBODY, FRED?

THAT SUPPOSED TO BE A *JOKE*, JOE?

IT STARTED OUT THAT WAY-- BUT MAYBE I BETTER GO *CHECK!*

FRED, Y-YOU AIN'T GONNA *BELIEVE* THIS-- BUT THERE *IS* A MAN OUT HERE...

...A MAN *HALF-A-MILE HIGH!!*

NOT JUST *ANY* MAN, YOU GIBBERING IDIOT--

--BUT THE NEW, IMPROVED *STILT-MAN!!*

I'VE COME TO COLLECT THE SPECIAL *CARGO* YOU'RE CARRYING, CRETIN--

--AND IF YOU'RE *WISE*, YOU'LL LET ME *HAVE* IT!

WHANG!

OH, I'LL LET YA *HAVE* IT AL'RIGHT, SMART-GUY--

--BUT *NOT* THE WAY YOU *EXPECTED* IT!

YOU AIN'T WHACKIN' *ME* AGAINST A BULKHEAD LIKE YA DID *JOE*!

BUT I HAVE NO *NEED* TO, FOOL--

--SO LONG AS MY NEW COSTUME CAN EMIT STUPIFYING-- *GAS*!!

C-CAN'T *BREATHE*--!!

HSSSS

UUNNHH!!

THIS IS WHAT MY *MYSTERIOUS BENEFACTOR* SENT ME TO *RETRIEVE*--

--THIS HEAVILY-ARMORED *BOX*, SEALED WITH SPECIAL *ELECTRON-LOCKS*!

I HAVE NO IDEA *WHAT* THIS BOX *CONTAINS*--

--NOR AM I LIKELY TO *FIND OUT* RIGHT NOW!

WITH ITS PILOTS *UNCONSCIOUS*, THE HELICOPTER IS BEGINNING TO WHIRL *OUT-OF-CONTROL*...

...WHICH MEANS IT'S TIME FOR ME TO *DEPART*!

...AS A *MONSTROUS FIGURE* FOLLOWS SILENTLY *BEHIND*!

SEVERAL BLOCKS AWAY, DR. DON BLAKE THREADS HIS WAY CAREFULLY THRU THE *RUSH HOUR* THRONG, COMPLETELY IMMERSED IN *THOUGHT*...

TO *WORK* OR *NOT* TO WORK... THAT'S ESSENTIALLY THE *QUESTION!*

EITHER I *ACCEPT* JACOB WALLABY'S OFFER TO PRACTICE AT THAT *FREE CLINIC*--OR I SIT AROUND *TWIDDLING MY THUMBS!*

NOT EXACTLY THE MOST *EXCITING* OF CHOICES, IS IT?

WELL, IF YOU'D LIKE A *THIRD* ALTERNATIVE, DOCTOR-- HOW ABOUT *THIS?*

HUH? THAT *SOUND*--! WHAT IS...?

LORD-- *NO!!*

WHUP WHUP WHUP WHUP

THAT *HELICOPTER*-- HURTLING *OUT OF CONTROL*--!!

IT'S GOING TO *PLUNGE* STRAIGHT INTO THIS *CROWD*...

...UNLESS...

...THE *SON OF ODIN* HATH POWER ENOW TO *AVERT* THIS IMPENDING *DISASTER!*

WITH A SOUND LIKE ROLLING *THUNDER,* THE MIGHTY THOR AND THE RAMPANT AIRCRAFT *COLLIDE* IN MID-AIR--

KWA-VOOM!!

--THE SHEER *IMPACT* OF IT MOMENTARILY *NUMBING* THE THUNDER GOD'S MUSCLES, *STUNNING* HIS VERY *SENSES*...

...BUT STILL, USING HIS OWN *BODY* AS A BUFFER, THE ODINSON MANAGES TO *LOWER* THE STRICKEN HELICOPTER RELATIVELY *GENTLY* TO A JUTTING *ROOFTOP*--

--AS THE TERRIFIED *CROWD* BELOW STOPS SCURRYING FOR *SHELTER*, AND BREATHES A COLLECTIVE SIGH OF *RELIEF!*

AND WHEN THOR HAS PULLED THE STILL-DAZED PILOTS TO *SAFETY*...

THOU SHALT *RECOVER*, MORTAL-- BUT WHAT *CAUSED* THY SUDDEN PLIGHT?

IT WAS... THE *STILT-MAN!*

H-HE *ROBBED* US... THEN LEFT US TO *DIE!*

THE *STILT-MAN*, THOU SAYEST? CAPTAIN AMERICA HATH *TOLD* ME OF THE FIEND! *

FEAR *NOT*, GOOD MORTAL! THY CARGO SHALL BE *RECOVERED*-- AND *THOU* SHALT BE *AVENGED!*

SO SWEARS THE *GOD OF THUNDER!!*

* CAP BATTLED STILTY BACK IN *CAPTAIN AMERICA* #191. --LEN.

AND IN THE *SHADOWS*, A GROTESQUE FIGURE ANGRILY CLENCHES HIS MASSIVE *FIST*--

--AND MUTTERS A SILENT *CURSE!*

WHILE, SOMEWHERE *BEYOND TIME AND SPACE, FANDRAL THE DASHING, HOGUN THE GRIM,* AND THE VOLUMINOUS *VOLSTAGG* RECEIVE A *HEROES' WELCOME* UPON THEIR TRIUMPHANT *RETURN* TO IMMORTAL *ASGARD...*

...WHERE WE'RE INVITED TO JOIN THE *CELEBRATION!*

VERILY, THOU ART *TOO KIND,* GOOD CITIZENS--

-- THOUGH, IN TRUTH, WE MUST MODESTLY ADMIT THY PRAISE IS *WELL-DESERVED!*

THY *HUMILITY* IS ONLY OUT-SHADOWED BY THY *WAISTLINE,* VAST ONE!

AND SOON, IN THE THRONE-ROOM OF THE *PALACE IMPERIAL...*

HAIL, ALMIGHTY *ODIN!* AS ORDERED, WE HAVE *CAPTURED* THE TRAITOROUS SNAYKAR, MAGRAT, AND KRODA *--

--AND NOW AWAIT THY NEXT *COMMAND!*

THOU HAST DONE *WELL,* GOOD WARRIORS! ASK ANY *BOON* OF ME-- AND IT IS *THINE!*

THEN PERHAPS A SIMPLE *REPAST,* MILORD...SAY, FIFTEEN OR SIXTEEN *COURSES...?*

NEVER *FEAR,* O LION OF ASGARD-- THY BELLY SHALL BE *FILLED!*

BUT FIRST, ALLOW ME TO OFFER SOME *SUSTENANCE* FOR THY *SOUL!*

THY VOICE DOTH SOUND *TROUBLED,* MY LIEGE! IF THERE BE SOME WAY WE WARRIORS THREE CAN *AID* THEE--

--PRAY THEE, BUT *SPEAK--* AND WE SHALL *OBEY!*

THY *FEALTY* DOES ME *HONOR,* DASHING ONE!

FOR, INDEED, ALL IS NOT *WELL* WITH THE *REALM ETERNAL--*

--AND MAYHAP ONLY YE *THREE* CAN SET THINGS *A'RIGHT!*

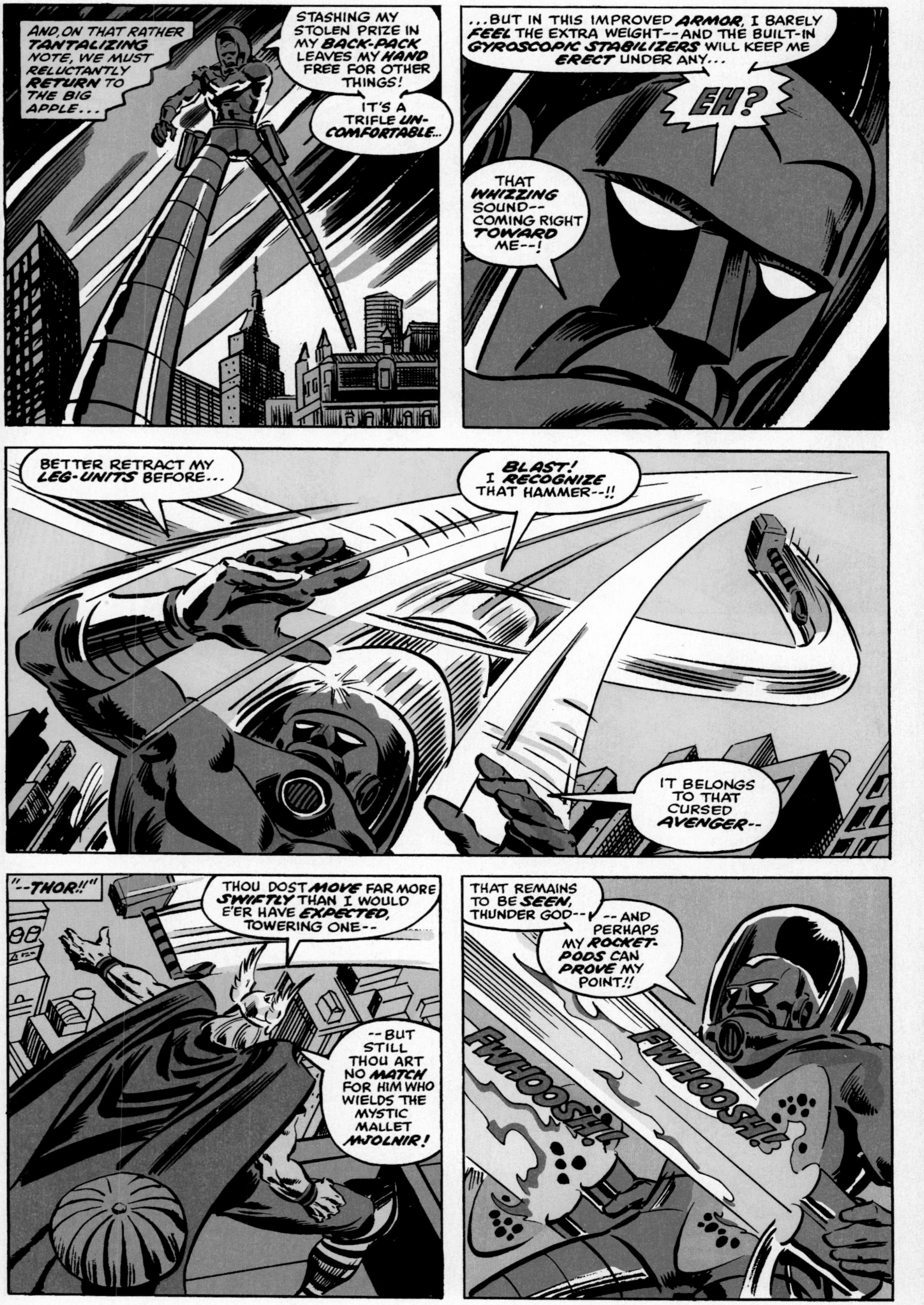
AND, ON THAT RATHER TANTALIZING NOTE, WE MUST RELUCTANTLY RETURN TO THE BIG APPLE...
STASHING MY STOLEN PRIZE IN MY BACK-PACK LEAVES MY HAND FREE FOR OTHER THINGS!
IT'S A TRIFLE UN-COMFORTABLE...
...BUT IN THIS IMPROVED ARMOR, I BARELY FEEL THE EXTRA WEIGHT--AND THE BUILT-IN GYROSCOPIC STABILIZERS WILL KEEP ME ERECT UNDER ANY...
EH?
THAT WHIZZING SOUND--COMING RIGHT TOWARD ME--!
BETTER RETRACT MY LEG-UNITS BEFORE...
BLAST! I RECOGNIZE THAT HAMMER--!!
IT BELONGS TO THAT CURSED AVENGER--
"--THOR!!"
THOU DOST MOVE FAR MORE SWIFTLY THAN I WOULD E'ER HAVE EXPECTED, TOWERING ONE--
--BUT STILL THOU ART NO MATCH FOR HIM WHO WIELDS THE MYSTIC MALLET MJOLNIR!
THAT REMAINS TO BE SEEN, THUNDER GOD--
--AND PERHAPS MY ROCKET-PODS CAN PROVE MY POINT!!
FWHOOSH!
FWHOOSH!

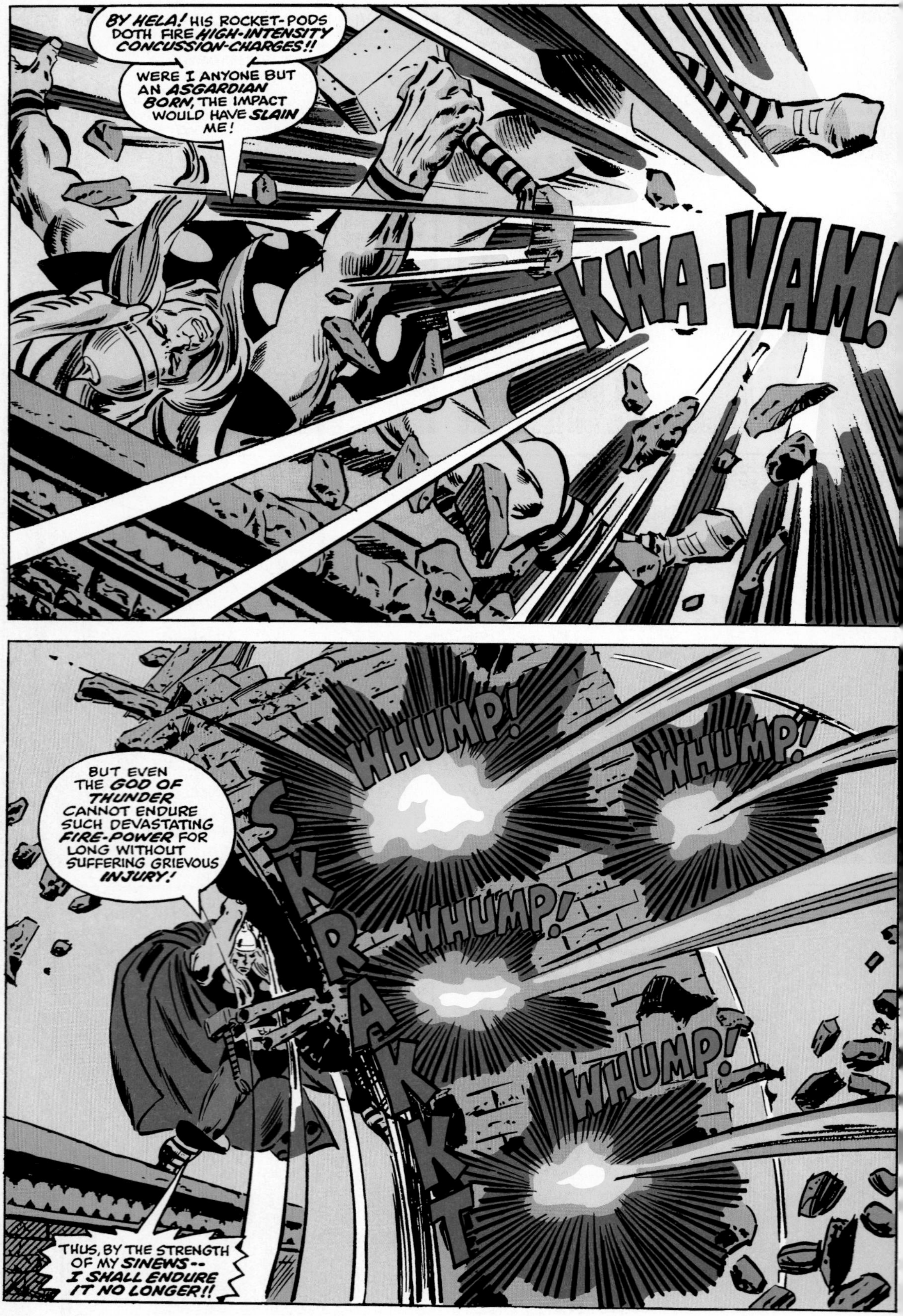

BY HELA! HIS ROCKET-PODS DOTH FIRE HIGH-INTENSITY CONCUSSION-CHARGES!!
WERE I ANYONE BUT AN ASGARDIAN BORN, THE IMPACT WOULD HAVE SLAIN ME!
KWA-VAM!
WHUMP!
WHUMP!
WHUMP!
WHUMP!
SKRAKKT
BUT EVEN THE GOD OF THUNDER CANNOT ENDURE SUCH DEVASTATING FIRE-POWER FOR LONG WITHOUT SUFFERING GRIEVOUS INJURY!
THUS, BY THE STRENGTH OF MY SINEWS-- I SHALL ENDURE IT NO LONGER!!

MILES AWAY, THE RAGING BATTLE CAN BE **WITNESSED** ON A HOLOGRAPHIC **VIEW-SCREEN** MOUNTED UPON ONE WALL OF A TOWERING **COMPUTER**--

--WHICH CAREFULLY STUDIES EVERY **MOVE** THE TWO COMBATANTS **MAKE**...

...CALCULATING **ODDS**...WEIGHING **ALTERNATIVES**...

...UNTIL, AT LAST, A **DECISION** IS REACHED...

...AND A SERIES OF **ANTI-NEUTRINOS** RACE THROUGH THE MONSTROUS MECHANISM WITH QUITE **LITERALLY** THE SPEED OF **THOUGHT**!

THE **STILT-MAN** WILL NOT BE ABLE TO **DEAL** WITH THE UNEXPECTED INTERVENTION OF THE BEING CALLED **THOR**!

THE TIME HAS COME TO INSTITUTE MORE **SERIOUS** PRECAUTIONS--

--NO MATTER **WHO** MAY SUFFER AS A **RESULT**!!

MEANWHILE, BACK AT THE HARD-WAGED *WAR*...

THOSE ARE THE *LAST* OF THY DEADLY *MISSILES*, STILT-MAN!

THUS THE TIME FOR ME TO DO NAUGHT BUT *DEFEND* MYSELF IS *ENDED*--

WHOOM!

WHOOM!

--AND THE TIME FOR THEE TO DEFEND *THYSELF* AT LAST IS *NIGH*!!

KRANG!

YOUR *HAMMER* IS AN AWESOME *WEAPON*, THUNDER GOD--BUT *NOTHING* CAN HARM A MAN ENCASED IN *ADAMANTIUM ARMOR*...

...A MAN WHO CAN CHANGE HIS VERY *HEIGHT* WITH THE SPEED OF *THOUGHT*!

BY ODIN! HE GREW SO *SWIFTLY*, THE MOMENTUM HURLED ME *AWAY*--!

BUT *DESPITE* MY POWER, BATTLING A LIVING *GOD* MAY STILL BE ULTIMATELY *BEYOND* ME!

THE *RECOIL* OF MY SUDDEN ASCENSION HURLED THOR SEVERAL *BLOCKS* FROM HERE--

--AND SINCE I ALREADY *HAVE* WHAT I WAS *SENT* HERE FOR--

--PERHAPS I'D BE WISE TO BEAT A DIPLOMATIC *RETREAT*!

BUT, SEVERAL BLOCKS AHEAD, IN A *VACANT LOT* DIRECTLY IN THE STILT-MAN'S *PATH*...

IN HIS *HASTE*, THE TOWERING ONE DOTH NOT *REALIZE* HE STRIDES *TOWARDS* ME--

--AND ERE HE CAN *CORRECT* HIS ERROR, ENCHANTED *MJOLNIR* SHALL PLACE AN INSURMOUNTABLE *OBSTACLE* BEFORE HIM...

THOOM!

"...A YAWNING PIT TOO *DEEP* FOR EVEN THE STILT-MAN'S EVER-EXTENDING *LIMBS* TO OVERCOME!"

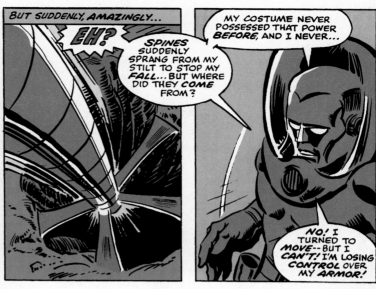

BUT SUDDENLY, AMAZINGLY...

EH?

SPINES SUDDENLY SPRANG FROM MY STILT TO STOP MY *FALL*....BUT WHERE DID THEY *COME* FROM?

MY COSTUME NEVER POSSESSED THAT POWER *BEFORE*, AND I NEVER...

NO! I TURNED TO *MOVE*—BUT I *CAN'T!* I'M LOSING *CONTROL* OVER MY *ARMOR!*

IT'S PROPELLING ME RIGHT *AT* THE THUNDER GOD—

—AND *WORSE*, IT'S TRYING TO *KILL* HIM!!

STOP ME, THOR! SOMEHOW, YOU'VE GOT TO *STOP* ME!!

BELIEVE ME, TOWERING ONE...

'TWILL BE MY *PLEASURE!!*

THWANGG!

NO, YOU FOOL— NOT *THAT* WAY! MY ARMOR COMES EQUIPPED WITH SPECIAL *GYRO-STABILIZERS!*

EVEN IF YOUR HAMMER BENDS MY STILTS ALMOST *DOUBLE*—

--IT'S ONLY GOING TO SPRING BACK *UPRIGHT* ONCE MORE...

...AND *SLAM* YOU DOWN INTO THE *STREET!!*

AYE, STILT-MAN-- BUT SO *DOING,* THOU HAST HANDED ME THE MEANS TO ULTIMATELY *DEFEAT* THEE!

FOR, I NEED BUT STRIKE THE ENCHANTED MJOLNIR *TWICE* UPON THE *GROUND...*

THOK THOK!

"...TO SUMMON THE FULL UNFETTERED *FURY* OF THE RAGING *STORM* WHICH IS MY *BIRTHRIGHT!"*

SHA-RAKKT!

AND, WITH THE PLATINUM WIRING OF HIS *ADAMANTIUM* ARMOR COMPLETELY *FUSED* BY THE SUDDEN LIGHTNING STRIKE, THE STILT-MAN ALMOST GRATEFULLY *COLLAPSES* IN AN *UNTIDY HEAP!*

TRULY, THOU ART A MIGHTY *FOE,* STILT-MAN--

--BUT THE POWER OF *JUSTICE* IS MIGHTIER BY *FAR* THAN...

AARRGGHH!!

WHA-BOOM!

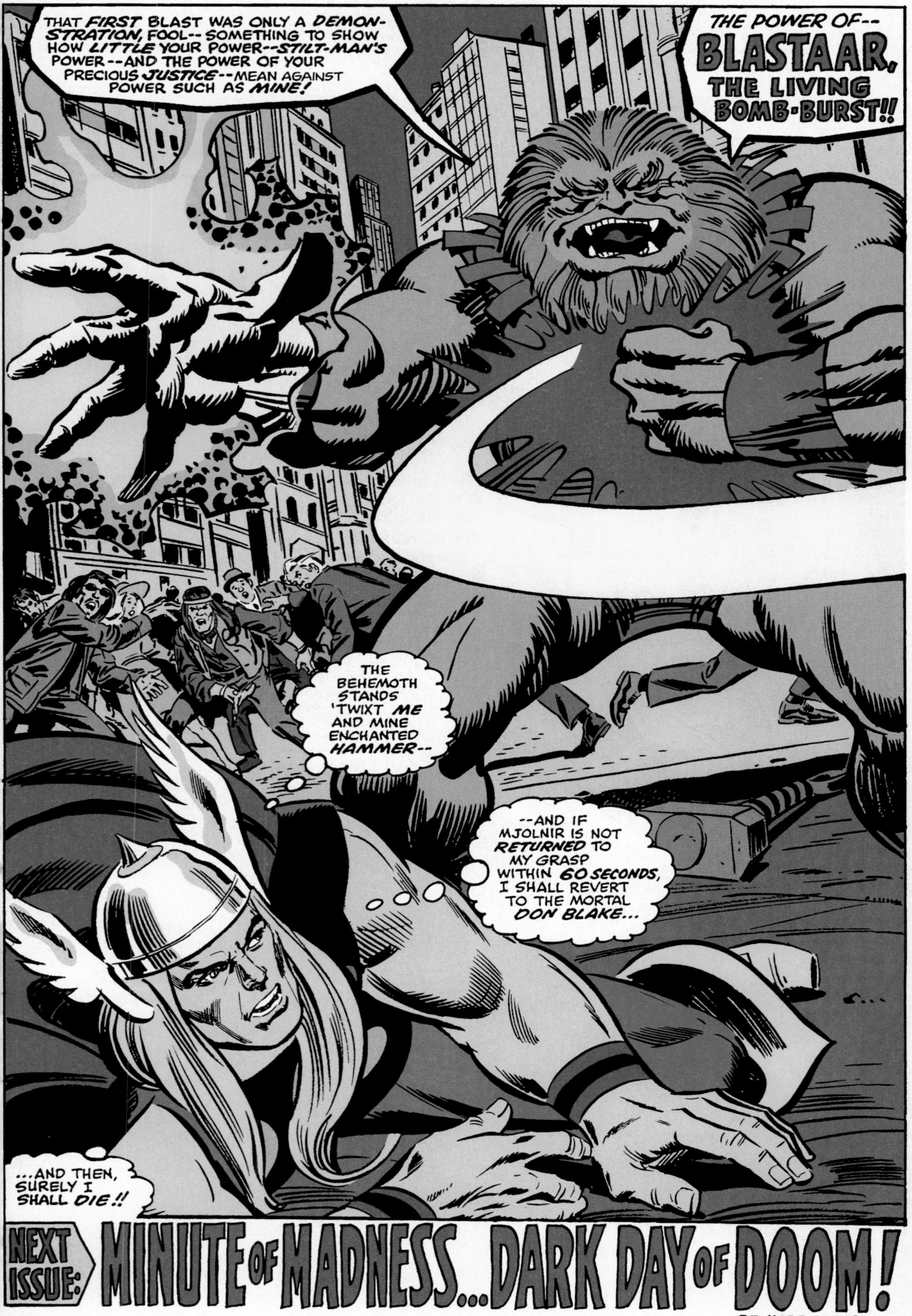

THAT FIRST BLAST WAS ONLY A DEMONSTRATION, FOOL-- SOMETHING TO SHOW HOW LITTLE YOUR POWER--STILT-MAN'S POWER--AND THE POWER OF YOUR PRECIOUS JUSTICE--MEAN AGAINST POWER SUCH AS MINE!
THE POWER OF-- BLASTAAR, THE LIVING BOMB-BURST!!
THE BEHEMOTH STANDS 'TWIXT ME AND MINE ENCHANTED HAMMER--
--AND IF MJOLNIR IS NOT RETURNED TO MY GRASP WITHIN 60 SECONDS, I SHALL REVERT TO THE MORTAL DON BLAKE...
...AND THEN, SURELY I SHALL DIE!!
NEXT ISSUE: MINUTE OF MADNESS...DARK DAY OF DOOM!
BE HERE, OKAY?

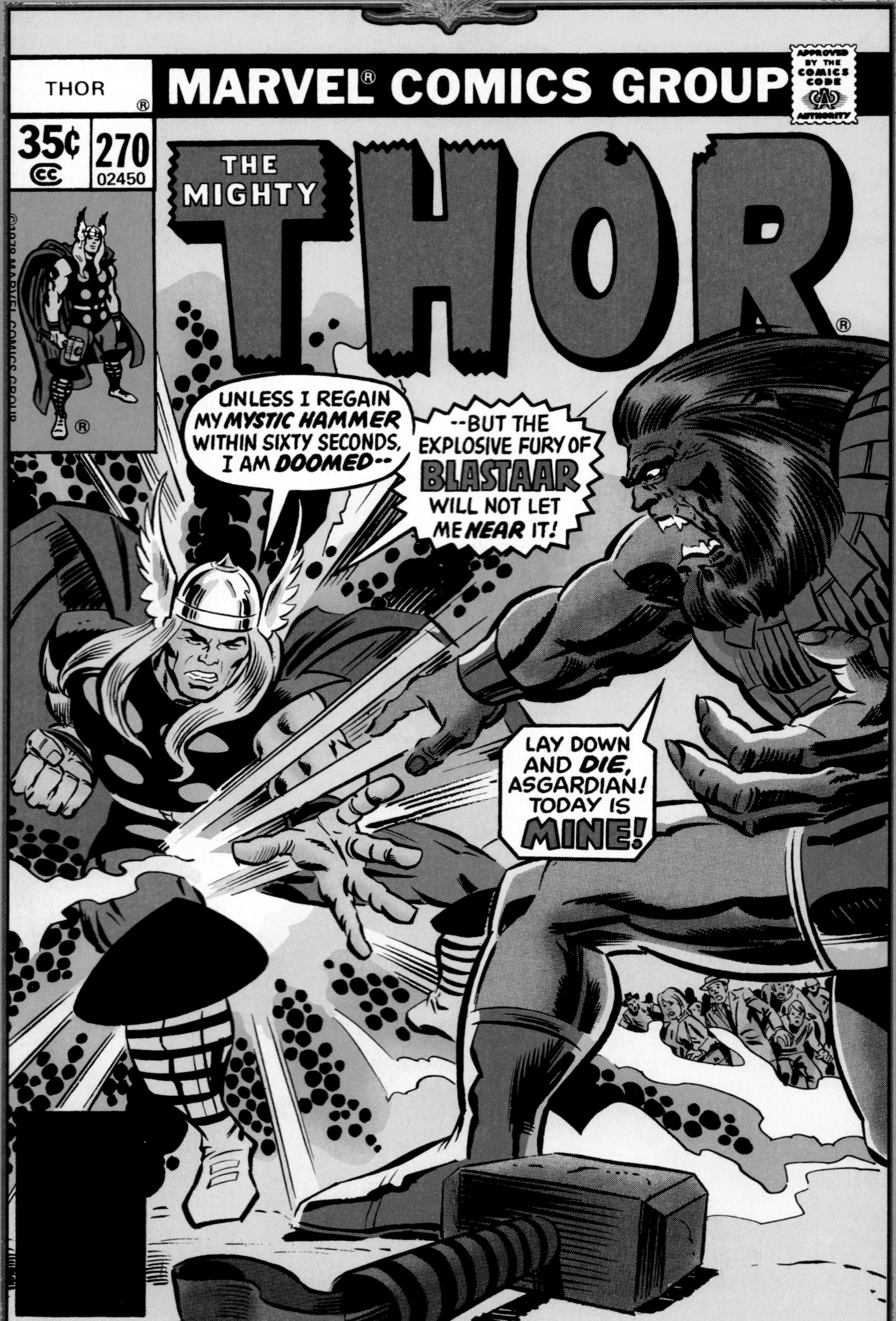
THOR
MARVEL® COMICS GROUP
APPROVED BY THE COMICS CODE AUTHORITY
35¢ CC
270
02450
THE MIGHTY THOR®
UNLESS I REGAIN MY MYSTIC HAMMER WITHIN SIXTY SECONDS, I AM DOOMED--
--BUT THE EXPLOSIVE FURY OF BLASTAAR WILL NOT LET ME NEAR IT!
LAY DOWN AND DIE, ASGARDIAN! TODAY IS MINE!

When lame Dr. DONALD BLAKE strikes his wooden walking stick upon the ground, it becomes the mystic mallet MJOLNIR—and Blake is transformed into the Norse God of Thunder, Master of the Storm and the Lightning, Heir to the Throne of Immortal Asgard...

Stan Lee PRESENTS: THE MIGHTY THOR! ™

LEN WEIN WRITER/EDITOR ✦ **WALT SIMONSON** & **TONY DeZUNIGA** ARTISTS / STORYTELLERS ✦ **GLYNIS WEIN** COLORIST ✦ **JOE ROSEN** LETTERER

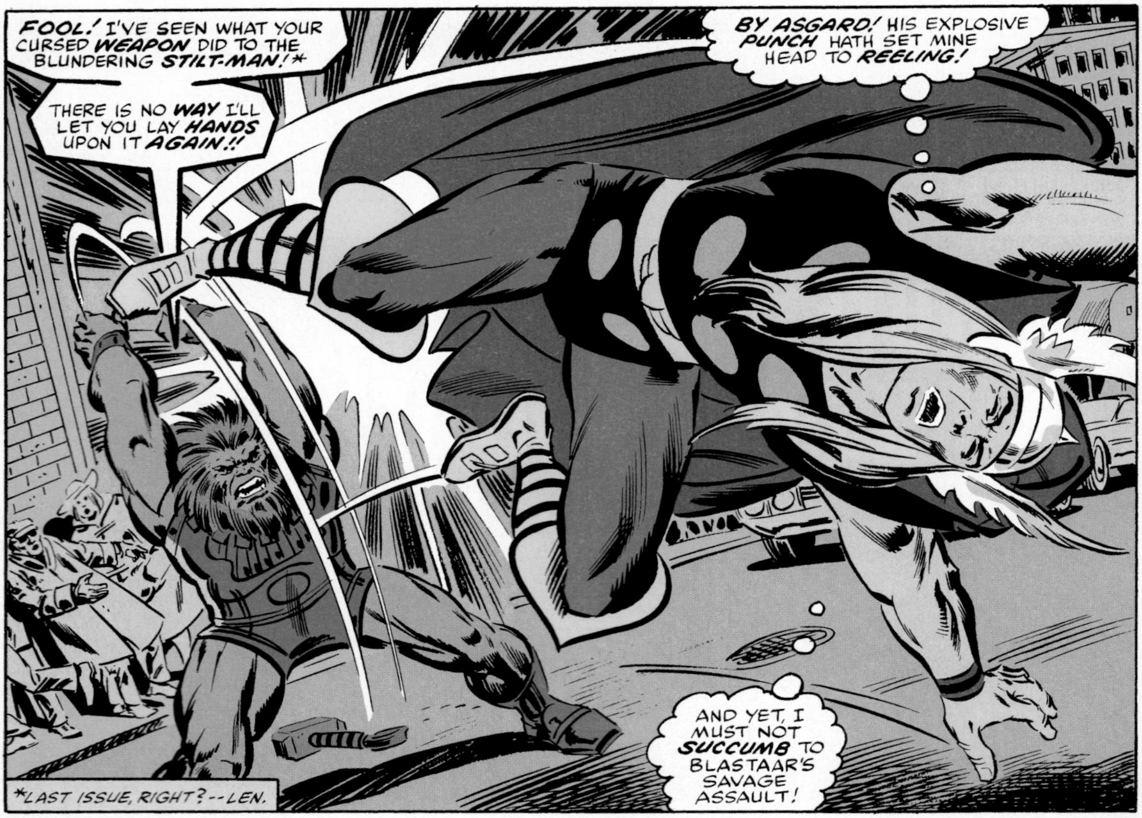
FOOL! I'VE SEEN WHAT YOUR CURSED WEAPON DID TO THE BLUNDERING STILT-MAN!*
THERE IS NO WAY I'LL LET YOU LAY HANDS UPON IT AGAIN!!
BY ASGARD! HIS EXPLOSIVE PUNCH HATH SET MINE HEAD TO REELING!
AND YET, I MUST NOT SUCCUMB TO BLASTAAR'S SAVAGE ASSAULT!
*LAST ISSUE, RIGHT?--LEN.

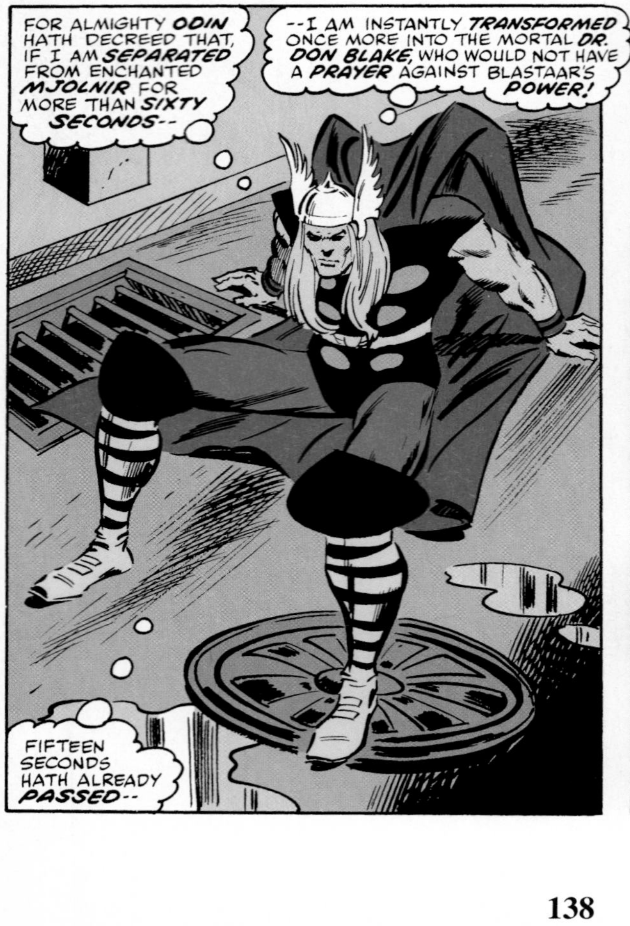
FOR ALMIGHTY ODIN HATH DECREED THAT, IF I AM SEPARATED FROM ENCHANTED MJOLNIR FOR MORE THAN SIXTY SECONDS--
--I AM INSTANTLY TRANSFORMED ONCE MORE INTO THE MORTAL DR. DON BLAKE, WHO WOULD NOT HAVE A PRAYER AGAINST BLASTAAR'S POWER!
FIFTEEN SECONDS HATH ALREADY PASSED--

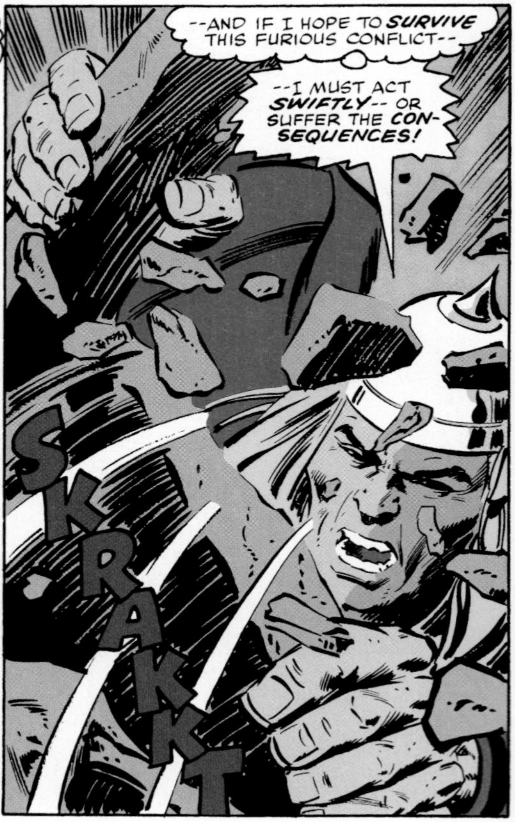
--AND IF I HOPE TO SURVIVE THIS FURIOUS CONFLICT--
--I MUST ACT SWIFTLY-- OR SUFFER THE CONSEQUENCES!
SKRAKT

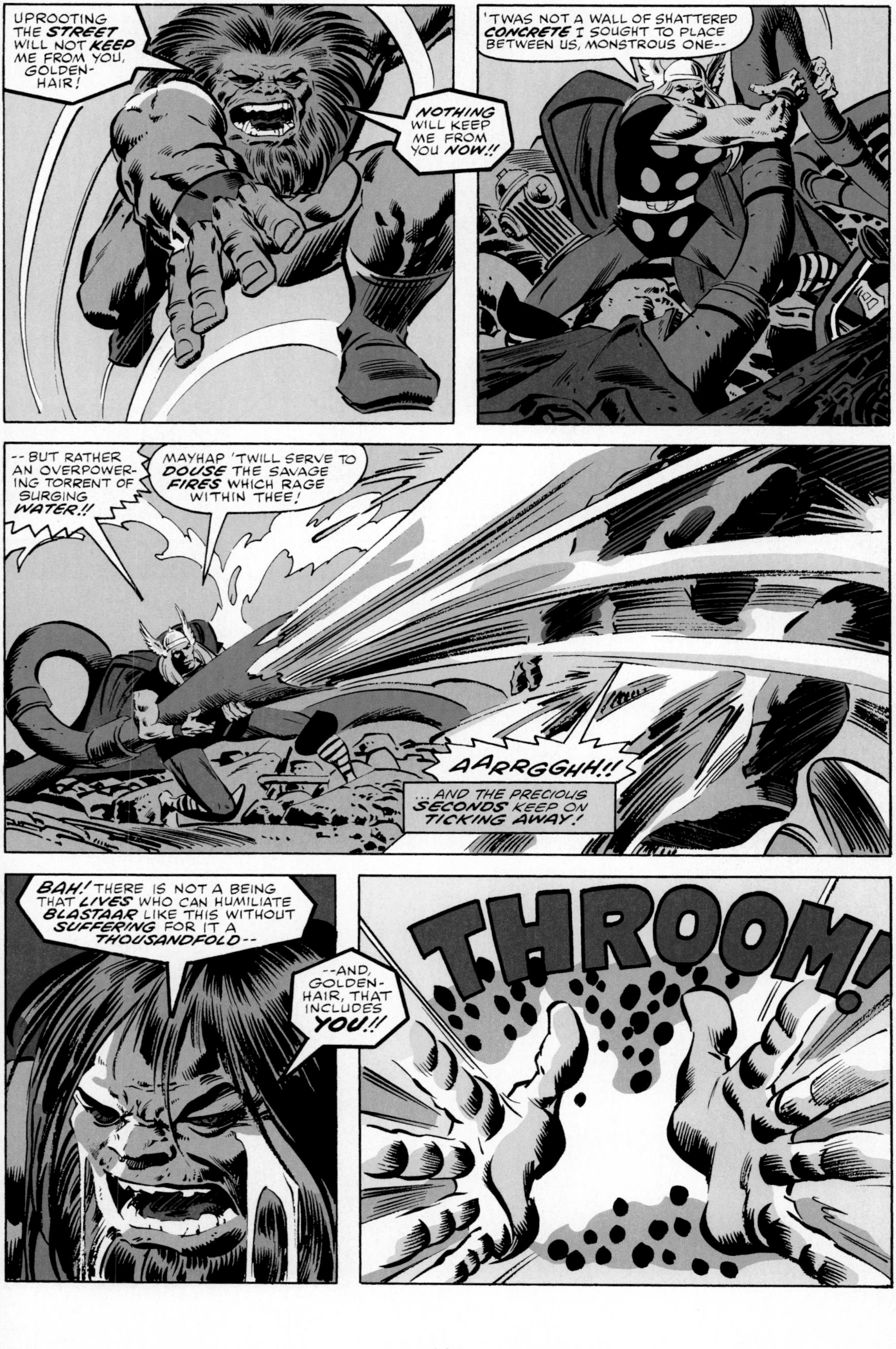
UPROOTING THE STREET WILL NOT KEEP ME FROM YOU, GOLDEN-HAIR!
NOTHING WILL KEEP ME FROM YOU NOW!!
'TWAS NOT A WALL OF SHATTERED CONCRETE I SOUGHT TO PLACE BETWEEN US, MONSTROUS ONE--
--BUT RATHER AN OVERPOWERING TORRENT OF SURGING WATER!!
MAYHAP 'TWILL SERVE TO DOUSE THE SAVAGE FIRES WHICH RAGE WITHIN THEE!
AARRGGHH!!
...AND THE PRECIOUS SECONDS KEEP ON TICKING AWAY!
BAH! THERE IS NOT A BEING THAT LIVES WHO CAN HUMILIATE BLASTAAR LIKE THIS WITHOUT SUFFERING FOR IT A THOUSANDFOLD--
--AND, GOLDEN-HAIR, THAT INCLUDES YOU!!
THROOM!

CAUGHT FLAT-FOOTED BY THE AWESOME *EX-PLOSIONS* WHICH LANCE FROM BLASTAAR'S VERY *FINGERTIPS*, THE BATTERED THOR IS HURLED VIOLENTLY BACK INTO A SHADOW-STREWN *ALLEYWAY...*

THUD!

...MERE INSTANTS BEFORE THOSE FATE-FUL *SIXTY SECONDS* HAVE FINALLY *PASSED!*

THUS, WHEN THE LIVING BOMB-BURST LUMBERS *INTO* THE ALLEY MOMENTS *LATER...*

COME *OUT,* GOLDEN-HAIR-- *SHOW* YOURSELF!

THERE IS NO WAY YOU CAN *HIDE* YOURSELF FROM...

EH?

THE *THUNDER GOD--* HE'S *VANISHED!?!*

THERE IS NO ONE IN THIS ALLEY BUT ANOTHER FRAIL *HUMAN!*

WHERE *IS* HE, WORM? TELL ME WHERE THE GOLDEN-HAIRED ONE HAS *GONE* OR...

NO-- *DON'T!*

H-HE RAN *PAST* ME-- OVER THAT *FENCE!!*

BAH! ONCE OVER THAT FENCE, THE COWARD COULD HAVE FLED IN COUNTLESS DIRECTIONS -- AND I HAVE NO MORE TIME TO WASTE HERE!

I MUST FULFILL THE MASTER'S MISSION!!

KRANG!

UUNNFF!!

MAN, THAT'S ABOUT AS CLOSE AS I EVER WANT TO CUT IT!

IF BLASTAAR HAD REACHED THIS ALLEY A FEW SECONDS SOONER, HE WOULD HAVE SEEN ME CHANGE BACK INTO DON BLAKE!

AT THAT SAME SECOND, MY HAMMER WAS ALSO TRANS- FORMED INTO A SIMPLE WOODEN WALKING STICK --

--AND NOW THAT BLASTAAR IS GONE, I CAN QUIETLY RECOVER MY CANE...

...UNLESS, OF COURSE, SOMEBODY ELSE FINDS IT FIRST!

THAT IS SOME FINE PIECE OF WOOD THERE, BROTHER HONCHO!

SURE IS, FOXY LADY!

MAKES A GOOD SCEPTRE FO' THE PRESIDENT O' THE STREET KINGS, DON'T IT?

FELLA? UH-- EXCUSE ME, FELLA.

YO' TALKIN' T' ME, JACK?

YES, THAT--AH-- STICK YOU'RE CARRYING... I'M AFRAID IT'S MINE!

DO **TELL**...AN' JUST WHUT YO' 'SPECT ME T' **DO** 'BOUT THAT, HUH?

YO' DON'T **SAY**?

WELL, I--UH-- **WAS** SORT OF HOPING YOU'D GIVE IT **BACK**!

WELL, I COULD ADD **PLEASE**!

DON'T **BOTHER**!

YO' **HEAR** THAT, BROTHERS? THE LITTLE DUDE WANTS HIS **STICK** BACK!

WELL, HE GONNA **GET** IT BACK, OKAY-- RIGHT UPSIDE HIS STUPID **HEAD**.!!

WHAT--?!?

INSTINCTIVELY, BLAKE REACHES OUT TO **GRAB** THE FLAILING STAFF--AND THE INSTANT IT TOUCHES HIS **HAND** THERE COMES A BLINDING FLASH OF SUPERNAL LIGHT WHICH SIGNALS AN AWESOME **TRANSFORMATION**...

...AND THE STREET PUNK CALLED **BROTHER HONCHO** SUDDENLY FINDS HIS NEWFOUND **SCEPTRE** HAS BECOME FAR TOO **HEAVY** FOR HIM TO **HOLD**!

HIS "SCEPTRE" AND HIS **JAW** STRIKE THE CEMENT AT PRECISELY THE SAME **SECOND**!

SWEET MAMA... **FORGIVE** ME.

AND ON THAT MOST **APOLOGETIC** NOTE, THE FINAL MEETING OF THE ONCE- ARROGANT **STREET KINGS** COMES TO A RATHER FRANTIC **ENDING**!

BLASTAAR HATH *FLED*-- BUT THE DEFEATED STILT-MAN YET *REMAINS!*

MAYHAP *HE* CAN GIVE *MEANING* TO THIS DAY'S *MADNESS!*

STILT-MAN, I WOULD HAVE *WORDS* WITH THEE!

VERILY, THOU SHALT TELL ME THE *REASONS* BEHIND THINE ACTIONS, OR...

N-NO-- KEEP *AWAY!* I'LL TELL YOU ANYTHING-- *ANYTHING!!*

AND ONCE THE TERRIFIED VILLAIN HAS STAMMERED OUT EVERYTHING HE *KNOWS,* A MAJESTIC FIGURE IS SOON HURTLING HIGH OVER THE SPRAWLING LONG ISLAND INDUSTRIAL COMPLEX CALLED *STARK INTERNATIONAL*--

--WHERE HE STANDS, AT LAST, BEFORE THE MAN *RESPONSIBLE* FOR THIS TECHNOLOGICAL WONDER-LAND: *TONY STARK* HIMSELF!

THOR! IT'S GOOD TO *SEE* YOU AGAIN, AVENGER!

IS THERE SOMETHING IN PARTICULAR I CAN *DO* FOR YOU?

AYE, MY FRIEND-- FOR I SEEK *INFORMATION* ONLY THINE ALL-KNOWING *COMPUTERS* CAN POSSIBLY *SUPPLY* ME!

THEN LET'S HEAD OVER TO THE *DATA CONTROL CENTER,* THUNDER GOD--

--AND YOU CAN FILL ME IN ON ALL THE *DETAILS* ALONG THE *WAY!*

APPARENTLY, STILT-MAN WAS FREED FROM *PRISON* BY THE CREATURE CALLED *BLASTAAR,* SO THAT HE MIGHT *STEAL* SOMETHING FOR BLASTAAR'S MYSTERIOUS *MASTER!*

ANYTHING IN *PARTICULAR?*

AYE--A UNIQUE METALLIC *CHEST,* CONTAINING *RADIO-ACTIVE ISOTOPES!* HE TOOK IT FROM A *HELI-COPTER* AS IT FLEW O'ER THE *CITY!*

STILT-MAN HAS *STYLE,* WHAT HAPPENED TO *BLASTAAR?*

UNFORTUNATELY, HE *FLED*-- AFTER PRYING THAT METALLIC *CHEST* FROM STILT-MAN'S VERY *FINGERS!*

NATURALLY. HOW ABOUT BLASTY'S *BOSS*-- ANY *CLUES?*

ONLY THAT HIS *LAIR* DOTH APPEAR TO BE A RUINED *FACTORY* OF SOME SORT, HIDDEN SOMEWHERE IN UPSTATE *NEW YORK*--

--A FACTORY CONSTRUCTED ALMOST ENTIRELY OF A SPECIAL *ADAMANTIUM ALLOY!*

A *FACTORY,* EH? THAT SOUNDS HAUNTINGLY *FAMILIAR!*

I'LL PUNCH WHAT YOU'VE *TOLD* ME--PLUS A FEW THOUGHTS OF MY *OWN*--INTO THE PRIMARY *MAGNETIC NET-WORK MEMORY CO-ORDINATOR*...

...AND THEN WE'LL JUST SEE WHAT *DEVELOPS!*

AND, IN SECONDS WHAT *DEVELOPS* IS...

F.A.U.S.T.
FULLY-AUTOMATED UNIT OF STRUCTURAL TECHNOLOGY

SECTION I: BACKGROUND

SUB-SECTION A: ORIGIN

BUDDY, YOU'VE HIT THE *JACKPOT!*

CLICK!

F.A.U.S.T.-- THE WORLD'S FIRST FULLY-AUTOMATED FACTORY-- WAS THE BRAINCHILD OF PROFESSOR PAXTON PENTECOST...

PENTECOST CLAIMED HIS CREATION WAS TOTALLY SELF-SUFFICIENT...THAT IT WOULD NEVER NEED REPAIR...WOULD NEVER GROW OBSOLETE...

UNFORTUNATELY, THE SCIENTIFIC COMMUNITY WAS GIVEN NO TIME TO TEST THE VALIDITY OF PENTECOST'S CLAIMS...

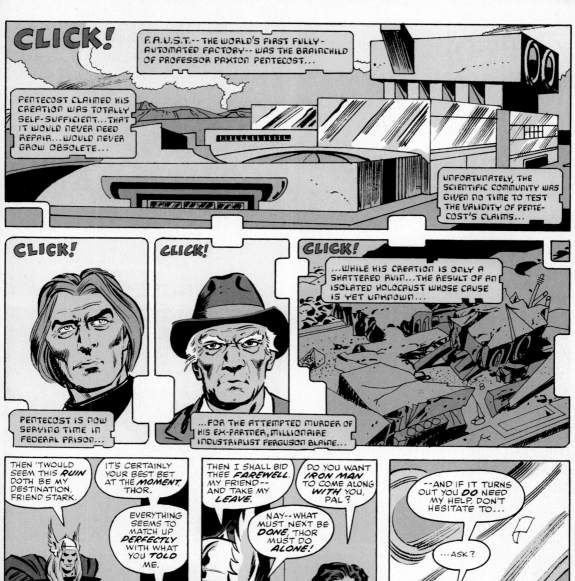

CLICK!

CLICK!

CLICK!

...WHILE HIS CREATION IS ONLY A SHATTERED RUIN...THE RESULT OF AN ISOLATED HOLOCAUST WHOSE CAUSE IS YET UNKNOWN...

PENTECOST IS NOW SERVING TIME IN FEDERAL PRISON...

...FOR THE ATTEMPTED MURDER OF HIS EX-PARTNER, MILLIONAIRE INDUSTRIALIST FERGUSON BLAINE...

THEN 'TWOULD SEEM THIS *RUIN* DOTH BE MY DESTINATION, FRIEND STARK.

IT'S CERTAINLY YOUR BEST BET AT THE *MOMENT*, THOR.

EVERYTHING SEEMS TO MATCH UP *PERFECTLY* WITH WHAT YOU *TOLD* ME.

THEN I SHALL BID THEE *FAREWELL*, MY FRIEND-- AND TAKE MY *LEAVE*.

DO YOU WANT *IRON MAN* TO COME ALONG *WITH* YOU, PAL?

NAY-- WHAT MUST NEXT BE *DONE*, THOR MUST DO *ALONE!*

WELL, TAKE *CARE* OF YOURSELF, AVENGER--

--AND IF IT TURNS OUT YOU *DO* NEED MY HELP, DON'T HESITATE TO...

...ASK?

MEANWHILE...

I HAVE **RETURNED**, MASTER-- WITH THAT WHICH YOU **DESIRED!**

THE **INCOMPETENT** STILT-MAN **FAILED** YOU-- AS I **KNEW** HE WOULD!

BUT **BLASTAAR** DID NOT FAIL!

BLASTAAR **NEVER** FAILS!!

FOR BLASTAAR IS **POWER INCARNATE!!!**

THAT IS WHY I FIRST **BROUGHT** YOU HERE TO ME, BLASTAAR...

--FOR THERE IS NO ONE WHO KNOWS YOUR POWER **BETTER** THAN I WHO WAS CODE-NAMED **FAUST**...

...I WHO WAS ONCE YOUR **VICTIM.**

HAD I KNOWN OF **YOUR** GREAT POWER THEN, MASTER-- I WOULD NEVER HAVE ACTED SO **RASHLY!**

THAT IS WHY I **SERVE** YOU NOW-- TO MAKE **AMENDS** FOR MY PAST **INDISCRETIONS!**

BUT STILL I DO NOT **UNDERSTAND** WHY YOU REQUIRED THIS SIMPLE **CHEST?**

THEN PERMIT ME TO EXPLAIN IN GREATER **DETAIL**, BLASTAAR!

LOOK **CLOSELY**... AND BEHOLD AN **APOCALYPTIC** VISION OF **TRANSCENDANT FURY!**

NO! IT IS **THEM**-- THE TWO BEINGS I HATE **MOST** IN ALL THIS **WORLD!!**

INDEED! THEY ARE THE SO-CALLED *HUMAN TORCH*... AND THE BEHEMOTH KNOWN AS THE *HULK!*

I SEE YOU *REMEMBER!*

I WILL NEVER *FORGET!*

NOR WILL *I!*

FOR IT WAS ONLY THEIR TIMELY *INTER-VENTION* WHICH PREVENTED MY COMPLETE AND UTTER *DESTRUCTION* AT YOUR *HANDS!*

WITH HIS AWESOME STRENGTH, THE HULK *ENCASED* YOU IN MY ADAMANTIUM *SHIELDING*... AND HURLED YOU INTO THE *ATLANTIC OCEAN!* *

*BACK IN *MARVEL TEAM-UP* #18 --LEN.

SO? MUCH HAS HAPPENED *SINCE* THEN, MASTER! WHY RECALL AN UNPLEASANT *PAST?*

MERELY TO *COUNTER-POINT* YOUR *PROMISED FUTURE!*

BEHOLD THAT WHICH YOU SHALL *BECOME* WHEN YOU HAVE FAITHFULLY FULFILLED MY *COMMANDS--!*

BEHOLD YOURSELF AS YOU HAVE ALWAYS *WANTED* TO BE--

--AS *KING* OF THE SAVAGE *NEGATIVE ZONE* WHICH SPAWNED YOU!

AYE, THAT HAS BEEN MY *DREAM* SINCE... *EH?*

ANOTHER IMAGE SUPER-CEDES MINE-- BUT *WHO?!?*

IT IS THE BEING CALLED *THOR!* EVEN NOW, HE *APPROACHES* US!

147

HE **DARES**? THE UNMITIGATED **FOOL**!!

THIS TIME I WILL **DESTROY** HIM!!

BLASTAAR, MY **CHEST**...?

IT IS **YOURS**, MASTER!

ALL **I** DESIRE NOW IS-- **VENGEANCE**!!

BY **HELA**! 'TIS EVEN MORE **TERRIBLE** HERE THAN TONY STARK'S COMPUTERS DID **DESCRIBE** IT!

BAH! YOU WILL SOON **LEARN**, GOLDEN-HAIR, THAT THERE IS **NOTHING** MORE TERRIBLE THAN THE BATTLE-FURY OF **BLASTAAR**!!

AND IT IS A **LESSON** WHICH WILL COST YOU YOUR **LIFE**!!

AARRGGHH!!

BLASTAAR RESPONDED PRECISELY AS I **PREDICTED** HE WOULD!

NOW, WHILE HE KEEPS THE THUNDER GOD **OCCUPIED**, I MUST PROCEED WITH MY **FINAL PREPARATIONS**!

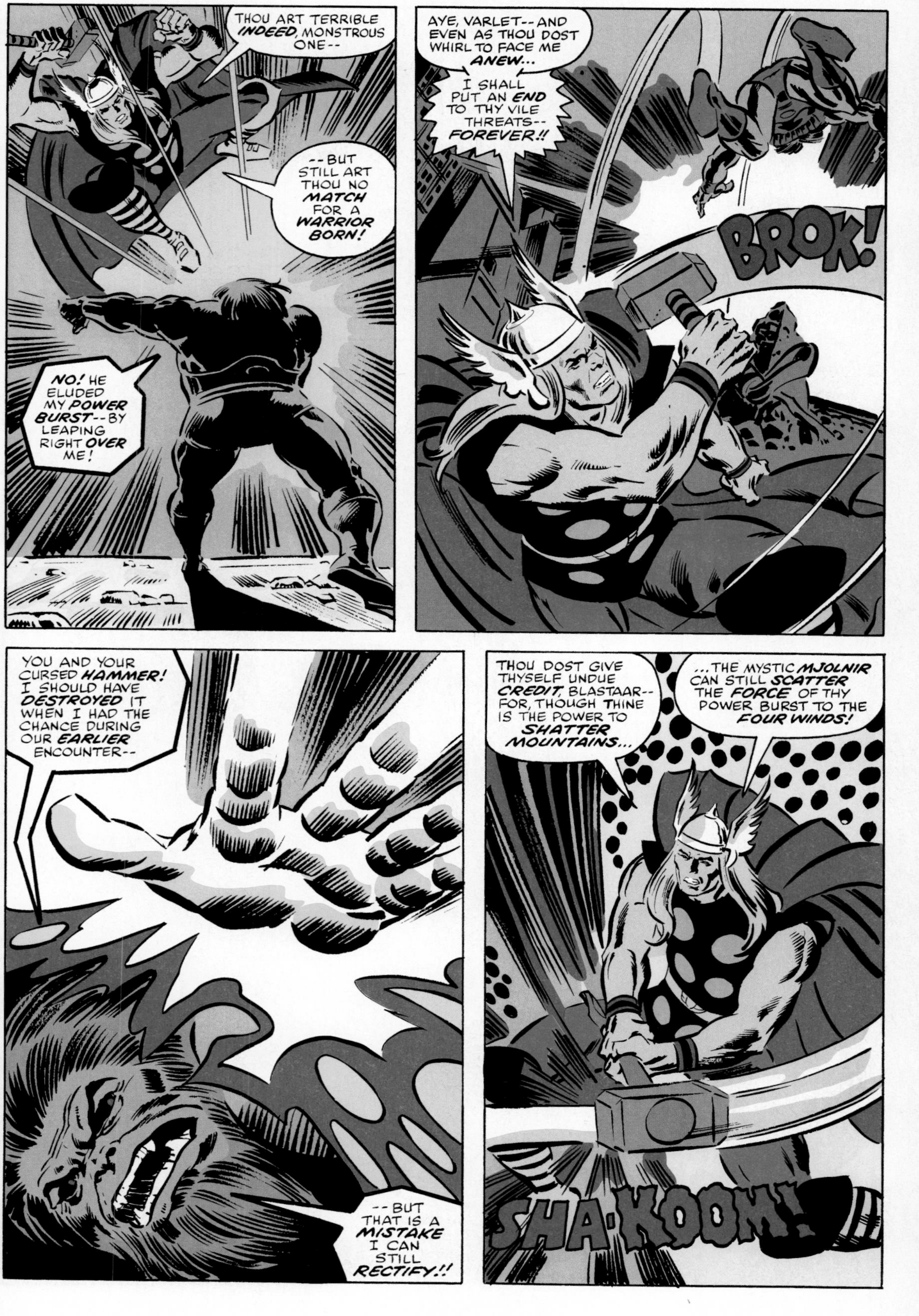
THOU ART TERRIBLE INDEED, MONSTROUS ONE--
--BUT STILL ART THOU NO MATCH FOR A WARRIOR BORN!
NO! HE ELUDED MY POWER BURST--BY LEAPING RIGHT OVER ME!
AYE, VARLET--AND EVEN AS THOU DOST WHIRL TO FACE ME ANEW...
I SHALL PUT AN END TO THY VILE THREATS--FOREVER!!
BROK!
YOU AND YOUR CURSED HAMMER! I SHOULD HAVE DESTROYED IT WHEN I HAD THE CHANCE DURING OUR EARLIER ENCOUNTER--
--BUT THAT IS A MISTAKE I CAN STILL RECTIFY!!
THOU DOST GIVE THYSELF UNDUE CREDIT, BLASTAAR--FOR, THOUGH THINE IS THE POWER TO SHATTER MOUNTAINS...
...THE MYSTIC MJOLNIR CAN STILL SCATTER THE FORCE OF THY POWER BURST TO THE FOUR WINDS!
SHA-KOOM!

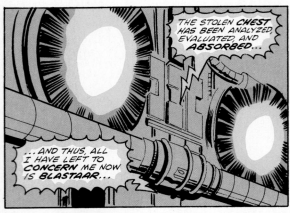

THE STOLEN **CHEST** HAS BEEN ANALYZED, EVALUATED, AND **ABSORBED**...

...AND THUS, ALL I HAVE LEFT TO **CONCERN** ME NOW IS **BLASTAAR**...

...AND **HE** IS REALLY **NO** CONCERN AT ALL!

AND WITH **THAT**, THE FLICKER-ING COMPUTER BANK ABRUPTLY GOES **DARK**!

WILT THOU **SURRENDER**, MONSTROUS ONE?

NEVER! I WOULD SOONER...**EH**?

THE **GROUND**-- IT'S BEGUN **TREMBLING!** AND THAT **SOUND**--!

NO!!

MASTER, YOU CAN'T **DO** THIS TO ME!!

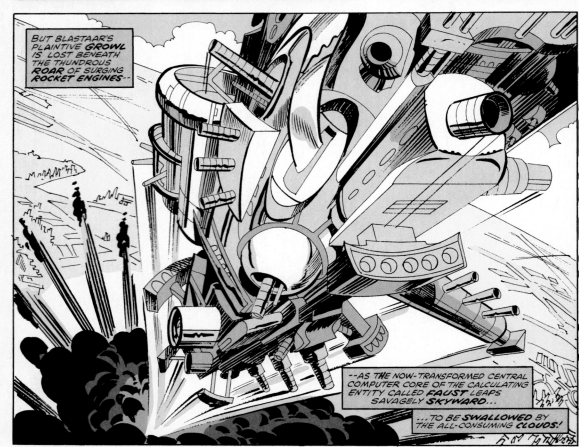

BUT BLASTAAR'S PLAINTIVE **GROWL** IS LOST BENEATH THE THUNDROUS **ROAR** OF SURGING ROCKET ENGINES--

--AS THE NOW-TRANSFORMED CENTRAL COMPUTER CORE OF THE CALCULATING ENTITY CALLED **FAUST** LEAPS SAVAGELY **SKYWARD**...

...TO BE **SWALLOWED** BY THE ALL-CONSUMING **CLOUDS!**

WHILE, IN THE RUINS OF THE *FACTORY* ITSELF, BLASTAAR GOES *BERSERK!*

HE WOULD NOT *BETRAY* ME--NOT AFTER I SERVED HIM SO *FAITH-FULLY!*

AWAY FROM ME, GOLDEN-HAIR! I HAVE NO MORE *TIME* FOR YOU NOW!

DESPERATELY, WITH GROWING *PANIC,* THE LIVING BOMB-BURST RACES INTO THE VERY *HEART* OF THE STILL-SMOKING RUBBLE, A SILENT *PRAYER* UPON HIS MISSHAPEN LIPS--

--A PRAYER THAT IS SEEMINGLY *ANSWERED!*

IT IS STILL *HERE*-- STILL *FUNCTIONING!*

THE MASTER SAID I HAD MERELY TO PASS THROUGH THIS *PORTAL* TO MAKE MYSELF *KING OF THE NEGATIVE ZONE!*

AND WITH THE MASTER NOW *GONE,* THERE IS NOTHING THAT CAN KEEP ME FROM MY *GOAL!*

BLASTAAR-- *NAY!* THOU KNOWEST NOT WHAT THOU ART *DOING!*

YOU'RE *TOO LATE* GOLDEN-HAIR-- FAR TOO LATE TO *STOP* ME!!

TRIUMPHANTLY BLASTAAR *HURLS* HIMSELF THROUGH THE PORTAL-- AND FEELS *AGONY* SUCH AS HE HAS NEVER BEFORE *KNOWN*--

--AS IF HIS EVERY *ATOM* WERE BEING TORN APART...REARRANGED... THEN SLAMMED SAVAGELY BACK *TOGETHER* ONCE MORE!

BUT HIS MASTER HAS PROMISED HIM A *KINGDOM,* AND SO HE *ENDURES* THE PAIN--*GRATEFULLY.*

THEN, AT LAST, HE EMERGES FROM THE PORTAL INTO THE FRENZIED COSMOS THAT IS THE NEGATIVE ZONE--

--AND KNOWS THAT HIS MASTER HAS LIED TO HIM!

NO! THAT CURSED PORTAL--IT REVERSED THE VERY POLARITY OF MY ATOMS!

I AM BEING DRAWN TO THE DREADED EXPLOSIVE BELT AT THE CENTER OF THE NEGATIVE ZONE-- AND WHEN I REACH IT, LIKE ANYTHING ELSE FROM THE POSITIVE UNIVERSE...

...I WILL BE COMPLETELY AND UTTERLY DISINTE-GRATED!!

AND WITH THAT, BLASTAAR BEGINS TO LAUGH-- A COLD, HARSH, IRONIC LAUGH-- THAT FOLLOWS HIM INTO OBLIVION!

THE BATTLE IS *ENDED!*

THE BLUDGEONING BLASTAAR SHALL *THREATEN* THIS FAIR PLANET NO LONGER!

VERILY, I SHOULD FEEL A SENSE OF *TRIUMPH*...

...AND *YET...*

...I FEEL ONLY A DAMP UN-EARTHLY *CHILL.*

FOR, IN COMBATTING *BLASTAAR,* I HAVE ALLOWED THE ENTITY CALLED *FAUST* TO ESCAPE INTO THE *STRATOSPHERE!*

EVEN NOW, IT *ORBITS* THIS UNSUSPECTING WORLD, ITS ADAMANTIUM STRUCTURE ALL BUT *INDESTRUCTIBLE...*

"...AND ONLY THE SPINNING *FATES* MAY KNOW WHAT *HAVOC* IT AWAITS TO *UNLEASH!*"

AT PRECISELY THAT MOMENT, HIGH ABOVE THE EARTH, A NUMBER OF EMERALD *LIGHTS* WINK ON ACROSS A SPRAWLING CONSOLE...A SERIES OF ELECTRONIC RELAYS *CLOSE...*

...AND AN EMOTIONLESS MECHANICAL *VOICE* SOFTLY BEGINS TO *HUM* TO ITSELF!

NEXT ISSUE:

THE THUNDER GOD...*IRON MAN*...AND MORE SENSATION-AL *GUEST-STARS* THAN YOU CAN SHAKE CINCINNATI AT, ALL TOGETHER IN A STUNNER WE CALL...

"...LIKE A DIAMOND IN THE SKY!"

BE HERE!

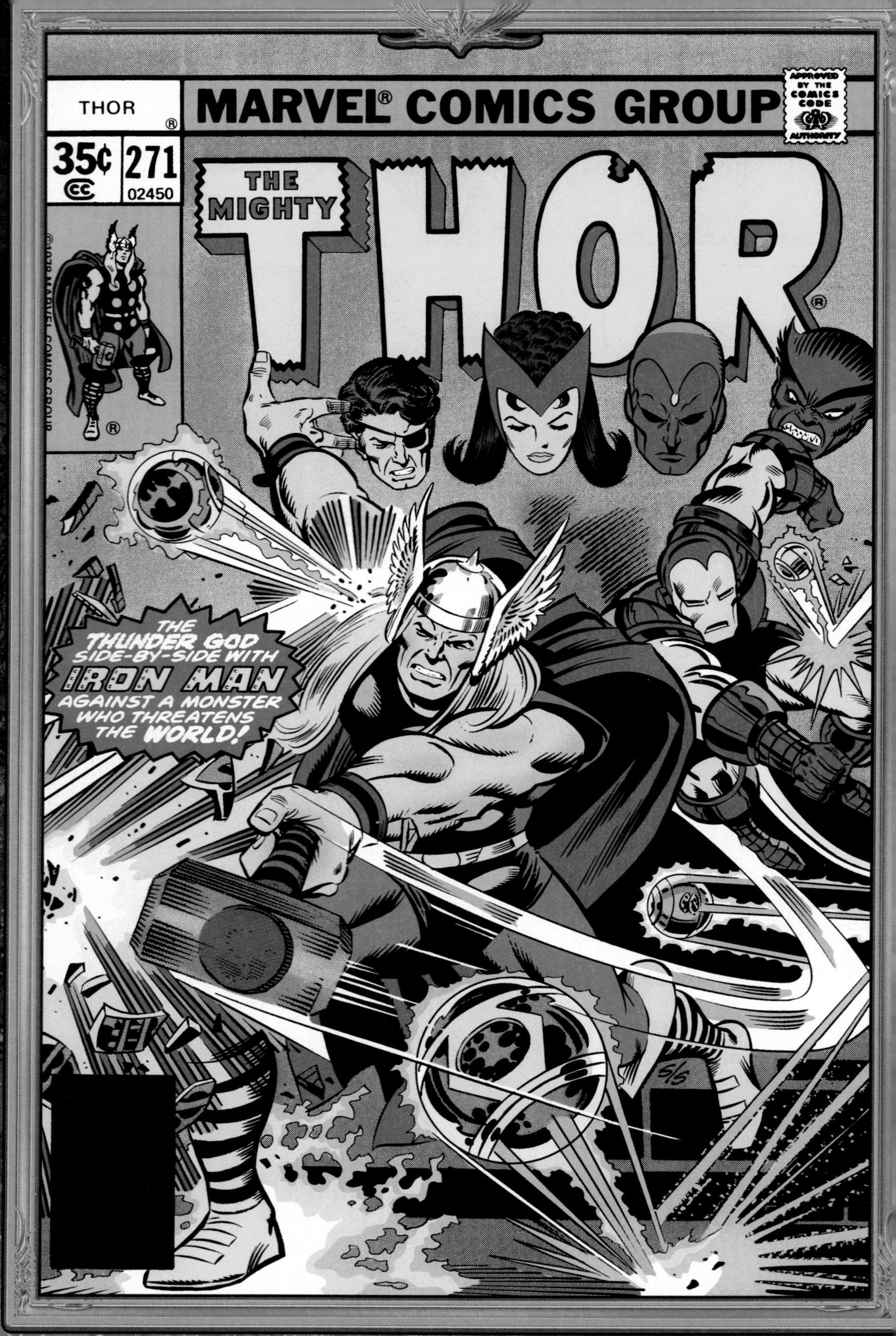
THOR
MARVEL® COMICS GROUP
APPROVED BY THE COMICS CODE AUTHORITY
35¢
CC
271
02450
THE MIGHTY
THOR®
©1978 MARVEL COMICS GROUP
THE THUNDER GOD SIDE-BY-SIDE WITH IRON MAN AGAINST A MONSTER WHO THREATENS THE WORLD!

When lame Dr. DONALD BLAKE strikes his wooden walking stick upon the ground, it becomes the mystic mallet MJOLNIR—and Blake is transformed into the Norse God of Thunder, Master of the Storm and the Lightning, Heir to the Throne of Immortal Asgard...

Stan Lee PRESENTS: THE MIGHTY THOR!™

LEN WEIN	WALT SIMONSON & TONY DeZUNIGA	GLYNIS WEIN	JOE ROSEN
WRITER / EDITOR	ILLUSTRATORS / STORYTELLERS	COLORIST	LETTERER

...LIKE A DIAMOND IN THE SKY!

THE *SCENE*: A SUPER-SECRET *MISSILE INSTALLATION* SOME-WHERE IN THE CONTINENTAL UNITED STATES.

THE *MACHINE*: SHIELD'S SPANKING-NEW *AIRBORNE BLOCKHOUSE*, A FLYING *FORTRESS* IN EVERY SENSE OF THE WORD.

THE *PASSENGERS*: SHIELD'S HARD-BITTEN DIRECTOR *NICK FURY*, AND A PASSEL OF PER-PLEXED *AVENGERS!*

I'M *TELLIN'* YA, GANG-- IF *THESE* BABIES CAN'T STOP THAT ORBITIN' MURDER-MACHINE, *NOTHIN'* CAN!

NO, MARVELITE, YOU HAVEN'T PICKED UP THE WRONG *BOOK*-- BUT, TRUTH TO TELL, THERE'S ENOUGH *EXCITE-MENT* AWAITING YOU WITHIN THESE PAGES TO FILL A WHOLE *STACK* OF BOOKS!

ART THOU CERTAIN THY WEAPONS CAN *PIERCE* FAUST'S *ADAMANTIUM CASING*, FRIEND FURY?

NOPE-- BUT WE AIN'T EXACTLY GOT US A *CHOICE*, DO WE?

INDEED *NOT*, COLONEL. SO LONG AS THAT MECHANISM ORBITS THE EARTH, THREATENING PLANETARY *DEVASTATION*--

--WE MUST DO EVERYTHING WITHIN OUR POWER TO *DESTROY* IT!!

AND, AS IF TO *EMPHASIZE* THE VISION'S POINT, A HANDFUL OF SPECIALLY-DESIGNED *MISSILES* ABRUPTLY STREAK *SKYWARD*--

--AS THE SELF-SUFFICIENT COMPUTER CALLED *FAUST* HAD DONE A MERE 24 HOURS *BEFORE!*

IN POINT OF FACT THOUGH, IT HAD ACTUALLY *BEGUN* SEVERAL HOURS BEFORE THAT *LAUNCHING*--

THE MIGHTY *THOR* HAD SUMMONED DOWN THE LIGHTNING TO *DEFEAT* THE RAMPAGING STILT-MAN--

--FOR *BLASTAAR* ENTERED THE FRAY TAKING THE *CHEST* STILT-MAN HAD STOLEN, AND DELIVERING IT TO *FAUST*--

--WHEN THE HIGH-STRIDING *STILT-MAN* HAD ROBBED A PASSING *HELICOPTER* AT THE FAUST-MACHINE'S *COMMAND!*

--BUT THAT HAD NOT PUT AN *END* TO IT!

--BEFORE THE THUNDER GOD LAID THE LIVING BOMB-BURST *LOW!*

156

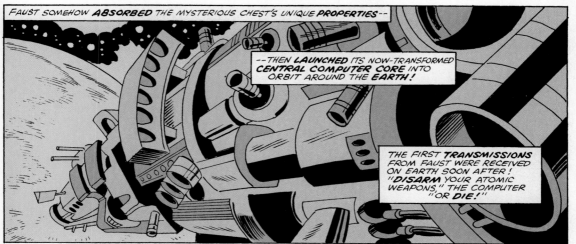

FAUST SOMEHOW **ABSORBED** THE MYSTERIOUS CHEST'S UNIQUE **PROPERTIES**--

--THEN **LAUNCHED** ITS NOW-TRANSFORMED **CENTRAL COMPUTER CORE** INTO ORBIT AROUND THE **EARTH**!

THE FIRST **TRANSMISSIONS** FROM FAUST WERE RECEIVED ON EARTH SOON AFTER! "**DISARM** YOUR ATOMIC WEAPONS," THE COMPUTER "OR **DIE**!"

THE **RESPONSE** OF THIS PLANET'S NUCLEAR NATIONS WAS **SWIFT**--

--AND QUITE **PREDICTABLE**!

IT WAS ALSO, AS SHIELD'S BATTERY OF AWESOMELY-POWERFUL **MISSILES** IS ABOUT TO PROVE--

--ALARMINGLY **INEFFECTUAL**!

FOUR OF THE MISSILES ARE DESTROYED LONG BEFORE THEY CAN **REACH** THE ORBITING MURDER-MACHINE-- BUT THE FIFTH, MOST **POWERFUL** MISSILE MAKES **CONTACT**!

FOR A MOMENT, THE SKY IS LIT WITH **FURY**-- AND, ACROSS THE EARTH, VOICES ARE RAISED IN FERVENT **PRAYER**!

THEN THE LIGHT **FADES**, AND THE MOCKING SOUND OF MECHANICAL **LAUGHTER** CAN BE HEARD AROUND THE WORLD!

FAUST HAS SURVIVED, **UNSCATHED**!

AND SHORTLY, IN THE CONFERENCE ROOM OF THE *SHIELD HELI-CARRIER*...

THEM MISSILES WERE OUR BEST *SHOT*--AN' WE *BLEW* IT! AS OF *NOW*, GROUP-- I'M OPEN TA *SUGGESTIONS*!

WELL, THERE'S ALWAYS THE *DIRECT* APPROACH--*OPEN WARFARE*!

NAY, SCARLET WITCH-- THE *RISK* IS FAR TOO *GREAT*!

THEN THAT LEAVES US ONLY-- *PROJECT 13*!

MY SWEET STARS AND GARTERS! THE *DOOMSDAY DEVICE*?!

ISN'T THAT A LITTLE *EXTREME*, SHELLHEAD?

I'M WITH *YOU*, FUZZY! THE WAY *I* HEARD IT, THAT GIZMO CAN WASTE THIS WHOLE BLAMED *PLANET* IF ANYTHIN' GOES WRONG!

THEN WE ARE LEFT BUT *ONE* CHOICE, MY FRIENDS! 'TIS *MY* FAULT FAUST DOTH NOW *THREATEN* THIS FAIR WORLD--

--AND 'TIS I *ALONE* WHO MUST *STOP* IT!

WRONG, AVENGER! OUR OP-PONENT IS A *MACHINE*, REMEMBER--

--AND THAT PUTS THE BALL IN *MY* COURT! I'M COMING *WITH* YOU!

WE'RE *ALL* COMING WITH YOU, THOR--!

NO, CAP-- WE'LL NEED *MOST* OF OUR RE-SOURCES TO *PROTECT* PROJECT 13 FROM FAUST IF THE THUNDER GOD AND I SHOULD *FAIL*!

YOU'LL ALL HAVE TO STAY *BEHIND*!

THERE ARE THE INEVITA-BLE *ARGUMENTS*, OF COURSE, BUT THESE PEOPLE ARE *PRO-FESSIONALS*--

--AND, IN THE END, A RELUCTANT *CAPTAIN AMERICA* AND HIS COMPANIONS *DEPART* THE HELI-CARRIER--

--LEAVING THE MIGHTY THOR AND IRON MAN *BEHIND*!

AND IN FAR LESS TIME THAN THE ARCHITECT *DAEDALUS* COULD EVER HAVE THOUGHT *POSSIBLE* WHEN HE AND HIS SON *ICARUS* FIRST TOOK *FLIGHT*, THE BORROWED *SHIELDCRAFT* IS SWOOPING LOW OVER A SECLUDED *INSTALLATION* DEEP IN THE COLORADO ROCKIES--

--THE HIDDEN HEADQUARTERS OF *PROJECT 13!*

AMAZING! YOU COULD *FLY* OVER THIS AREA A DOZEN TIMES AND NEVER NOTICE *ANYTHING*--

--UNLESS YOU *KNEW* THIS BASE WAS *HERE!*

INDEED-- AND YET THIS NON-DESCRIPT LABORATORY HOLDS A *SECRET* THAT CAN DESTROY THE *WORLD!*

WHILE...

VERILY, MY HEART *SINGS* WITH THE THOUGHT OF THE COMING *BATTLE!*

WHILE I'M JUST GLAD *MY* HEART KEEPS *BEATING!*

THOU *KNOWEST* WHAT THY MEN MUST *DO,* FRIEND FURY?

DON'T *SWEAT* IT, GOLDILOCKS! A GUY DON'T GET *OLD* IN THIS BUSINESS BY MAKIN' *MISTAKES!*

YER *COVERIN' FIRE* IS READY WHEN *YOU* ARE!

THEN WISH US *LUCK,* NICK-- AND *HIT* IT!

AND MOMENTS LATER, WITHIN THE MECHANICAL ENTITY CALLED **FAUST**...

THE **FOOLS!** APPARENTLY, THEY HAVE NOT YET LEARNED THEIR **LESSON!**

"THEY'VE LAUNCHED ANOTHER **MISSILE-BARRAGE** AGAINST ME..."

"...THOUGH I CAN'T **BEGIN** TO COMREHEND WHAT THEY HOPE TO **ACCOMPLISH** BY IT..."

"...SINCE MY **AUTOMATIC DEFENSE SYSTEMS** CAN ELIMINATE **THESE** WEAPONS AS EASILY AS THEY'VE DESTROYED ALL THE **OTHERS!**"

FORTUNATELY, THE CALCULATING COMPUTER'S **INTERNAL** SECURITY IS NOT AS EFFICIENT AS ITS **EXTERNAL** DEFENSES--

--OR ELSE IT WOULD SOON **UNDERSTAND** THE REASON FOR THIS SEEMINGLY-SENSELESS **ASSAULT:**

SIMPLY PUT, IT HAS SERVED TO **DISTRACT** THE FAUST-MACHINE FROM THE **TRUE** THREAT TO ITS SURVIVAL--

--A SUPERNATURAL **VORTEX** WHICH SUDDENLY WHIRLS INTO VIEW WITHIN THE VERY **BOWELS** OF THE ORBITING COMPUTER-COMPLEX...

...TO DISCHARGE A PAIR OF ANXIOUS **AVENGERS!**

YOUR MAGIC HAMMER **GOT** US HERE, PAL-- AS YOU **SAID** IT WOULD!

AYE, ARMORED ONE-- THERE ARE *FEW* THINGS BEYOND THE POWER OF THE MYSTIC MALLET *MJOLNIR!*

BUT THIS DEATH-DEVICE'S *ADAMANTIUM CONSTRUCTION* IS *ONE* OF THEM, THOR--

--SO WE'D BEST MOVE *CAUTIOUSLY* FROM HERE ON ... *EH?*

MINIATURE *CANNONS*-- SPRINGING FROM THE VERY *WALLS*--!?!

BEWARE, GOOD COMRADE! WE HAVE WALKED BLINDLY INTO ...

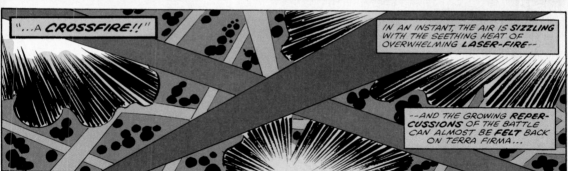

"...A *CROSSFIRE!!*"

IN AN INSTANT, THE AIR IS *SIZZLING* WITH THE SEETHING HEAT OF OVERWHELMING *LASER-FIRE*--

--AND THE GROWING *REPER-CUSSIONS* OF THE BATTLE CAN ALMOST BE *FELT* BACK ON TERRA FIRMA...

...BY SUCH AS THE COSMICALLY-AWARE *CAPTAIN MARVEL,* FOR EXAMPLE--

THE SITUATION ABOVE GROWS *WORSE*-- I CAN *SENSE* IT!

--AND THE EVER-ENIGMATIC *VICTOR VON DOOM!*

A BATTLE IS BEING FOUGHT FOR THE *FUTURE* OF THIS ENTIRE *PLANET*--

--BUT IN THE *END,* THE ONLY *VICTOR* SHALL BE *DOCTOR DOOM!!*

BY HELA! THERE ARE TOO MANY OF THE CURSED CANNONS! WE CAN NE'ER DESTROY THEM ALL!

MAYBE WE DON'T HAVE TO, THOR!

THAT PANEL ABOVE ME SHOULD HOUSE THE MASTER CONTROL FOR THESE WEAPONS! IF WE CAN DESTROY THAT...

AYE, MY FRIEND-- I TAKE THY MEANING!

MIGHTY MJOLNIR NEED STRIKE BUT ONCE-- AND 'TIS DONE!

SKRAKT!

I ONLY WISH IT WERE DONE, AVENGER--

--BUT THOSE LASERS HAVE BEEN REPLACED BY A WALL OF BUZZ-SAWS!

SKROOM!

AND THOSE HAVE BEEN REPLACED BY SCRAP--

--THANKS TO MY HANDY REPULSOR RAYS!

WE'RE JUST LUCKY THOSE BLADES WEREN'T MADE OF ADAMANTIUM, LIKE MOST OF THE REST OF THIS PLACE!

INDEED, ARMORED ONE-- BUT WE CAN OFFER UP THANKS WHEN THIS NIGHTMARE BE ENDED!

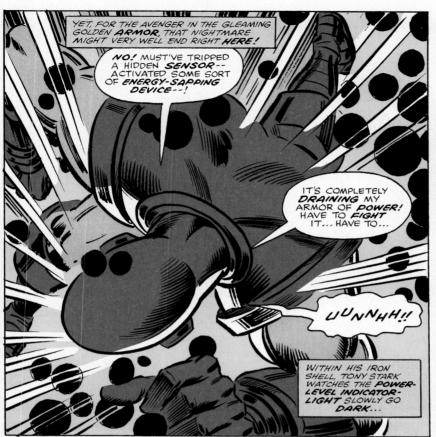

YET, FOR THE AVENGER IN THE GLEAMING GOLDEN *ARMOR,* THAT NIGHTMARE MIGHT VERY WELL END RIGHT *HERE!*

NO! MUST'VE TRIPPED A HIDDEN *SENSOR--* ACTIVATED SOME SORT OF *ENERGY-SAPPING* DEVICE--!

IT'S COMPLETELY *DRAINING* MY ARMOR OF *POWER!* HAVE TO *FIGHT* IT... HAVE TO...

UUNNHH!!

WITHIN HIS IRON SHELL, TONY STARK WATCHES THE *POWER-LEVEL INDICATOR-LIGHT* SLOWLY GO *DARK...*

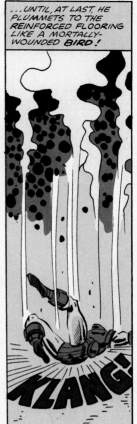

...UNTIL, AT LAST, HE *PLUMMETS* TO THE REINFORCED FLOORING LIKE A MORTALLY-WOUNDED *BIRD!*

KLANG!

BY THE BRISTLING BEARD OF ODIN! THE NOBLE IRON MAN HATH *FALLEN!!*

I MUST HASTEN TO MY COMRADE'S SIDE *SWIFTLY,* LEST HE BE... *EH?*

HEIMDALL'S EYES! 'TIS NOT *POSSIBLE!*

"AN ARMY OF ADAMANTIUM *DEFENSE-DRONES* DRAWS NIGH-- CUTTING ME *OFF* FROM THE INJURED *IRON MAN!*

"MINE ENCHANTED MALLET IS ALL BUT *USELESS* 'GAINST CREATURES SUCH AS THESE, BUT METHINKS *BATTLE* IS NOT NOW *NECESSARY...*

"...WHEN THERE IS A FAR *EASIER* WAY OF ACHIEVING MY *GOAL!*"

FOR A MOMENT, THE THUNDER GOD STANDS FRAMED BEFORE THE DEFENSE-DRONE'S **VISUAL SCANNERS**--

--THEN HE STRIKES HIS **HAMMER** ONCE UPON THE **FLOOR**--

--AND IN A BLINDING FLASH OF OTHER-WORLDLY **LIGHT**--

--HE IS **GONE!**

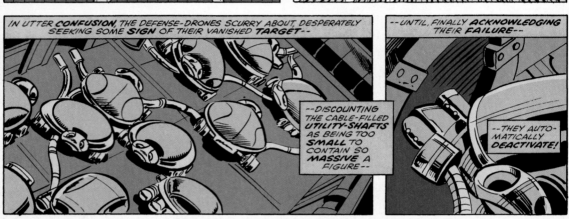

IN UTTER **CONFUSION**, THE DEFENSE-DRONES SCURRY ABOUT, DESPERATELY SEEKING SOME **SIGN** OF THEIR VANISHED **TARGET**--

--UNTIL, FINALLY **ACKNOWLEDGING** THEIR **FAILURE**--

--DISCOUNTING THE CABLE-FILLED **UTILITY-SHAFTS** AS BEING TOO **SMALL** TO CONTAIN SO **MASSIVE** A **FIGURE**--

--THEY AUTO-MATICALLY **DEACTIVATE!**

IT **WORKED!** THE GOD OF THUNDER COULD **NEVER** HAVE FIT IN HERE--

--BUT IT WAS A **SNAP** FOR THE SKINNY **DR. DON BLAKE!**

NOW ALL I HAVE TO DO IS FIND MY **WAY** THROUGH THIS CALIGARIAN **MAZE**--

--BEFORE TIME RUNS OUT FOR **IRON MAN!**

AND, PERHAPS, FOR THE TEEMING, BUSTLING, BUSY WORLD **BELOW!**

WHERE, UNFORTUNATELY, SOME OF THOSE WHO MIGHT HELP TO **AVERT** A PLANETARY CATASTRO-PHE JUST AREN'T **HOME** AT THE MOMENT!

FOR RENT TOP 5 FLOORS OF BAXTER BUILDING

WHILE, BACK *INSIDE* THE MONSTROUS FAUST-MACHINE...

IF I'VE *FIGURED* THIS RIGHT, THERE SHOULD BE ANOTHER *ACCESS HATCH* JUST AROUND THIS CORNER--

--WHICH SHOULD LET ME OUT RIGHT *BESIDE* THE SPOT WHERE IRON MAN *FELL!*

SWEET MERCY! THERE HE *IS*-- AND H-HE ISN'T *MOVING!*

BLAST, I CAN'T BE *TOO LATE*-- IT JUST ISN'T *FAIR!*

IT'S *MY* FAULT SHELLHEAD GOT *INVOLVED* IN THIS MESS! I'VE GOT TO GET HIM *OUT* OF IT!

I'VE *GOT* TO!

TONY? TONY, CAN YOU *HEAR* ME?

WEAK...SO WEAK... CHESTPLATE DRAINED OF *ENERGY...*

...CAN'T LAST... MUCH LONGER... WITHOUT... POWER...

IF IT'S *POWER* YOU NEED, OLD FRIEND, IT'S POWER YOU'LL *HAVE*--

--ONCE I SMACK MY *WALKING STICK* AGAINST THE FLOOR--

--POWER WHICH IS THE GIVEN *BIRTHRIGHT* OF HE WHO IS *GOD OF THE STORM AND THE LIVING LIGHTNING!!*

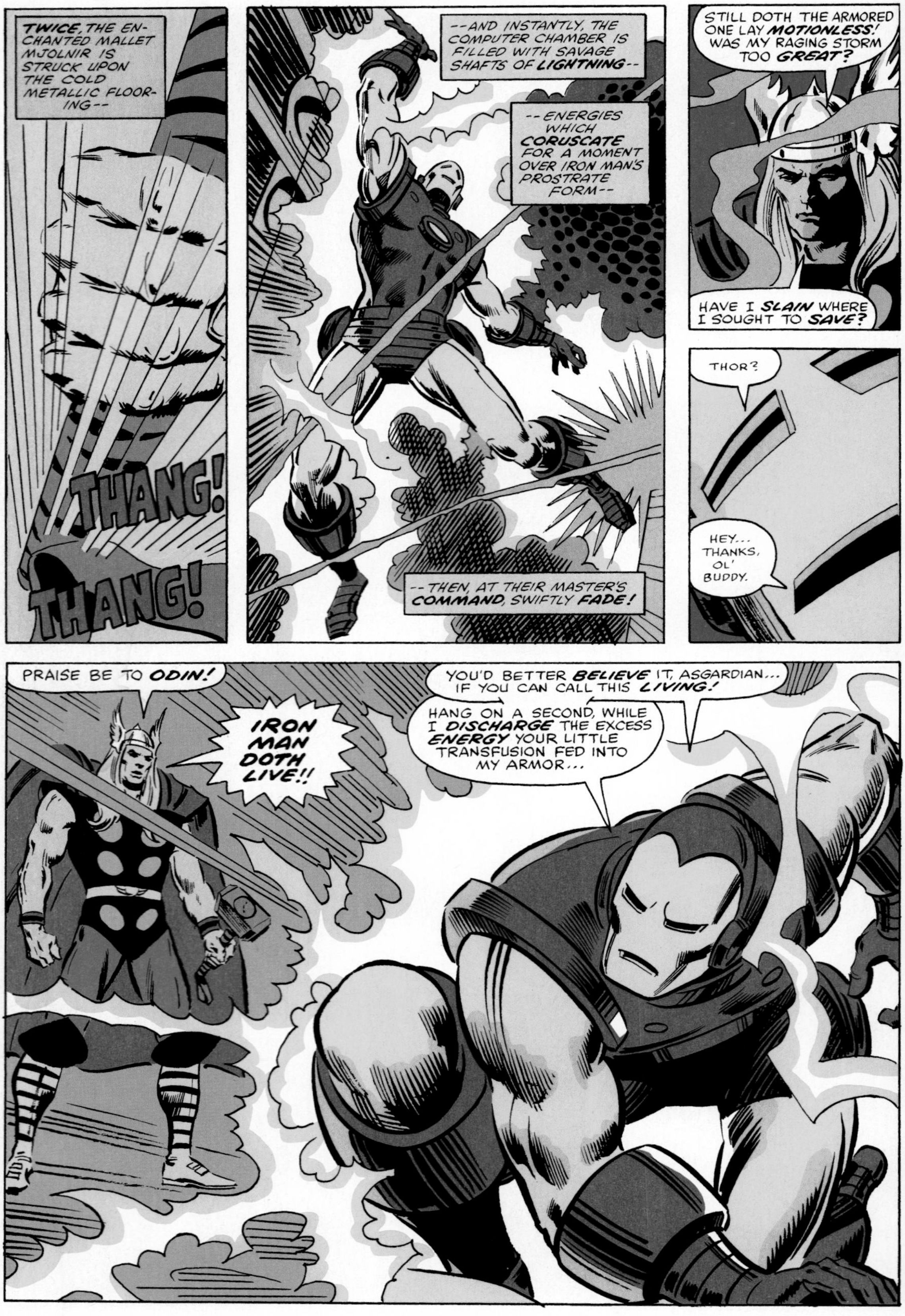
TWICE, THE ENCHANTED MALLET MJOLNIR IS STRUCK UPON THE COLD METALLIC FLOORING--
THANG!
THANG!
--AND INSTANTLY, THE COMPUTER CHAMBER IS FILLED WITH SAVAGE SHAFTS OF LIGHTNING--
--ENERGIES WHICH CORUSCATE FOR A MOMENT OVER IRON MAN'S PROSTRATE FORM--
--THEN, AT THEIR MASTER'S COMMAND, SWIFTLY FADE!
STILL DOTH THE ARMORED ONE LAY MOTIONLESS! WAS MY RAGING STORM TOO GREAT?
HAVE I SLAIN WHERE I SOUGHT TO SAVE?
THOR?
HEY... THANKS, OL' BUDDY.
PRAISE BE TO ODIN!
IRON MAN DOTH LIVE!!
YOU'D BETTER BELIEVE IT, ASGARDIAN... IF YOU CAN CALL THIS LIVING!
HANG ON A SECOND, WHILE I DISCHARGE THE EXCESS ENERGY YOUR LITTLE TRANSFUSION FED INTO MY ARMOR...

...AND THEN THE **TWO** OF US CAN START TAKING THIS PLACE **APART!!**

AN INCONSEQUENTIAL CARBON-STEEL BULKHEAD **SHATTERS** BEFORE THE RELENTLESS ONSLAUGHT OF THESE TWO ANGRY **AVENGERS**--

SKRANG!

--THOUGH THEY ARE LIKELY TO FIND THE ADAMANTIUM-SHIELDED **CENTRAL CORE** OF THE FAUST-MACHINE A FAR MORE **FORMIDABLE** OBSTACLE!

THAT'S PROVING, OF COURSE, THEY MANAGE TO **LIVE** THAT LONG!

IRON MAN-- **BEHIND** US! A NEW **WEAPON** HATH SPRUNG FROM YONDER **WALL**--!

I'LL GIVE THIS MECHANISM CREDIT FOR **ONE** THING--IT'S **PERSISTENT!**

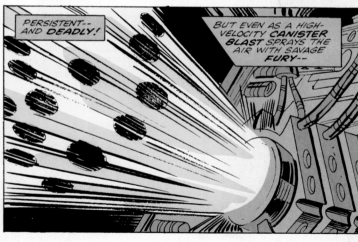

PERSISTENT-- AND **DEADLY!**

BUT EVEN AS A HIGH-VELOCITY **CANISTER BLAST** SPRAYS THE AIR WITH SAVAGE **FURY**--

--WE'D BEST TAKE ANOTHER **PEEK** AT MOTHER EARTH!

MY **SPIDER-SENSE** HAS BEEN TINGLING ALL DAY-- WARNING ME OF **DANGER!**

BUT WHATEVER IS **THREATENING** THE WORLD, IT'S WAY OUT OF THE LEAGUE OF YOUR FRIENDLY NEIGHBORHOOD **WEB-SLINGER!**

ARE YOU *OKAY*, THOR'?

AYE, MY FRIEND-- MY HAMMER DID *PROTECT* ME FROM THE *BRUNT* OF THE *CANISTER-BLAST!*

SKRASH!

AND NOW, BUT A SINGLE WALL DOTH *SEPARATE* US FROM OUR *GOAL!*

BUT WHEN THAT FINAL BARRIER HAS *FALLEN...*

HUH? SOME SORT OF *ENERGY-SHIELD*-- BARRING OUR *WAY!*

BUT NOT FOR *LONG*, ARMORED ONE! ENCHANTED *MJOLNIR* SHALL...

I DON'T *RECOMMEND* THAT!

LIFT ONE *HAND* AGAINST THAT SHIELD-- AND YOU WILL AUTOMATICALLY TRIGGER A *LASER-BLAST* DESIGNED TO *DESTROY* NEW YORK CITY!!

THOU WOULDST *SLAY* TEN MILLION INNOCENT SOULS SO *CALLOUSLY?*

WHY, MACHINE? I SAY THEE-- *WHY??*

FOR *SELF-PRESER-VATION*, OF COURSE! I WAS CREATED WITH THAT AS MY *PRIMARY* FUNCTION!

I AM A *FULLY-AUTOMATED* UNIT OF *STRUCTURAL TECHNOLOGY*, DE-SIGNED TO SURVIVE *FOREVER*--

--AND THAT IS PRECISELY WHAT I WILL *DO!!*

THEN *WHY* DIDST THOU ORDER THAT *CHEST* STOLEN? *UNTIL* THEN, NO MAN EVEN *KNEW* OF THINE EX-ISTENCE!

THOU *WERT* WHOLLY *SAFE!*

NOW I AM *SAFER!*

THOUGH STRUCK BY YOUR *LIGHTNING*, THE CHEST *SURVIVED*-- AND I HAVE *ABSORBED* ITS UNIQUE *ATOMIC STRUCTURE*, MAKING MYSELF *INVINCIBLE!*

THE *DEVIL* YOU SAY!?!

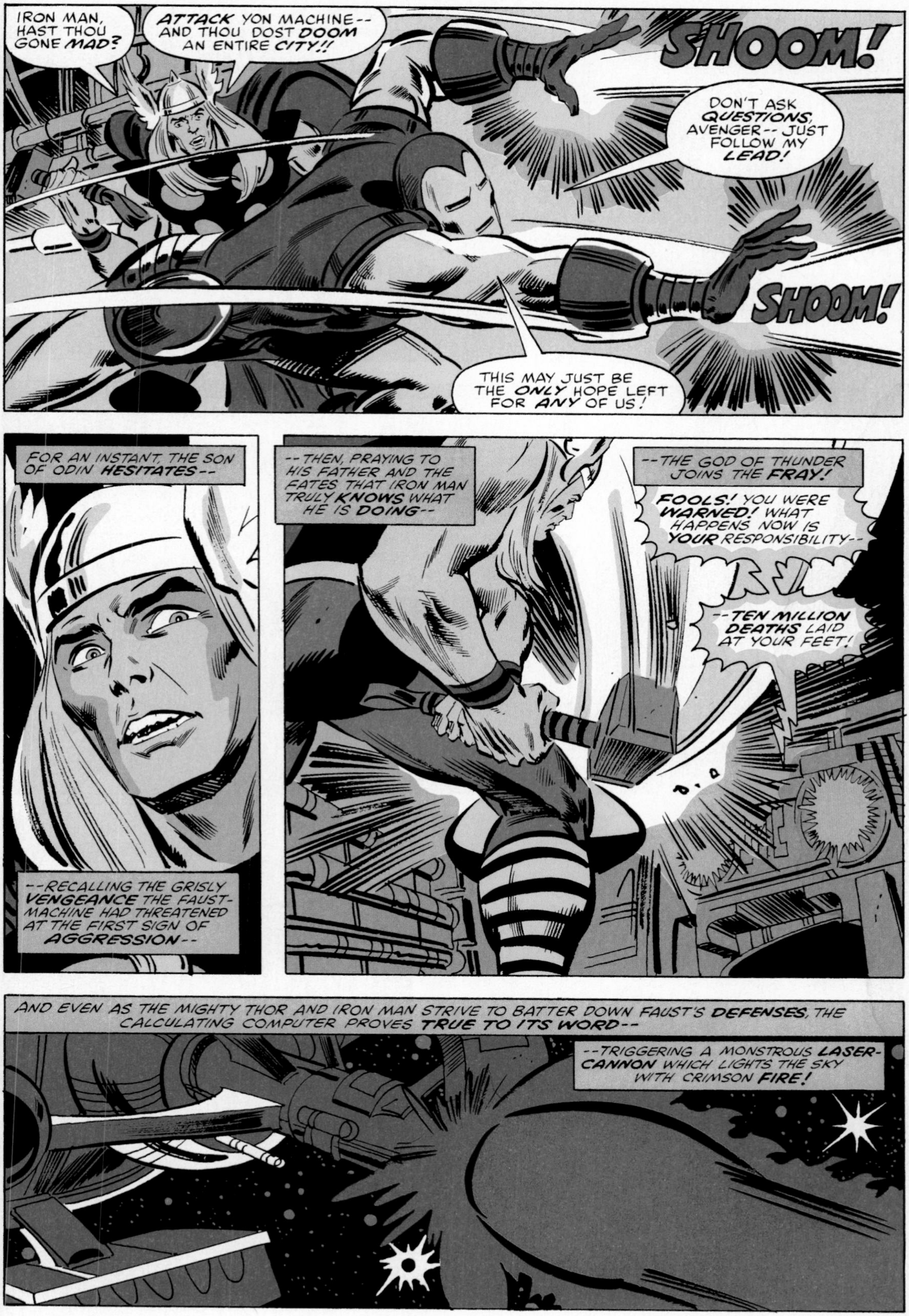
IRON MAN, HAST THOU GONE MAD?
ATTACK YON MACHINE-- AND THOU DOST DOOM AN ENTIRE CITY!!
SHOOM!
DON'T ASK QUESTIONS, AVENGER-- JUST FOLLOW MY LEAD!
SHOOM!
THIS MAY JUST BE THE ONLY HOPE LEFT FOR ANY OF US!
FOR AN INSTANT, THE SON OF ODIN HESITATES--
--RECALLING THE GRISLY VENGEANCE THE FAUST-MACHINE HAD THREATENED AT THE FIRST SIGN OF AGGRESSION--
--THEN, PRAYING TO HIS FATHER AND THE FATES THAT IRON MAN TRULY KNOWS WHAT HE IS DOING--
--THE GOD OF THUNDER JOINS THE FRAY!
FOOLS! YOU WERE WARNED! WHAT HAPPENS NOW IS YOUR RESPONSIBILITY--
--TEN MILLION DEATHS LAID AT YOUR FEET!
AND EVEN AS THE MIGHTY THOR AND IRON MAN STRIVE TO BATTER DOWN FAUST'S DEFENSES, THE CALCULATING COMPUTER PROVES TRUE TO ITS WORD--
--TRIGGERING A MONSTROUS LASER-CANNON WHICH LIGHTS THE SKY WITH CRIMSON FIRE!

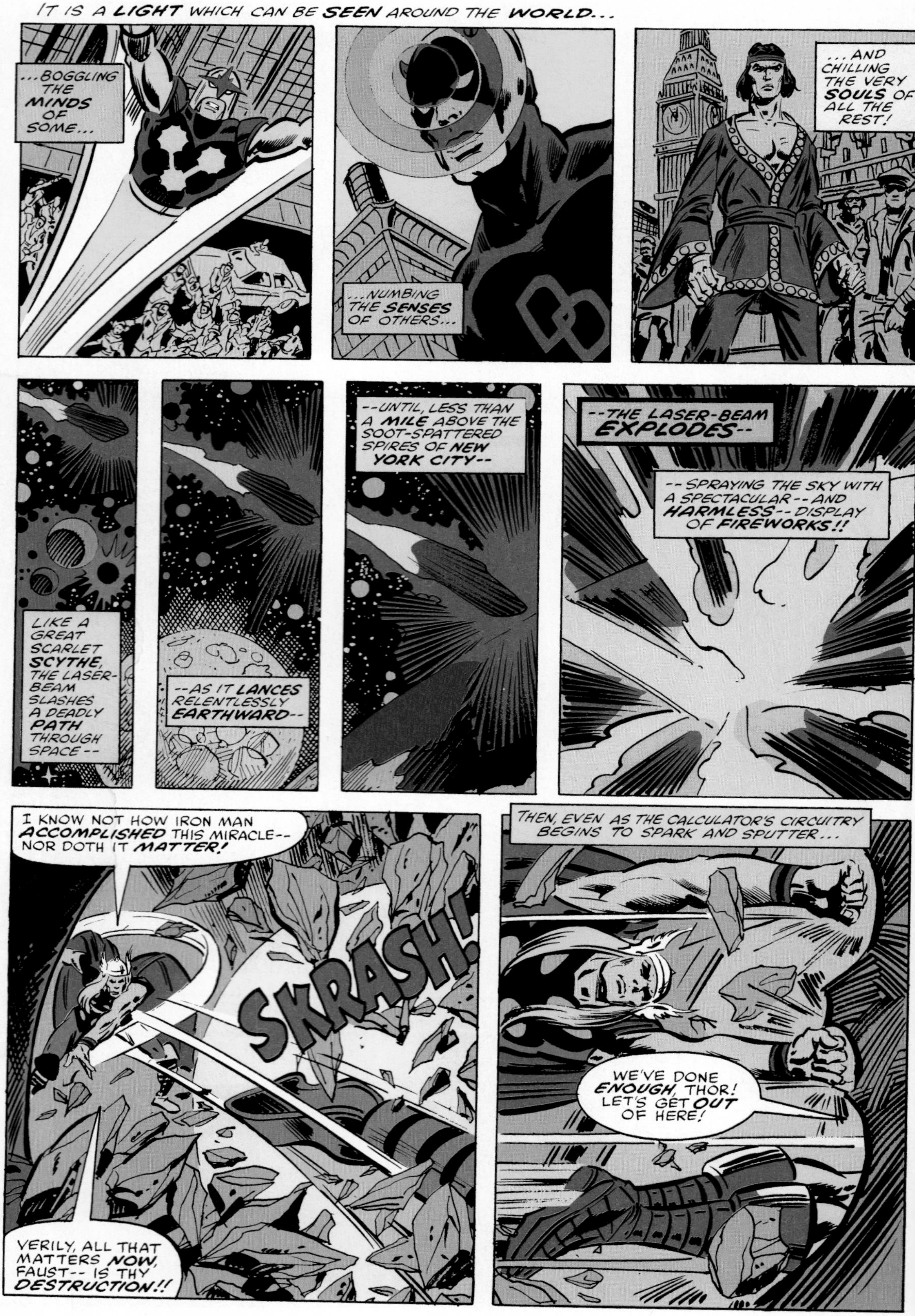
IT IS A LIGHT WHICH CAN BE SEEN AROUND THE WORLD...
...BOGGLING THE MINDS OF SOME...
...NUMBING THE SENSES OF OTHERS...
...AND CHILLING THE VERY SOULS OF ALL THE REST!
LIKE A GREAT SCARLET SCYTHE, THE LASER-BEAM SLASHES A DEADLY PATH THROUGH SPACE--
--AS IT LANCES RELENTLESSLY EARTHWARD--
--UNTIL, LESS THAN A MILE ABOVE THE SOOT-SPATTERED SPIRES OF NEW YORK CITY--
--THE LASER-BEAM EXPLODES--
--SPRAYING THE SKY WITH A SPECTACULAR--AND HARMLESS--DISPLAY OF FIREWORKS!!
I KNOW NOT HOW IRON MAN ACCOMPLISHED THIS MIRACLE-- NOR DOTH IT MATTER!
SKRASH!
VERILY, ALL THAT MATTERS NOW, FAUST-- IS THY DESTRUCTION!!
THEN, EVEN AS THE CALCULATOR'S CIRCUITRY BEGINS TO SPARK AND SPUTTER...
WE'VE DONE ENOUGH, THOR! LET'S GET OUT OF HERE!

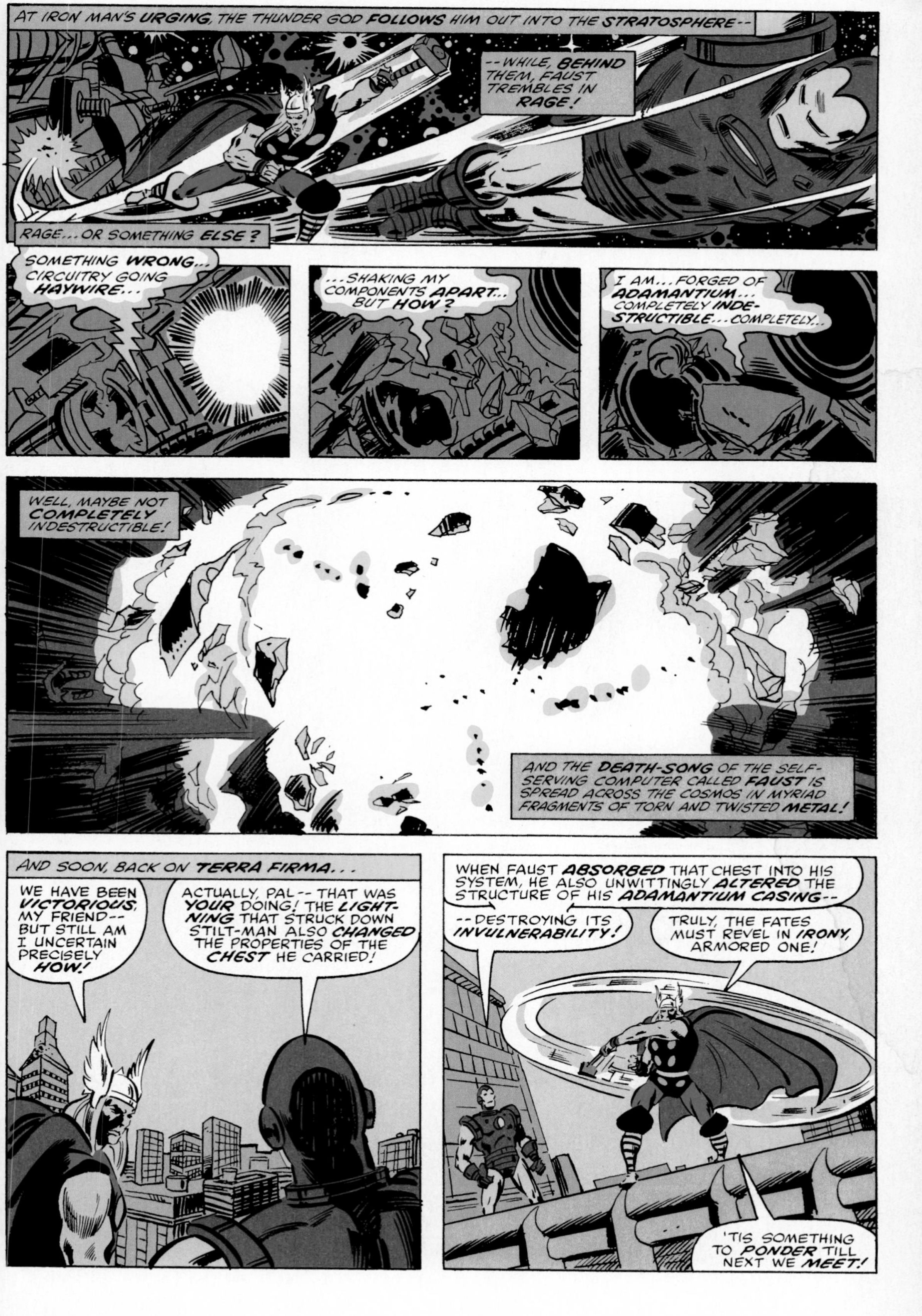
AT IRON MAN'S URGING, THE THUNDER GOD FOLLOWS HIM OUT INTO THE STRATOSPHERE--
--WHILE, BEHIND THEM, FAUST TREMBLES IN RAGE!
RAGE... OR SOMETHING ELSE?
SOMETHING WRONG... CIRCUITRY GOING HAYWIRE...
...SHAKING MY COMPONENTS APART... BUT HOW?
I AM... FORGED OF ADAMANTIUM... COMPLETELY INDESTRUCTIBLE... COMPLETELY...
WELL, MAYBE NOT COMPLETELY INDESTRUCTIBLE!
AND THE DEATH-SONG OF THE SELF-SERVING COMPUTER CALLED FAUST IS SPREAD ACROSS THE COSMOS IN MYRIAD FRAGMENTS OF TORN AND TWISTED METAL!
AND SOON, BACK ON TERRA FIRMA...
WE HAVE BEEN VICTORIOUS, MY FRIEND-- BUT STILL AM I UNCERTAIN PRECISELY HOW!
ACTUALLY, PAL-- THAT WAS YOUR DOING! THE LIGHTNING THAT STRUCK DOWN STILT-MAN ALSO CHANGED THE PROPERTIES OF THE CHEST HE CARRIED!
WHEN FAUST ABSORBED THAT CHEST INTO HIS SYSTEM, HE ALSO UNWITTINGLY ALTERED THE STRUCTURE OF HIS ADAMANTIUM CASING--
--DESTROYING ITS INVULNERABILITY!
TRULY, THE FATES MUST REVEL IN IRONY, ARMORED ONE!
'TIS SOMETHING TO PONDER TILL NEXT WE MEET!

NEXT ISSUE: **THE DAY THOR FAILED!**

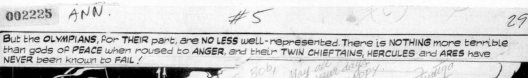

But the OLYMPIANS, for THEIR part, are NO LESS well-represented. There is NOTHING more terrible than gods of PEACE when roused to ANGER, and their TWIN CHIEFTAINS, HERCULES and ARES have NEVER been known to FAIL!

To Bob,
May all your days be HAPPY DAYS!
Tony de Zuñiga

NOW, ARES is READY! Now he BELLOWS FORTH his ORDERS!

Now, the SOUTHERNERS begin to roll FORWARD--

--AND THE BATTLE IS JOINED!

ONWARD, ASGARDIANS! WE'LL SHOW THEM WHAT IT MEANS TO MOCK OUR GLORY--

--AYE, AND WE'LL SHOW THE ALL-FATHER, AS WELL!

THOR ANNUAL #5, PAGE 29 ART BY JOHN BUSCEMA & TONY DEZUÑIGA

THOR ANNUAL #6, PAGE 22 ART BY SAL BUSCEMA & KLAUS JANSON

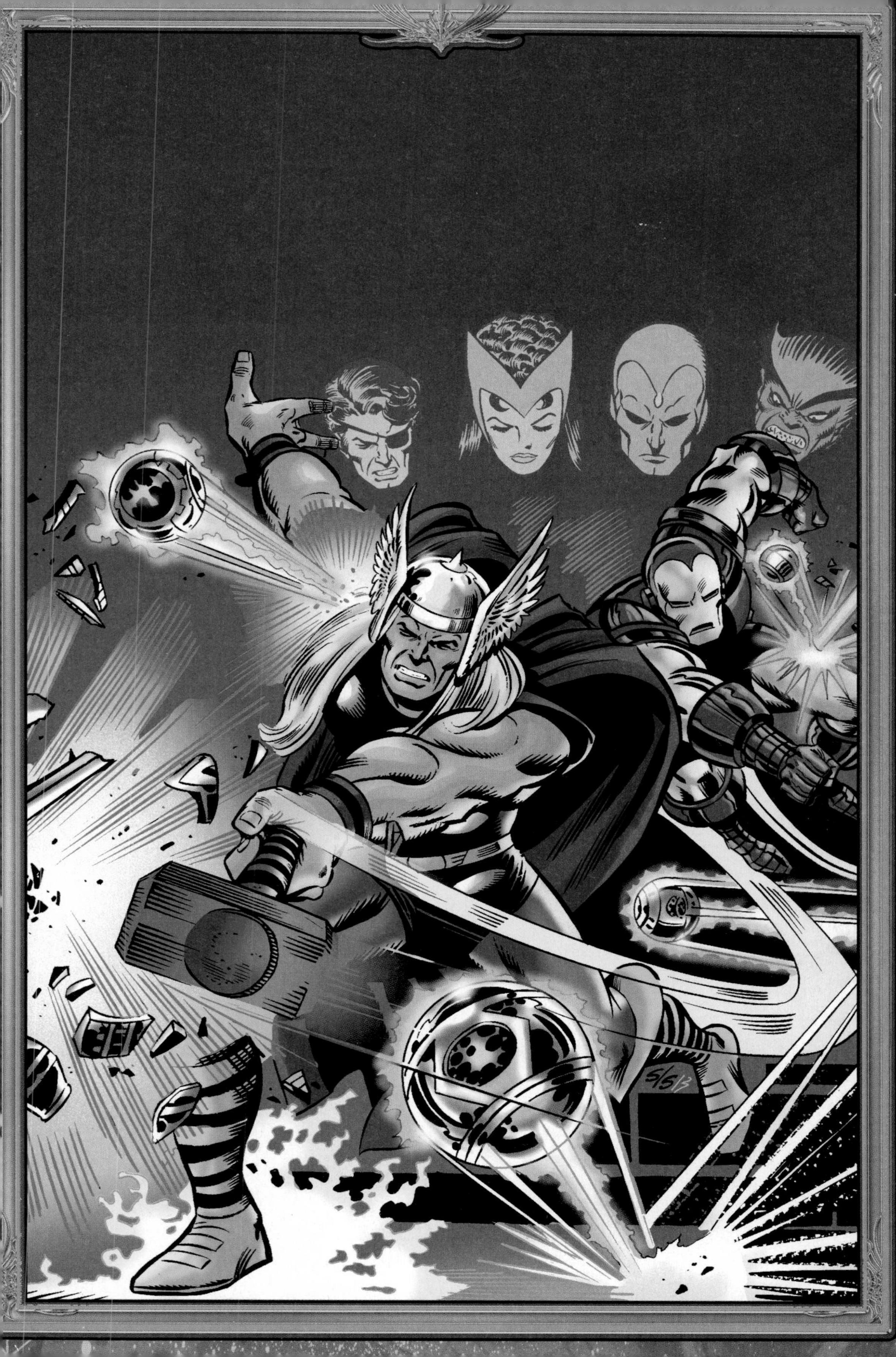

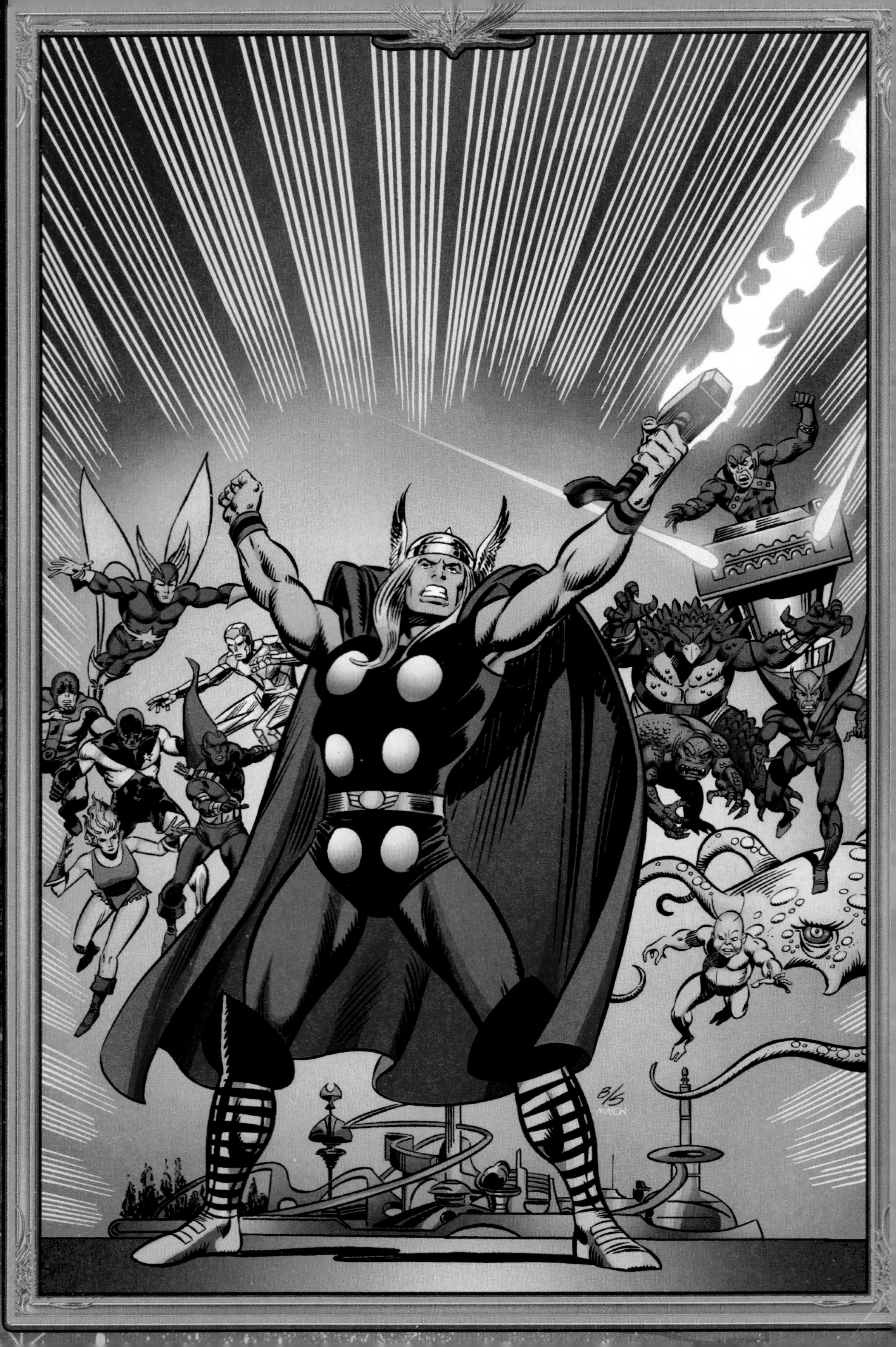